Introduction to Christian Education

Introduction to Christian Education

by Eleanor Daniel • John W. Wade • Charles Gresham
foreword by Lawrence O. Richards

STANDARD PUBLISHING
Cincinnati, Ohio 88591

Textbooks by Standard Publishing:

The Christian Minister
Sam E. Stone
Introduction to Christian Education
Eleanor Daniel, John W. Wade, Charles Gresham
Ministering to Youth
Methods for Youth Ministry
David Roadcup, editor
The Church On Purpose
The Church On Target
Joe S. Ellis
The Faith . . . Once Delivered
William J. Richardson, editor

Library of Congress Cataloging in Publication Data

Daniel, Eleanor Ann.
Introduction to Christian education.

Includes bibliographies and indexes.
1. Christian education. I. Wade, John William, 1924-. II. Gresham, Charles. III. Title.
BV1471.2.D26 1987 268 87-18069
ISBN 0-87403-211-3

A division of STANDEX INTERNATIONAL Corporation.
Printed in U.S.A.

Foreword

An "Introduction" is probably the most difficult of books to write, in any field. We can't presuppose that the reader or student will know anything at all about the subject. Yet we dare not be superficial in our treatment and leave the learner with only a host of vague impressions. To add to the normal difficulties, it's hard to take the work of a number of individuals and integrate that work into a whole that reflects a common philosophy and excellence.

Because I know how hard it is to do these things well, I have appreciated the opportunity to read this volume in manuscript. I've had the enriching pleasure of knowing several of the authors personally, and now the added pleasure of hearing their voices, speaking from the solid biblical perspective of restorationism.

A number of things about this *Introduction to Christian Education* invite approval. The authors have rightly seen that we must begin thinking about Christian education by exploring the nature of the church. Understanding the church—our relationship with Christ as its living head and with one another as members of God's family—is basic to effective educational ministry. Often in the body of the book beyond the initial chapters the authors return to related issues, and in these sections the work is uniformly excellent.

The authors have also shown consistent scholarship that is

fully aware of both historic and contemporary contributions to our understanding of educational ministry. Historical background is invariably provided where it is important to gain perspective, and each section shows a good choice of bibliographical material. Focusing on readings in these suggested resources, as the author suggests, is a good approach for conducting a course. The guidance the references provide will also be valuable to the local church practitioner.

One of the great tensions felt in the church today is never quite resolved, and probably cannot be. This is the tension between what is ... and what might be. Some will find the detailed examination of contemporary educational programs in the church troublesome; they will doubt that we can squeeze the wine of the theology the book espouses into the older wineskins of the contemporary institution. At the same time, revolutionary kinds of changes are seldom helpful and often harmful. It seems to me that the authors have wisely chosen to explore the potential for good of what *is*, and not to describe for this kind of work the "might be" we all dream of. Still, the tension does exist. And because many of us may have to continue to live with that tension, it is helpful to explore how to make the best of what is possible for us now.

I believe that we can expect more educational ministry taking place in neighborhood settings. These non-formal settings and their potential will require exploration, perhaps as another study by these same authors based on the same solid theological assumptions.

All in all, I am pleased to express my appreciation to Standard and to each of the authors for what is certainly one of the very best introductions to Christian education available.

Lawrence O. Richards

Contents

For the Teacher

Introduction to Christian Education is an overview of the educational task of the church. But it is more than an academic exercise—it is intended to be a practical primer in Christian education.

This book is a revision of a text that first appeared in 1980. The original book was the result of the efforts of seven writers who reflected their particular academic interests and practical experiences in their chapters. Despite their differences, these authors were consistent in demonstrating a strong biblical base for the practice of Christian education.

Though the principles set forth in the original edition remained sound and valuable to the Christian educator, it was time for revision and updating. Much of the book remains the same. Some chapters are totally new work. Other chapters have been expanded. One chapter was omitted. A few chapters have been placed in a different sequence in the book because the new position seems more logical. Bibliographies have been updated. All in all, however, the book presents the same basic approach to Christian education as the 1980 edition.

An introductory course in Christian education could use this text to accomplish three objectives:

1. Provide an overview to beginning students of what Christian education is and how it is accomplished.

2. Lay foundations for further study in Christian education.
3. Encourage students to understand how Christian education relates to their respective vocational choices.

The course could be divided into four sections corresponding to the four parts of the book: foundations, materials and methods, administration, and extra-church organizations.

The first part, Foundations of Christian Education, should emphasize precise definitions and identification of genuinely biblical education. Four to six weeks may be devoted to this section. This section may best be taught with readings and by having each student write a short paper examining the nature of teaching in the church.

Part Two, Materials and Methods for Christian Education, will require at least six weeks to develop. Projects coupled with readings will contribute to adequate expansion of this section. The projects suggested at the end of each chapter provide practice of concepts discussed in the chapter.

Audiovisual materials should be selected carefully to develop the concepts in the chapters on materials and methods. Training filmstrips from the International Center for Learning are helpful resources for this section. So are the films available from the National Training Institute and the videotapes from Lowell Brown Enterprises and the International Center for Learning. The teacher will also find helpful overhead transparencies and lesson plan forms in the "Training Successful Teachers" kit from Standard Publishing.

Involve the students in examining curriculum materials and preparing Bible lessons for various age levels. Demonstrate the wide variety of visuals available. A field trip to observe adequate buildings and facilities would add interest.

The third section, Administration of Christian Education, will require two or three weeks to develop. Practical projects, suggested at the end of each chapter, should be coupled with the readings. Assign interviews with educational leaders or invite a minister and a minister of education to share in a question-and-answer period in class.

The final section deals with extra-church organizations. Although the section is brief (a week or two will suffice), the reading is important. Another short paper on a topic of interest would be appropriate if time permits.

Building a Christian education file is a worthwhile term project. I require the student to set up his filing system and add at least a hundred items to it. A well-established file will be a valuable tool for the future.

Above all else, work at modeling effective teaching—the kind of teaching outlined in the text. Balance the course with reading, films, projects, discussion, outside resource people, and lecture. Help the student to experience effective teaching. He will teach in much the same way he has been taught.

Dr. Eleanor Daniel
Cincinnati Bible Seminary

Contributors

Eleanor Daniel is professor of Christian education at the Cincinnati Bible Seminary in Cincinnati, Ohio, teaching at both the graduate and undergraduate levels. Her academic credits include an A.B. and M.A. in Christian education from Lincoln Christian College and an Ed.M. and Ph.D. in educational psychology from the University of Illinois. She has served as minister of education in Ohio, Illinois, Michigan, and Oklahoma, and has taught at Midwest Christian College, Lincoln Christian College, and the University of Illinois.

Gerald Denny is a preaching minister in Urbana, Illinois. He holds the A.B. and M.A. degrees from Lincoln Christian College and an Ed.M. in educational psychology from the University of Illinois. He has served in educational ministries in Indiana, Illinois, and Georgia, and has taught for one year at Lincoln Christian College.

W. Edward Fine is minister of education at Central Christian Church, St. Petersburg, Florida. He holds an A.B. from Milligan College. He has also preached in Florida and has served as a public school administrator in Tennessee and Florida.

Charles Gresham is professor of Bible and Christian education at Kentucky Christian College, Grayson, Kentucky. His academic background includes an A.B. from Manhattan Christian College, and the M.R.E. and Ed.D. degrees from Southwestern Baptist Theological Seminary. He has preached and has served on the faculties of Midwest Christian College, Dallas Christian College, Manhattan Christian College, and Emmanuel School of Religion, in addition to Kentucky Christian College.

Ann Myers is an instructor in medical education at Southern Illinois University Medical School. She holds the B.S. and M.S. degrees from Illinois State University and has completed all but the dissertation for a Ph.D. in educational psychology at the University of Illinois. She has directed a ministry to the mentally handicapped at a church in Illinois.

Chris Templar is professor of Christian education at Johnson Bible College, Knoxville, Tennessee. Her academic credentials include the A.L.B.C. from London Bible College, B.D. from Trinity Evangelical Divinity School, and Ed.D. from Southern Baptist Theological Seminary. She has served as a Christian school teacher in the United States, a missionary in Indonesia, and a church worker in England.

John W. Wade is professor of Christian education at Atlanta Christian College, East Point, Georgia. He holds A.B. degrees from Cincinnati Bible College and Butler University and M.A. degrees from Southwest Christian Seminary and the University of Cincinnati. He previously taught at Cincinnati Bible College and served on the editorial staff of the Standard Publishing Company.

Part One

FOUNDATIONS OF CHRISTIAN EDUCATION

Section Outline

1. Beginning With the Church
   - A. The Nature of the Church
   - B. The Mission of the Church
   - C. The Church's Mission and the Teaching Task
   - D. The Church's Mission and Its Practical Application

2. The Bible Speaks: Biblical and Theological Foundations
   - A. The Nature of the Bible
   - B. The Bible and Christian Education
   - C. Biblical Theology as Content

3. The Lessons of History
   - A. Christian Education in the Early Church
   - B. Christian Education in the Medieval Church
   - C. Renaissance and Reformation
   - D. Christian Education in America
   - E. The Early Twentieth Century
   - F. The Current Scene

4. Communicating the Word to the World
   - A. Demographic Trends
   - B. Social Trends

5. Developing a Philosophy of Christian Education
   - A. Why a Philosophy of Christian Education?
   - B. Components of a Philosophy of Christian Education
   - C. Five Approaches to Christian Education

Christian education is not merely the use of methods. Nor is it limited to the Sunday morning Bible school. It is "the school of the church," giving careful consideration to all phases of the church's life and work. Even more, Christian education is "education for Christian living." As such, it should provide the necessary guidance for the total lifestyle of the Christian.

Since Christian education is crucially related to both the ministry of the church and the life of the individual Christian, it must be built upon secure foundations. These foundations not only undergird educational procedures, but they also provide the content and perspective of the total educational process.

The first section of this book explores the foundations that guide current educational programs and practices. The section begins with a discussion of the nature and mission of the church—the context of Christian education. It explores the biblical and historical information that relates to Christian education. The final chapters describe the present social scene, which affects the educational process, and set forth a beginning philosophy of Christian education.

Those who would give serious consideration to various phases of Christian education should realize that Christian education is more than *education*—that is, a process by which learning takes place. It is *Christian*—the process serves some greater purpose that is caught up in the meaning of the word "Christian." *Christian education* must be viewed from a particular perspective. This perspective is gained only from a study of these foundational areas.

CHAPTER 1

Beginning With the Church

As you read, think about these questions:
—What is meant by *church education?*
—What is the biblical understanding of the church's nature and purpose?
—How does our understanding of the church's nature and purpose help us in Christian nurture?
—What is meant by *institutionalization?*

Christian education is church education—that is, education that takes place in the church.

This important fact has often been overlooked. Historically, institutions other than the church (for example, the public school) were expected to do what only the church and home can do—educate for Christian living. Many parachurch organizations and other agencies that were originally established to nurture Christians (Sunday school and Christian Endeavor, for example) have tended to work parallel with the church rather than carry out the mission of the church. "Church work" has been too often given over to separate agencies rather than seen as the work of the church through these agencies.

Because of the influence of theological liberalism in the early part of this century, religious educators came to be influenced more by secular education than the Bible. Religious education came to have little relationship to the historic Christian faith, and its literature lacked sufficient biblical and theological emphasis. Such religious education became character education, bore little relationship to the church, and was "uninterested in exploring the biblical evidence for the rootage of teaching in the nature of the church."[1]

But the Bible is clear. It presents Jesus as the head of the church and both the builder and foundation of the church. This Jesus, after His death and resurrection (by which He made the church possible), sent the apostles into the world to preach and teach. Preaching would bring about obedient response and commitment, and teaching would ensure that obedient response and commitment would lead to spiritual maturity and growth. These two ministries became the effective means of the church's rapid growth throughout the inhabited world. "They never stopped teaching and proclaiming the good news that Jesus is the Christ," recorded Luke, the first church historian.[2]

If Christians are to be faithful to God, they must recognize that Christian education is a vital ministry of the church. But to take this educational ministry seriously, they must understand the nature and mission of the church as revealed through Scripture.

The Nature of the Church

Popular concepts of the church often have little relationship to what the New Testament reveals. Many think of the church as a physical building where certain meetings are held. But the New Testament doesn't even mention church buildings. When it does equate building to church, as Paul does in 1 Corinthians 3, it speaks figuratively. The church is God's building for which certain leaders have laid the foundation (in gospel preaching and through missionary outreach) and others have built on it (by continued preaching and teaching).

The prevalent concept of the church as hierarchical—that is, that its essence is seen in its ordained leadership—is just as erroneous. The idea that "where the bishop is, there is the church" is not found in the New Testament. This idea reached its zenith in the papacy of the Middle Ages, saddling the church with tradition and corruption that necessitated its reform.

Even the Reformation of the sixteen century was not complete. Though certain biblical insights were recovered, the acceptance of existing church-state relationships and other erroneous ideas led Protestantism to view the church in denominational terms. Though the church was no longer ruled over by the Roman bishop, it was now the Reformed Church of Switzerland or some other entity of a geographical or sectarian nature. The church was divided according to geography or adherence to certain religious tenets.

Over and against these concepts of the church's nature is the concept found in the New Testament. The church is Christ's. He is its head, founder, and authority. "On this rock [the truth of Jesus' messiahship and deity, confessed by Peter] I will build my church," Jesus proclaimed.[3] Paul, the great preacher and church-planter, acknowledges this fact: "And he [Christ] is the head of the body, the church; he is the beginning and the firstborn from among the dead, so that in everything he might have the supremacy."[4] The church centers in Christ, not in human leadership or sectarian creed.

But the church is made up of people. Peter, who first confessed Jesus to be the Christ and heard His answer, understood this. He wrote, "You also, like living stones, are being built into a spiritual house to be a holy priesthood, offering spiritual sacrifices acceptable to God through Jesus Christ. . . . But you are a chosen people, a royal priesthood, a holy nation, a people belonging to God, that you may declare the praises of him who called you out of darkness into his wonderful light. Once you were not a people, but now you are the people of God."[5]

The church is people. It is *personal*, not hierarchical or denominational. The Greek word *ecclesia*, translated "church," means an assembly of people, of "called-out-ones." The church is a community of persons who have submitted to the authority of Jesus Christ.

The New Testament also presents the church as people in *relationship*. When the church began in Jerusalem, Peter presented Jesus as Savior and Lord. When individuals obeyed Jesus Christ in baptism, they were "added to their number." This body of people continued in fellowship, as well as in the apostles' teaching, the breaking of bread and prayers.[6]

Fellowship means "partnership." The relationship is first vertical—"Our fellowship is with the Father and with his Son,

Jesus Christ," and then horizontal—"We proclaim to you what we have seen and heard, so that you also may have fellowship with us."[7] Paul wrote that all Christians are members of the one body and "should have equal concern for each other."[8] This relationship of caring and concern transcends all distinctions—racial, social, and sexual. "There is neither Jew nor Greek, slave nor free, male nor female, for you are all one in Christ Jesus."[9]

The Mission of the Church

The church is the body of Christ. It continues the servanthood of Jesus in this world. It responds to His direction for function and purpose. What Jesus Christ began to do, His church continues to do.

Jesus Christ, God's only Son, came in human flesh to accomplish what sinful man could never achieve for himself—redemption and reconciliation. The resurrection of His physical body is evidence of the reality of that atoning work. The church was created by outpouring and inspired direction of the Holy Spirit. It exists in order to "continue to do and teach" that which Jesus began. In response to Jesus Christ, the church carries forth His mission "to the ends of the earth" and "to the very end of the age."[10]

The risen Lord was specific about the nature and extent of that mission. In His appointment with the eleven disciples on a mountain in Galilee, He spoke in unequivocal terms:

> All authority in heaven and on earth has been given to me. Therefore go and make disciples of all nations, baptizing them in the name of the Father and of the Son and of the Holy Spirit, and teaching them to obey everything I have commanded you. And surely I will be with you always, to the very end of the age.[11]

The mission of the church is to make disciples of all nations. "Discipling"—as the process was carried out in the book of Acts—involved both preaching and teaching. The gospel was preached, and that "good news" was centered on Christ's redeeming work. Response was immediate. The inspired message brought conviction of sin, awakened and focused faith in Christ, and led to active obedience in baptism. Upon such faith and obedience, these disciples were "added to the church" and became partners with other believers in the community of faith.[12]

Within the fellowship of the Christian community, the believers devoted themselves to the apostles' teaching, which conveyed the Lord's commandments. When a person becomes a disciple of Christ, he enters into a new relationship as a son or daughter of the living God, a joint heir with Jesus Christ.[13] The disciple also becomes a willing, dutiful student who not only learns God's will, but also does God's will.[14]

The Church's Mission and the Teaching Task

The "Great Commission," by emphasizing teaching and nurture, sets the pattern for Christian education. It establishes the authority of the risen Jesus that underlies all Christian activity, and sets forth a program of enlistment and discipleship that emphasizes initial commitment and continued learning. The scope of Christian teaching is outlined by the statement, "teaching them to obey everything I have commanded you." Christian education is to include "the sum total of Christ's commandments concerning man's duty both to God and to man, and is to secure Christian action."[15]

The church's mission can be further seen by noting how the apostles carried it out. From the first, they recognized teaching as an important function. Disciples in Jerusalem continued in the apostles' teaching, and the apostles were accused by the Sanhedrin of filling Jerusalem with their teachings. Peter and John were teaching people in the temple and were commanded "not to speak or teach at all in the name of Jesus."[16] In spite of such warnings and threats, the apostles continued to teach: "Day after day, in the temple courts and from house to house, they never stopped teaching and proclaiming the good news that Jesus is the Christ."[17]

The apostle Paul also applied the term "teacher" to his calling.[18] Paul is shown to be teaching eleven times in the book of Acts. He presents himself as a teacher four times in his epistles. He and Barnabas taught at Antioch for a year, and they are mentioned in a group of "prophets and teachers" of the local church.[19] On his second missionary journey Paul remained in Corinth "a year and a half, teaching them the word of God."[20] He continued teaching for two years in the school of Tyrannus in Ephesus.[21] In his closing ministry in Rome, Paul lived for two years in a rented house, "and welcomed all who came to see him. Boldly and without hindrance he preached the kingdom of God and taught about the Lord Jesus Christ."[22]

The apostles themselves clearly stated how important teaching is. Paul lists pastors and teachers among the "gifts" given to the church by the risen Lord in order "to prepare God's people for works of service, so that the body of Christ may be built up."[23] A spiritual leader (an elder) must be "able to teach" and "must hold firmly to the trustworthy message as it has been taught, so that he can encourage others by sound doctrine and refute those who oppose it."[24] The spiritual leader must know the correct doctrine and be skillful in teaching it. Those who have proven their teaching ability are to be especially honored.[25]

As Paul's representative, Timothy was told to teach those in Ephesus. Timothy was to take "the things you have heard me say" from Paul, and entrust them to faithful men who "will also be qualified to teach others."[26] Such directives showed the place of teaching in the early church and also ensured that the task would be continued by future generations.

The Church's Mission and Its Practical Application

An understanding of the mission of the church is relevant to a study of the church's teaching function. Over the centuries, the church has tried various methods of carrying out this essential task.

At any given time in history, Christians fulfill essential tasks by developing certain programs and activities. These are often relevant, meaningful, and successful for a while, but historical and cultural changes occur and the programs become irrelevant and nonproductive. But by this time the programs have also become familiar and even cherished. Many people are not willing to change or eliminate them—they are considered "sacred" and treated not as expedients, but as essentials. As a result, what sociologists call *institutionalization* occurs.

Institutionalization generally develops in four stages. The first stage is that period when people are searching for a solution to the demands and needs of the moment. Once they agree upon a solution, the *institution* (the techniques, program, or organization that will solve the problem) is established. The second stage is the "efficiency stage," in which the potential values of the institution are realized. Steps are taken to preserve the original pattern intended by the group that established the institution. The third stage is formalism. Rules are established, chains of command developed, set forms or rituals developed, and material structures built to implement and maintain the institution. The fourth stage is one of disorganization, occurring when the mechanisms of the institution no longer work as originally intended. Individuals are little impressed by the ideals of the institution; they become indifferent and uncooperative. The original goals are no longer fulfilled and the institution is discarded or radically altered.

One can easily relate this overall pattern to the church. But while the church is transcultural and timeless, its institutions are not. At any given time and in any given culture, the church produces agencies, programs, and techniques (institutions) to accomplish its universal and eternal tasks. These institutions should never become ends in themselves or be confused with the nature of the church. Since they are all man-made and culturally determined (including Sunday school and evangelistic techniques), they should always be "subjected to continuous rigorous sociological and theological analysis to determine their effectiveness as instruments of the church."[27]

In this way, the church's nature is not confused with a particular method of fulfilling its purpose within a given cultural and historical context. The church itself, the fellowship of God's people, must be the norm by which all expedients are judged, according to Snyder:

> In the final analysis, church structure is a question of the community of God's people using their God-given intelligence and creativity to manufacture useful tools to help extend the Church's witness, while always remembering that these man made tools stand under God's judgment and must never be worshiped.[28]

An understanding of the nature and mission of the church is essential for the development of relevant strategies and the avoidance of institutionalization. The church is God's instrument for bringing His world back under His sovereignty. It was meant to penetrate every society, throw down every evil stronghold, and bring people spiritually captive to the Lord of hosts. The church must strive to employ a strategy that He will honor and bless by productive results.

Gene Getz suggests that such a strategy can be developed only when the strategy is founded on sound principles. Three "lenses" are suggested to correct the blurred vision of the present church's ministry. One is the "lens of history," which reveals the past efforts of Christendom and the tragic failures of institutionalization. Another is the "lens of contemporary culture," which provides understanding of today's world and implications for the church's ministry in it. The third and most important lens is the "lens of Scripture," which sets forth the nature of the church, its mission in the world, and basic principles governing the essential tasks of the church's mission. Getz concludes:

> Once we develop a proper perspective biblically, historically, and culturally, we must develop a contemporary strategy based particularly on New Testament principles; we must determine current needs in our own local church, formulate relevant objectives and goals, devise contemporary forms and structures, and use every legitimate resource to be a New Testament church in contemporary culture.[29]

Summary

Christian education is the teaching function of the church. It can be understood only within the context of the church. It has validity only if the church is a nurturing community. The church *is* that kind of community. It must teach, just as it must preach, if it is to be like the church revealed in the New Testament. Any church that neglects teaching has lost something indispensable to its nature as a church. However, the church is also defective when it allows the structures and methods by which it attempts to teach to become institutional idols. The church is *people*, not programs. Such people, however, must use their God-given talent to devise programs in order to achieve the divine purposes for which they exist. This is the proper order—divine *purpose*, committed *people*, practical and relevant *programs*.

Christian education begins with the church.

Selected Bibliography

Allen, Roland. *The Spontaneous Expansion of the Church*. Grand Rapids, MI: Wm. B. Eerdmans Publishing Co., 1962.

Costas, Orlando. *The Church and Its Mission: A Shattering Critique From the Third World*. Wheaton, IL: Tyndale House Publishers, 1974.

Ellis, David J. and W. Ward Gasque. *In God's Community: Essays on the Church and Its Ministry*. Wheaton, IL: Harold Shaw, 1978.

Ellis, Joe S. *The Church on Purpose*. Cincinnati, OH: Standard Publishing, 1982.

________. *The Church on Target*. Cincinnati, OH: Standard Publishing, 1986.

Fallaw, Wesner. *Church Education for Tomorrow*. Philadelphia: Westminster Press, 1960.

Getz, Gene. *Sharpening the Focus of the Church*. Chicago: Moody Press, 1974.

Grimes, Howard. *The Church Redemptive*. Nashville, TN: Abingdon Press, 1958.

Murch, James DeForest. *Christian Education in the Local Church*. Cincinnati, OH: Standard Publishing, 1943.

Richards, Lawrence O. *A New Face for the Church*. Grand Rapids, MI: Zondervan Publishing House, 1970.

Smart, James D. *The Teaching Ministry of the Church*. Philadelphia: Westminster Press, 1954.

Snyder, Howard A. *The Community of the King*. Downers Grove, IL: Inter-Varsity Press, 1977.

---

[1]James D. Smart, *The Teaching Ministry of the Church* (Philadelphia: Westminster Press, 1954), p. 12.

[2]Acts 5:42

[3]Matthew 16:18

[4]Colossians 1:18

[5]1 Peter 2:5, 9, 10

[6]Acts 2:41, 42

[7]1 John 1:3

[8]1 Corinthians 12:25

[9]Galatians 3:28
[10]Acts 1:8; Matthew 28:20
[11]Matthew 28:18-20
[12]See Acts 2:24-42 and other examples throughout the book of Acts.
[13]Galatians 3:26-28; John 1:12
[14]Matthew 7:24-27; James 1:22-27
[15]James DeForest Murch, *Christian Education in the Local Church* (Cincinnati, OH: Standard Publishing, 1943), p. 39.
[16]Acts 4:18
[17]Acts 5:42
[18]2 Timothy 1:11
[19]Acts 11:26; 13:1
[20]Acts 18:11
[21]Acts 19:9, 10
[22]Acts 28:30, 31
[23]Ephesians 4:11, 12
[24]1 Timothy 3:2: Titus 1:9
[25]1 Timothy 5:17
[26]2 Timothy 2:2
[27]Taken from *The Community of the King* by Howard A. Snyder. © 1977 by Inter-Varsity Christian Fellowship of the USA and used by permission of Inter-Varsity Press.
[28]*Ibid.*, p. 168.
[29]From *Sharpening the Focus of the Church* by Gene Getz. Copyright 1974, Moody Press, Moody Bible Institute of Chicago. p. 18. Used by permission.

CHAPTER 2

The Bible Speaks: Biblical and Theological Foundations

As you read, think about these questions:
—What is the nature of the Bible?
—What is meant by "The Bible is a revelation of reality"?
—How is the Bible revelative, normative, and foundational to Christian education?
—How is the Bible significant for educational content?

The personal nature of the church and its authority can be understood only through the Bible. The Bible alone reveals the Word of God—living in Jesus and proclaimed by His apostles. The Bible is the Word of God written or "inscripturated." To understand this is crucial to the church's educational task.

The Nature of the Bible

The Bible and Revelation

All revelation can be described by the biblical phrase, "the Word of God." Even what is termed "natural revelation" is a result of the Word of God, for when God initiated the creative process He did so by His Word. In the beginning, God said, "Let there be light;" God said, "Let the earth bring forth living creatures." And it was so. The psalmist poetically described God's creation as speaking about God:

The heavens declare the glory of God;
  the skies proclaim the work of his hands.
Day after day they pour forth speech;
  night after night they display knowledge. . . .
Their voice goes out into all the earth,
  their words to the ends of the world.[1]

The apostle Paul maintained that the world of nature clearly reveals God to mankind: "Since the creation of the world God's invisible qualities—his eternal power and divine nature—have been clearly seen, being understood from what has been made, so that men are without excuse."[2]

God has spoken not only in what has been created for man, but in man himself. The word of decision was spoken: "Let us make man in our image, in our likeness." Then God created man, "and man became a living being."[3]

Jesus Christ is the key even to this revelation through nature, for He is that Word who was with God and who was God, through whom all things were made.[4] "He is the image of the invisible God . . . By him all things were created: things in heaven and on earth, visible and invisible, whether thrones or powers or rulers or authorities; all things were created by him and for him."[5]

But God's special revelation is focused in Jesus Christ. In the Old Testament Scriptures we see God speaking "to our forefathers through the prophets at many times and in various ways," but in the New Testament Scriptures, He is speaking "by his Son."[6] The message of the Bible is God's drama of redemption. It begins with Adam, who acted disobediently, and concludes with the new Adam, whose obedient act removed the penalty of the first Adam's disobedience. God called a people to produce a community of faith through whom the oft promised Son would be born. Later God entered into a covenant with them through the mediation of Moses. When they violated the covenant, He promised a new covenant to be mediated through one greater than Moses. In this drama of redemption, God set forth a law having both moral and ceremonial aspects, to show how sinful man is. But "when the time had fully come" He sent His own Son, "born of a woman, born under law"[7] so that He might redeem all people by a sacrifice given once for all not upon a stone altar, but upon a Roman cross.

This drama, set forth on the stage of human history, is revealed in the Bible. The Bible is God's revelation, His self-disclosure. As such, the Bible is a trustworthy and adequate bearer of His revelation. Apart from the Bible we would not know that this special disclosure had occurred. The Bible is, therefore, the *indispensable* means of special revelation. (The Bible, however, does not record every event in the life of Israel, the life of Christ, or the church. As John says of his Gospel, "Jesus did many other miraculous signs in the presence of his disciples, which are not recorded in this book."[8] The same could be said of any other part of the Bible.)

The Bible is the special revelation of God put in permanent form. It records both God's deeds and God's words in understandable human words. The Word is there in the words of Scripture. Carl F. H. Henry writes:

> In the sense that Scripture sets before us both God's acts and words, saving events together with their meaning, special revelation becomes equivalent to the Bible. . . . This identification of written sentences and propositions with the special divine revelation—the recognition, that is, of the Word in the form of words—evangelical Christianity held to be not merely the historic Christian view, but an indispensable element in a proper biblical theology.[9]

There is no contradiction between the Word as written and the Word as personal. Though a book is not a person, a book often expresses a person's will, nature, or purpose. In a written record, the history of persons and events are captured and held, making the record both indispensable and authoritative.

The Bible and Inspiration

Revelation has to do with disclosure of content. Inspiration has to do with the guidance of those who are used by God in the revelatory process. "Men spoke from God as they were carried along by the Holy Spirit" is the way Peter describes this process.[10] Paul declares that "all Scripture is God-breathed and is useful for teaching, rebuking, correcting and training in righteousness, so that the man of God may be thoroughly equipped for every good work."[11] Here, Paul relates divine guidance ("God-breathedness") to the product—Scripture! Such guidance guarantees the authority and the benefit of these sacred writings. The writings are trustworthy because the content is disclosed by God and because the method of disclosure is peculiarly guided by the Spirit of God.

Both Peter and Paul referred to the Old Testament when they wrote about the authority of Scripture. Evidence points to the same kind of divine guidance for the New Testament. Jesus promised the apostles the Spirit of truth who would guide them into all truth.[12] The book of Acts presents the apostles as being guided in word and action by the Spirit. Paul was aware that he wrote by the power of the Spirit: "We have not received the spirit of the world but the Spirit who is from God, that we may understand what God has freely given us. This is what we speak, not in words taught us by human wisdom but in words taught by the Spirit."[13]

The Bible is the inspired Word of God. It reveals God's redemptive purpose for man as worked out in human history. Great redemptive acts, such as the exodus of Israel from Egypt and the achievements of Israel, are related and explained. This history reveals God's relationship first to a family (Abraham's), then to a nation (Israel), and finally to a person coming from that family and nation (Jesus of Nazareth), who is revealed as God incarnate. But the Bible is more than history, for it shows that the Lord of history has broken into history to manifest His power and purpose. This divinely disclosed content is our basis for understanding what God's people are to be and do in this present age.

The Bible and Christian Education

Christian education, as Sara Little asserts, "is a servant and not a master of revelation." Biblical revelation determines the educational task and guides the educational process. Since the Bible functions as the primary source and the only inerrant criterion for truth, all presumed facts and opinions must be tested by the inspired writings.

The Bible reveals reality, not mere abstract ideas. This reality demands a response. Lawrence O. Richards writes that God's truth must be heard as more than a message requiring only assent; when God's Word is seen as "a revelation of reality," human beings must come to terms with that reality. When an issue "involves a reconstruction of our understanding of reality, our way of living must also change."[14] Reality-orientation determines one's actions, as Richards illustrates:

> It is because of our reality-orientation that we look for doors to enter buildings rather than try to walk through walls. It is because of reality-orientation that we hesitate to cross the street in the face of onrushing traffic. Our perception of reality tells us that we cannot walk into walls without bruising and that a mistake in gauging the speed and distance on an oncoming automobile is likely to be our last mistake. *When we are fully convinced that something is rooted in reality, we modify our behavior to harmonize with it.*[15]

The truth of this view is apparent in the social and moral realm as well. Adoption of the "playboy philosophy" regarding sexual behavior follows one's assumption that man is mere animal. The use of falsehood, deception, or other purely manipulative devices in human relations is the result of perceiving human beings as things, or means to ends, not as persons who are ends in themselves. Richards is right: "Our response to people, to situations, to all of life, is based ultimately on our whole-person (conceptual and affective) orientation to reality."[16]

If the biblical revelation has come from God who created and ordered all things, then that revelation is by nature a revelation of reality. Reality is not the result of man's construction, but of God's creation. The most accurate perceptions of reality, then, come as man's attempts at understanding are guided by the revealed Word of God. Such perceptions demand decision. The Christian who perceives reality guided by the revelation of God must live in harmony with it.

An understanding of the nature of biblical revelation has tremendous implications for the Christian educator. Biblical revelation is normative and foundational; that is, it sets the standards and provides a basis for all Christian education, including both the content that is taught and the methods by which it is taught. All educational factors must be in keeping with the reality presented in the Bible.

The Bible must be seen as a reality picture, not just as true information. Scripture must be presented as a revelation of reality that confronts one with choices in response to it.

This approach to Scripture can be summarized as follows:

1. God's Word in Scripture must always be understood as a revelation of reality.

2. God's Word must be taught requiring a decision, to produce action that is in harmony with the reality it reveals.[17]

Secular education (and too often, what has been called religious or Christian education) is designed to communicate information as "truth to be believed," not as a reality demanding decision. This information-oriented teaching/learning process does not deal with *values*, the "what is important to me" issue on which most accept or reject various points of view. The reality-oriented process does raise such issues.

Only an approach to teaching/learning that seeks to deal with learners' values in a context of open, honest, and loving personal relationships (as are provided in the Christian home and the fellowship of the church) is likely to bring learners to accept and live by the reality revealed in Scripture.

Biblical Theology as Content

The Bible is the standard for the approach taken in Christian education and the content of Christian education. In the Bible we find factual information that becomes the content of Christian teaching, but this information is not necessarily presented in systematic form. To collect, collate, systematize, understand, and apply biblical data is the task of the biblical theologian. Biblical theology is the result. These biblical concepts, thus arranged, become the basic content from which a curriculum for Christian education is developed.

Biblical revelation begins with *God* as Creator—perfect, self-revealing, loving, and saving. It involves *man*, created in God's image, but fallen from that perfect state and in need of redemption and reorientation of his life and thought. The Bible further reveals *Jesus, the incarnate Son of God*, who came into the world of reality to provide a real way out of man's predicament by His own atoning life, death, and resurrection. It reveals the *church*, a family of families, in which worship, fellowship, nurture, and outreach are the essential tasks and relationships of this new community of faith set in the world to accomplish God's purposes.

The Biblical Concept of God

God is revealed in Scripture as Creator, Lord, and Redeemer. His triune nature as Father, Son, and Spirit is seen, not as the basis of speculative philosophy, but in His actions towards man, the crown of His creation. The Father created man in love and for fellowship, but His creation rebelled and sinned against Him. The Son came into the world as a man, as a servant, to redeem and reconcile mankind by His own sacrificial death. The Son was raised from the dead; through the Holy Spirit, He created the church, through which the ultimate purpose of God is to be accomplished. The Spirit led apostolic witnesses into all truth and inspired authentic gospel preaching and Christian teaching. He indwells and energizes individual believers in the body of Christ, the church.

This triune God created man, redeemed man, provided revelation for man, and became an example and substitute for man so that sin may be overcome in man's life. God commands His people to teach and nurture their children so that they may live obediently in relation to Him. He has created the nurturing contexts of family and church to carry out this process.

The Biblical Concept of Man

Man is revealed in Scripture as separate from all other created beings because he alone is created in God's image. Man is created to subdue and rule his world. Man is created male and female. Human sexuality is part of that goodness pronounced by God upon His work. Man is created for fellowship—the human fellowship of family and society, and divine fellowship with God.

But man has succumbed to temptation, sinned against God, and fallen from his high position. Such sin, through prideful autonomy, has affected all of humanity and the material world as well. Alienation and separation have become universal human experiences both in relation to God and in relation to others. As a sinner, man stands in need of a Redeemer. Because he is flawed from God's original intention, man is in need of a perfect example.

In the perfect manhood of Jesus, the incarnate Son of God, man's need is met, man's sin atoned for, and man's broken fellowship restored. It is in Jesus that flawed humanity sees its perfect pattern and goal. Christian teaching is designed to bring prodigals "to themselves" and speed them on the way home to the Father to live as redeemed children.

The Biblical Concept of Salvation

Salvation is the theme of the biblical drama. Sin has ruined the human race. It must be overcome. But man, the sinner, cannot save himself; salvation can come only from the gracious God of love. The initiative was taken by God through the election of a family, a race, a nation. God set in motion the series of historical events we read about in the Old Testament. A covenant of law and words bound the nation of Israel to God.

But the covenant was temporary. A new covenant of grace, forgiveness, and loving relationship was promised. That new relationship was made possible by a Savior, Christ the Lord, coming into the world as the incarnate Son of God, born of a virgin. This person grew to manhood, gave himself to a messianic ministry of healing and service, and voluntarily went to His death on a cross to bear the sins of all who would accept Him as Savior and Lord. The resurrection of this dead Jesus gave assurance that His atoning work has been accepted by the Father. With His ascension into Heaven, Jesus began His mediatorial and intercessory work as high priest, "able to save completely those who come to God through him."[18] This same Jesus will come a second time and gather His own from the four corners of the earth—the resurrected dead and the living who will be instantly changed[19]—to enjoy eternity with God.

But such salvation is not "cheap grace." The life of the Christian is a sanctified life in which holiness is demanded. Within the church, by means of the indwelling Spirit, the saved individual is to be a servant, a minister using the gifts he has been given to witness to others in word and deed about this great salvation.

Christian ethics is more than do-goodism. James Smart is right in his keen criticism of Christian education programs that perpetuate a "suffocating fog of moralism:"

> The Christian standard of conduct is not a natural possibility for any person; it is a supernatural possibility, to be realized only through the redemptive power of Jesus Christ working in human persons through the gospel. Therefore, to impress upon a child or youth or adult his duty to fulfill the Christian standard, to

> leave him ignorant of the truth of the gospel which alone makes him aware how that standard is to be fulfilled, is as absurd and exasperating as to order a man to shovel two feet of snow from a hundred feet of sidewalk and give him no shovel with which to do it. Moralism bores us because it confronts us with an impossibility. By the very nature of things, ethics are always insecure until they are firmly rooted in our understanding of truth.[20]

The Biblical Concept of the Church and Its Ministry

The church is revealed in the New Testament Scriptures as the community of the disciples of Jesus Christ, who have found peace and pardon from their sins. Entered by obedience to Jesus Christ, the partnership with God demands gratitude expressed in worship and service. It is a "gathered fellowship" to worship, learn, and grow in grace; it is a "scattered fellowship" to preach, teach, and serve.

Each Christian must minister in Christ's stead. The *foundational* ministry of the church includes all of God's people. But this ministry of the church is also *functional*. It involves various tasks—preaching, teaching, serving. Every Christian is not equipped to do *all* of these tasks. A variety of service gifts have been given by the one Spirit.[21] Each Christian is to minister, discovering and using his gift to glorify God and help the church grow. The church also has a *formal* ministry, an equipping ministry, revealed in the Scriptures. The Lord gave us apostles and prophets in apostolic days to provide the authoritative word of witness. He also gave us evangelists, pastors, and teachers in every age to share that Word with those without and within the fellowship.[22]

Summary

Through Christian teaching, God's revelation of reality is grasped and lives are changed to conform to reality. Through the teaching ministry of the church, lives are enriched and individuals are equipped to further the church's ministry in the world. Through Christian nurture, both within Christian families and the greater family of God, young people are led to faithful commitment to Jesus Christ and introduced into an ever-continuing cycle of outreach and growth. The biblical revelation of reality is the indispensable source and authoritative guide by which such Christian nurture occurs.

Selected Bibliography

Cully, Iris V. *Imparting the Word*. Philadelphia: Westminster Press, 1963.

Gaebelein, Frank. *The Pattern of God's Truth*. New York: Oxford University Press, 1954.

Henry, Carl F. H. (ed.). *Revelation and the Bible*. Grand Rapids, MI: Baker Book House, 1958.

LeBar, Lois E. *Education That Is Christian*. Westwood, NJ: Revell, 1958.

Richards, Lawrence O. *Youth Ministry: Its Renewal in the Local Church*. Grand Rapids, MI: Zondervan Publishing House, 1972.

Smart, James D. *The Teaching Ministry of the Church*. Philadelphia: Westminster Press, 1958.

Walker, Dean E. *The Authority of the Word*. Milligan College, TN: Milligan College, 1950.

Walvoord, John W. (ed.). *Inspiration and Interpretation*. Grand Rapids, MI: Wm. B. Eerdmans Publishing Co., 1957.

---

[1]Psalm 19:1, 2, 4
[2]Romans 1:20
[3]Genesis 1:26; 2:7
[4]John 1:1-3
[5]Colossians 1:15, 16
[6]Hebrews 1:1, 2
[7]Galatians 4:4
[8]John 20:30
[9]John W. Walvoord (ed.), *Inspiration and Interpretation* (Grand Rapids, MI: Wm. B. Eerdmans Publishing Co., 1957), p. 256.
[10]2 Peter 1:21
[11]2 Timothy 3:16, 17
[12]John 16:13
[13]1 Corinthians 2:12, 13
[14]YOUTH MINISTRY: ITS RENEWAL IN THE LOCAL CHURCH by Lawrence O. Richards. Copyright © 1972 by The Zondervan Corporation. p. 177. Used by permission.
[15]*Ibid.*, p. 178.
[16]*Ibid.*
[17]*Ibid.*, p. 182.
[18]Hebrews 7:25
[19]1 Thessalonians 4:13-17; 1 Corinthians 15:51, 52
[20]From *The Teaching Ministry of the Church*, by James D. Smart, p. 79. Copyright © MCMLIV by Walter L. Jenkins. Used by permission of The Westminster Press.
[21]Romans 12; 1 Corinthians 12
[22]Ephesians 4:7-13

CHAPTER 3

The Lessons of History

As you read, think about these questions:
—What are the three important institutions for Christian teaching in the early church?
—Why are the Renaissance and Reformation important to Christian education?
—Describe the strong religious emphasis in early American education.
—How influential was the Sunday school movement upon Christian education in the nineteenth century?
—What is meant by the term *church school?*
—Why is Christian education important to the local church?

Wherever there is a vital, dynamic religion, there is religious education. Such a religion establishes types of "schools" by which it can teach its basic beliefs and expected behaviors. The Christian community was, and is, a living religion. It demanded an educational ministry in the first century, and when it has been truest to its basic principles, it has demanded education throughout its history.

A historical study of Christian education provides a perspective for understanding the nature and practice of church education. It shows how, throughout history, the leaders of the Christian religion responded to the need for education in a way suitable to both their religion and their culture. One can learn what the men and women of different periods of Christian history felt was essential to perpetuate the faith. One can distill from their words and actions what objectives governed their teaching. The need for more effective nurture becomes apparent as the study progresses.

Christian Education in the Early Church

The biblical mandate to teach has been essential to the Judeo-Christian heritage since the time of Abraham. Such teaching was centered in the *family.* When other educational emphases were added through the specific provisions of covenant-law, the family continued to be the center. The temple, priests, rituals, symbolic feasts and fasts, and other matters were supplemental. Even after the exile and the dispersion of Jews throughout the Mediterranean world, the family continued to be the supreme educator. The family was the driving force of such new agencies as the synagogue and the late developing synagogue school of the first century B.C.

This strong emphasis upon religious education, carried on generation after generation in family, synagogue, and school, is a significant part of the historical and religious context of Jesus and the apostles. Jesus himself was a teacher. He was more, of course; but He was known to His contemporaries as *Rabbi,* Teacher. His methods were educational, not oratorical. His final command to His apostles was to "go and make disciples of all nations, . . . teaching them to obey everything I have commanded you."[1] The apostles taught as well as preached. Spiritual leaders were to be "able to teach,"[2] so that the instruction would be continued from generation to generation.

A second institution was the *worship service* in which the entire Christian community participated. Patterned after the synagogue service, the apostolic church strongly emphasized teaching and prayer. The apostles understood worship in teaching terms, not aesthetic terms. Even the Lord's Supper contributed to this teaching emphasis. The observance of the Lord's Supper was a teaching tool, a memorial, to spur remembrance and continued understanding of Jesus' redemptive work.

The service of worship grew in length and complexity

throughout the early Christian centuries. From the second century on it had two differentiated segments. The first of these was known as the *missa catechumenous*, or the mass of the catechumens. This was a teaching service patterned after the synagogue service of Judaism. Persons who were receiving instruction prior to baptism, known as catechumens, were allowed to participate in this portion of the service. It included the reading and interpretation of Scripture. These catechumens were known as "hearers." After this segment of the worship service, the "hearers" were dismissed and the baptized believers remained for the *missa fidelium*, the mass of the faithful. Here the Lord's Supper was celebrated.

The third institution, necessitated by a growing pagan influx, was the *catechumenate* that flourished in the early church from the second to the fifth centuries. Great numbers of adults from pagan backgrounds were attracted to the church by what they saw and heard. They were prepared neither morally nor intellectually for the demands of the Christian faith. The catechumenate, an adult education program, was devised to meet this need. There seems to have been a threefold purpose for this informal educational program: "to provide a period of moral probation during which the candidate's sincerity could be tested; to give instruction on the Bible and the doctrines of the church; and to admit the candidate into a limited but genuine Christian fellowship while he was preparing for baptism."[3] This program was related to the worship service, as described above, but careful instruction was often given at other times, either individually or in groups. (Pantaeus, the great Alexandrian teacher, speaks of coming to his Christian faith at "the rude bench of the catechumen.")

Origen described one program in Alexandria about A.D. 250. It followed these steps: (1) a preliminary examination of the candidate's moral character and occupation (many occupations were forbidden to Christians); (2) private instruction given to each candidate as seemed necessary; (3) admittance to and participation in the service of worship as a "hearer;" (4) additional instruction outside the worship services in informal classes; (5) further inquiry into the growth and development of the candidate, intellectually and morally; and (6) intensive instruction prior to baptism and church membership. Such programs varied from area to area.

Christian Education in the Medieval Church

From the middle of the fifth century until the beginning of the sixteenth century, Christian education languished. Several factors contributed to this dearth. The clergy began to dominate more and more, and little individual responsibility of the laity was stressed. Along with the growing practice of infant baptism, this trend undermined such an educational program as the catechumenate. The union of state and church tended to eliminate high moral and intellectual standards, since it erased any important differences between believers and unbelievers. Then, too, the dissolution of the Roman Empire under the deluge of barbarianism created an instability detrimental to educational development both in the church and in society. The institutional church continued to exist and even to "Christianize" the barbaric tribes, but Christian education suffered enormously. When Christian education waned, so did the church.

Yet the light of learning was not completely extinguished during those dark ages. Pockets of concern for education continued to exist in various parts of Europe. Charles the Great of Frankland and, later, Alfred of England attempted educational reforms that had beneficial effect, though mostly for the religious and civic leadership of the day. But even the laity received some informal Christian education. They observed and participated in worship, learning some parts of the service such as the creed, the Lord's Prayer, and the *Ave Maria*. Beginning in the tenth century, they watched religious drama that portrayed certain biblical and theological themes. As a result, a sort of popular theology developed that combined Christian doctrine and superstition.

These types of informal, popular Christian education contributed little to the spiritual growth of Christendom, but there was unprecedented institutional and hierarchical growth during this period.

For the nobility there were formal schools. Monastic orders established schools to prepare novices for monastic life. In certain areas, these schools were opened to the sons and daughters of nobility. Cathedral schools developed at the center of the diocese primarily for the training of priests, though these were often open to sons of noblemen as well. The curriculum in these schools centered around the traditional seven liberal arts: grammar, rhetoric, and logic composing the trivium; and arithmetic, music, geometry, and astronomy making up the quadrivium. To these were added theology and, in some instances, canon and civil law and medicine.

The general level of knowledge declined steadily, however, especially the study of Scripture, which was supplanted by a study of theology. Ignorance began to feed ignorance in terms of scriptural instruction.

Toward the close of the twelfth century, certain of the cathedral schools developed into medieval universities as they freed themselves from diocesan control through a guildlike organization of teachers and students. Such universities as Paris, Bologna, Oxford, and Cambridge gave birth to many other similar institutions during the later Renaissance period.

Many of the students at these universities were of the clergy. Unfortunately few of the clergy as a whole had been educated at the university level. As a result, the priesthood became woefully ignorant. For example, in 1222, only five of seventeen priests serving under the Cathedral of Salisbury could read the first sentence in the first prayer of the Canon of the Mass. Those who did attend the university had a strong liberal arts background, heavy emphasis in church tradition, and little or no Scripture. It was not until the Reformation that significant change could be seen. Even so, higher education began to become part of the tradition of Christian education.

Renaissance and Reformation

The Renaissance, beginning in the latter part of the thirteenth century, left an indelible mark on education in general. This "revival" or "rebirth" laid the foundation for the humanistic tradition in education. It exalted the individual, quickened interest in this world as well as the next, and recovered the ancient languages and the classical literature of Greece and Rome. It was a secular movement, in the main "stressing the delights of living, the ideal of liberty, the free exercise of criticism, and, among those who found Christian morality too binding, a freedom from moral restraints."[4]

Along with the Reformation, the Renaissance caused great

ferment in continental Europe, which penetrated every phase of life. The monolithic power of the Roman Church was broken, nationalism became the order of the day, and individualism grew quickly. The Reformation was distinctly religious, though certainly influenced by the Renaissance (particularly the Christian Renaissance of the North associated with Richard Groote and the Brothers of Common Life). Educationally, the Renaissance and Reformation established the humanistic tradition: Christian education must be concerned with human life, its past development and present opportunities, as well as with theology and ecclesiastical concerns.

The Reformation set forth three basic principles that have had far-reaching consequences in education. The first was the replacement of papal authority with the authority of the Scriptures. The second was the doctrine of "the priesthood of every believer," which stressed individual responsibility before God. The third principle, derived from the first two, demanded universal education. If each individual is responsible to God, he must understand that responsibility in terms of the Word. The Word could be understood only by those who were educated.

Martin Luther, Ulrich Zwingli, John Calvin, and other Reformation leaders encouraged civic leaders to establish schools for both boys and girls. In 1524, Luther addressed a letter to the Mayors and Councillors of all the German cities, urging the establishment of such schools both for the edification of the church and the advancement of civic life. John Bugenhagen, a colleague of Luther, led in the establishment of vernacular primary schools (schools conducted in the native language, not Latin) in northern German parishes. Phillipp Melanchthon, who served with Luther on the faculty of the University of Wittenberg, was instrumental in the establishment and upgrading of secondary education at the grammar school and university levels, where Christian humanism became the content of the curriculum.

In Switzerland, John Calvin was moving along the same lines as the Lutherans. In 1538, he proposed a plan for the school system of Geneva that began with elementary vernacular schools open to all. Secondary schools, called "colleges," were to be established; in these, humanistic and religious studies could be combined so that leaders for both state and church could be trained. John Knox, following Calvin's lead, encouraged the establishment of schools in Scotland based upon this plan. Comparable programs developed in the Netherlands, where Calvinism was also prominent. Thus the two great branches of the Protestant Reformation—Lutheranism and Calvinism—stressed the importance of Christian education.

Not only did the Reformation demand and develop a system of universal Christian education, but it also aided education by translating Scriptures into the vernacular and distributing these as widely as possible. Such translations were read in church, used in the home, and studied in the schools. The reformers recovered the lost art of preaching with the Bible as the basic content. They also began preaching in the language of the people. Such preaching brought revival and renewal to a church dying in formalism.

The recovery of biblical Christianity also led to reestablishment of the home as a center of education, as it had been in apostolic times. Here the Bible and catechisms based upon the Bible (like Luther's Shorter Catechism) were used to instruct children and youth in the basic tenets of the faith. Such home teaching was especially strong among the Dutch, the Scots, and the English Puritans.

Christian Education in America

American Colonial Education

The dominant educational theory and practice of American colonialism was transplanted from Europe. The English cavaliers of the southern American colonies brought the pattern of Anglicanism, which centered education in the family. Families provided for their children in tuition schools or by a tutor in the home, if they could; children of poor families received little educational opportunity.

In New England, Calvinistic Puritanism led to the establishment of elementary schools in every township, after the Calvinistic pattern. In addition, secondary education was also established with Latin grammar schools in the larger towns and the establishment of Harvard College in 1636. In New England, the religious impulse was strong, and there was church-state cooperation in bringing the schools into existence.

In the middle colonies, the diversity of the religious groups limited the provisions. Each religious group (many with different ethnic and language backgrounds—Dutch, Swedish, Moravian, English Catholic, English Quaker) provided whatever education it could in a parochial pattern. Since there was no impetus by the state or civil governments, as in New England, such provisions were frequently minimal.

Post-Revolutionary Developments

Independence from England and the formation of a new nation brought changes to the patterns of education that had developed among the colonies. The principle of the separation of church and state in the first amendment of the Constitution (especially as the principle was later espoused in state constitutions) eliminated the government support of particular religious groups. The principle was to have far-reaching consequences for American education, particularly Christian education.

Beginning in New England, where universal education was already an established pattern, the states one by one developed a system of public schools. But since these schools were open to all, the elimination of sectarian teaching (teaching that would favor one church group over another) resulted in "secularization," which meant "the withdrawal of the support from private and church schools and the elimination of religious controls over the public schools."[5] State after state wrote provisions into their constitutions prohibiting the use of tax funds for private or parochial schools.

Thus the churches could no longer depend upon the public schools to teach their particular religious tenets. The alternative was to continue to maintain a system of parochial schools supported by church funds (as the Roman Catholics, many Lutheran groups, and other smaller groups did), or to find some way to provide for the teaching of religion and the instilling of their specific beliefs and practices. Fortunately, the Sunday school had been introduced into American life, and these schools became the formal instrument by which most American Protestant groups were able to continue their religious instruction.

The Sunday School Movement

The origin of the Sunday school is attributed to Robert

Raikes, a reform-minded journalist of Gloucester, England, who became concerned about the plight of poor children who had no educational opportunities. In 1780, he began to collect these youngsters on Sunday (the only day they were free from work responsibilities) in order to give them general instruction. His "noble experiment" proved successful, and soon was repeated throughout Great Britain with tremendous results. Sunday school societies were established to aid these schools by paying the teachers and providing funds for curriculum materials.

These early schools were conducted throughout the day on Sunday, with time out to participate in religious services. Instruction in reading, writing, and arithmetic were combined with study of the Bible and the catechism. As *Time*, August 25, 1980, observed: "If they used the Bible it was a means to learn reading. And if they met on Sunday, that was because it was the only day they had free. For Raikes' proteges were children of England's new industrial poor. They had no schools. Six days a week, starting at age seven, they worked in the local pin mills, sometimes for 15 hours a day."

The Sunday school was transplanted to America as early as 1785, first as a charity school like its forerunner in England. The First Day Society, launched in Philadelphia just seven years after the end of the Revolutionary War, set about to instruct the offspring of "indigent parents" on Sunday.

Soon, however, the American Sunday school came to demonstrate a character of its own. By 1790, the Methodist Conference endorsed such educational ventures and encouraged Methodist preachers to promote them. In 1816, the Philadelphia Union was established to promote Sunday schools in that geographical area.

A class-oriented school could not survive long in a nation proud of its democratic equality. What had begun as a charitable exercise became a prep school for evangelical Christianity.

At the same time, the common school movement began to gather force. When public schools opened, the Sunday schools were released from the pressure of teaching reading and writing. Religious instruction alone became the main undertaking.

The nation expanded westward. Although the churches weren't pushing toward the frontier, the Sunday school did. As Lynn and Wright observe, "Log cabin pioneers, first on the frontier, had nature's garden, powder and shot, weather and Indian worries—and the Sunday school."[6] It was there largely because the American Sunday School Union, launched in 1824 by several city Sunday school unions, made sure it was. In 1830, the Union took on the staggering task of establishing "a Sunday school in every destitute place where it is practicable throughout the Valley of the Mississippi."[7] And the Mississippi Valley extended from Harrisburg, Pennsylvania, to the Rockies, from Canada to the Gulf of Mexico!

This grandiose *two-year* plan was staged with a three-man staff. Never would the task have been possible apart from the "union principle." The strategy was stated: to ignore doctrinal and political differences, to be undenominational in purpose and practice, but to establish Sunday schools on the frontier.

By the late 1830's and the 1840's many churches began to embrace the Sunday school as the means to provide religious instruction. Because the various denominations adopted the Sunday school as their own, the Sunday school movement grew rapidly in the following decades.

After the Civil War, the Sunday school movement began to find interdenominational cohesion through nationwide Sunday school conventions and associations. National conventions, held first in 1832, were resumed and met regularly. A world convention was held in 1889. Through these conventions, county, state, and eventually national Sunday school associations formed to promote Sunday school interest and to develop policies.

Two areas in which these conventions and associations were deeply concerned were the training of teachers and the development of curriculum. Most Sunday school teachers were volunteers recruited from local churches. Few had any specific training. Various proposals for Sunday school teacher training were set forth, inspired by the methods for training public school teachers. These ranged from reading courses to extensive city institutes for religious instruction.

Along with the need for trained teachers, the need for a curricular system was also felt. In 1872, the International Sunday School Convention adopted a uniform lesson plan and established a lesson committee to develop this plan. Though some denominational boards and publishers opposed the plan, it soon won general favor. An improved and modified uniform lesson plan is still widely used today. This plan provided one lesson graded for all ages in all schools. Such a systematic study of the Bible gave an opportunity for publishers to provide expositions and helps for the teacher. Though the plan greatly aided volunteer teachers and tended to standardize content, it has been under critical scrutiny for a number of years. Many denominations no longer use this system, preferring alternate approaches that they believe are more educationally sound.

From Sunday School to Church School

In the latter part of the nineteenth century, other needs became apparent that the Sunday school could not meet. Attempts were made to meet the expressional needs of youth through young people's societies, of which Christian Endeavor was the forerunner. This movement began in 1881 in the Williston Congregational Church, Portland, Maine, under the leadership of Francis Clark. Christian Endeavor, appealing to Christian youth's needs for combining study, expression, and service, grew rapidly across denominational lines and stimulated various denominations to begin their own youth programs.

Other church-related educational programs began in the late nineteenth century, including Christian camping and the campus ministry. The church also followed its students to the colleges, first through the interdenominational YMCA begun in the 1840's, then through the efforts of the individual denominations. Christian camping grew out of the camp meeting tradition of the nineteenth century and provided a means of Christian nurture and growth for youth. Organizations like the Salvation Army, YMCA, and the International Sunday School Association established camping programs that stimulated denominational programs.

After the turn of the century, such programs as daily Vacation Bible School and weekday religious education were established to supplement and expand the churches' educational program. Vacation Bible School began shortly before the turn of the century, but gained acceptance in 1901 in New York City under the leadership of Dr. Robert Boville. The movement grew so rapidly that within twenty years every Protestant denomination sponsored such schools. The movement that promoted weekday religious education began in Gary, Indiana, where the council of churches and the public school officials developed a "released-time plan" so that children could participate in religious instruction on a weekly basis. This program, guided by Myron Settles, soon spread throughout the nation.

At about this time, many leading religious educators were rediscovering Horace Bushnell's emphasis on the Christian family set out in his work *Christian Nurture*. In this classic work, Bushnell pleaded for recognition of the Christian family as the chief agency for both evangelism and education. The rise of the child psychology movement after the turn of the century vindicated much of Bushnell's emphasis. It promoted better teaching methods in the formal programs of Christian education, and also elevated the home to an important role in Christian education.

All of these educational emphases (and others such as the adult Sunday school class emphasis) arose independently of one another. The need for correlation and unification became apparent. The Religious Education Association (established in 1903 under the leadership of Dr. William Rainey Harper, president of the University of Chicago) appointed a committee to address this need. Dr. W. S. Athearn, professor of education at Drake University, headed this committee and authored the results of their deliberations under the title *The Church School*. This work, published in 1914, suggested that all the different facets of Christian education be correlated under a board or department of Christian education. This board would give oversight and supervision to a total program of education for the church. Thus, the religious education movement in America had evolved from a Sunday school to a church school. The Sunday school no longer carried the total weight of Christian nurture for the churches. Now a number of educational agencies and emphases were correlated to fulfill the church's mandate to teach and nurture.

The Early Twentieth Century

At the outset of the twentieth century, Christian education in general, and the Sunday school in particular, seemed destined to grow and to penetrate society. But it was not to be.

Two trends in the first quarter of the century greatly affected religious education. The first was the influence of theological liberalism that spread to America from Europe. Almost every Protestant denomination was affected. Invariably, the liberal segment captured the colleges and seminaries, mission boards, and educational boards of the denominations. The liberal position is difficult to pinpoint, for liberalism was more an attitude than a position. This liberal attitude (some called it the scientific attitude or the attitude of the open mind) tended to embrace the dogma of evolution, radical biblical criticism, and the social gospel, leading to some fairly general positions:

1. God was seen either as impersonal (as a social concept), or as a sentimental Father of love in whom there was no wrath or judgment.
2. The Bible was looked upon as a source book of religious inspiration, containing legend, myth, and folklore that emphasize a basic morality but not a supernatural absolute.
3. Christ was confessed as a great man, a wonderful moral teacher, but not deity in any unique sense. His death was not sacrificial or substitutionary, and His resurrection was often denied or explained as a mythical indication of some kind of human immortality.
4. The kingdom of God was not the supernatural role of God in the hearts of sinful men saved by Christ's vicarious atonement, but an earthly kingdom to be achieved by educational legislative reform. The concept of sin was often ignored entirely.

Many of the leaders of the religious education movement accepted the liberal position in part or totally. This affected both the philosophy and the procedures of religious education. Methods were borrowed from the progressive education movement, associated with John Dewey, with its interest in child-centeredness and the "social project." The progressive movement shared with religious liberalism its emphasis upon divine eminence, the inevitability of religious growth, the innate goodness of man, and the concept of the historical Jesus as only an ethical teacher and martyred prophet. Only an occasional voice was raised against this trend.

Liberalism's influence in religious education may be seen statistically. The decline was steady. From 1906 to 1916, there had been a 35 percent increase in Sunday school membership compared to a 19.5 percent increase in population. The next ten years (1916-1926) brought only a 6 percent increase in Sunday school membership. From 1926 to 1936, there was an 11 percent loss compared to a 2.2 percent gain in church membership and 10 percent gain in population. The individual denominational statistics are even more revealing. Between 1926 and 1936, the Methodists declined 34 percent, the Disciples of Christ 23 percent, and the Presbyterians 18 percent. Yet those who maintained a conservative biblical position grew. For example, the Assemblies of God showed a 300 percent growth in the same decade, while Pentecostal Holiness schools doubled.

A second trend was what could be called a growing ecclesiastical sectarianism. The nineteenth-century Sunday school movement was interdenominational and largely lay-controlled. Denominational boards and publishers were opposed to such control. To offset the influence of the International Sunday School Association and capture control for individual denominations, these leaders formed the Sunday School Council of Evangelical Denominations in 1906. When fighting between this organization and the International Sunday School Association reached a peak, a truce was declared and a joint committee was established looking toward merger. W. S. Athearn, a leader in the International Sunday School Association, led the two organizations to merge. The merger plans allowed for greater control by the denominational boards, but also maintained the older concepts of lay activity and control by local authority.

But when these two organizations merged into a new organization (known as the International Council of Religious Education), the denominational publishing agents set themselves to take control of the new organization. A professional spirit replaced the zealous humility that characterized the voluntarism of the lay leaders of the International Sunday School Association. This council has now, by merger, become the Division of Christian Education of the National Council of Churches of Christ in America, and is further alienated from formerly supportive evangelicals.

With liberalism and professionalism dominating the organization that had historically given direction to American religious education, Bible-believing groups were left without guidance. Some of these, like the Southern Baptists, were large enough to develop an excellent program of their own. Others depended upon whatever direction the older independent publishers such as Standard Publishing Company, David C. Cook, and Union Gospel Press could provide. New publishing ventures, such as Scripture Press, Gospel Light Publications, and R.B. Sweet Company were begun to meet some of these needs.

New interdenominational evangelical agencies were also established to meet some of these challenges. These parachurch organizations provided yeoman service during the years of disappointment and confusion. In 1942, the National Association of Evangelicals came into being as an interdenominational evangelical organization in which "cooperation without compromise" could be secured for Bible-believing individuals, churches, and denominations. Leaders of this organization proposed the reestablishment of a National Sunday School Association. This was accomplished in 1946. This agency, and its associated city, area, and state agencies, helped to reemphasize Christian education among evangelical groups.

The Current Scene

Since World War II, Christian education in general and the Sunday school in particular have been alternately lauded and criticized. Lynn and Wright note three dominant views of the Sunday school since the 1950's, each of which they assess as off base.[8]

The positive attitude was summed up by J. Edgar Hoover who praised the Sunday school as a "crime prevention laboratory."[9] The negative was put forth in a *Life* magazine article that called the Sunday school "the most wasted hour of the week."[10] The third attitude is simple disregard.

On the whole, the Sunday school has been strong when church leaders have supported it, kept its original purpose of revival in focus, and made lay leadership development a priority. But where the Sunday school has lost its focus, when leaders criticize more than support, or when lay leaders are ignored or poorly taught, it is weak. The same could be said of many Christian education programs that have developed over the years.

The most significant recent change in Christian education has been the phenomenal growth of the Christian school movement. The Association of Christian Schools International estimate that on an average one new Christian school is begun in the United States every day. While enrollment in Roman Catholic schools has declined, Protestant schools, especially those in evangelical churches, have increased dramatically in enrollment.

Certain societal trends seem sure to affect Christian education in the near future. One is the change in the family. A family can no longer be described as father, mother, and children. It may be father and children, mother and children, or a single person as well as the traditional pattern. This presents a challenge to the church to make Christian education meaningful, relevant, and appealing to those who do not fit the traditional descriptions so common in this society.

A second trend is the ferment in the public school. The growth of the Christian school movement is the result of growing unrest with the public sector of education. In addition to the Christian school movement, a new phenomenon, home schooling for children, has emerged recently. It is estimated that more than a million and a half children stay home from traditional schools to get instruction from their parents. That same mentality has brought formal Christian education programs into question and may well have its effect on the church in the near future.

A third trend is the emphasis upon lifelong learning for adults. The adult education movement challenges traditional Christian education that too often tends to teach adults as children are taught. Adults are volunteer learners who will subject themselves to any amount of effort if they are learning what is relevant to them and if the material is presented in an appealing manner. But they rarely get involved in a learning group that ignores their needs and learning style.

A fourth trend is leadership development. Refreshing new breezes seem to be blowing in Christendom: the lay leader seems again to be important. The church must meet this challenge in the overall Christian education program.

One can only suggest certain trends for the future of Christian education. Even among those mainline denominations that have historical association with the Division of Christian Education of the National Council of Churches, there is a healthier approach to the Bible and theology. Much has been written by such leaders as Randolph Crump Miller, James D. Smart, Lewis J. Sherrill, and others that point toward a renewal of biblical relevance for Christian education. In evangelical circles this relevance is taken even more seriously, for evangelical Christian educators such Lawrence O. Richards, Gene Getz, Edward Hayes, and many others are committed to the full authority of the Bible, and are attempting to restate what this biblical authority means for the church's educational task.

New methods have also been stressed. The behavioral sciences have helped in the development of new methods. Audio-visuals, group methods, and simulations are some of the newer methods used in vital programs of Christian teaching.

Millions are not involved in any kind of Christian education. The challenge they present is ever before us. Workers must be trained, teachers inspired, students recruited, and the best methods and programs employed. The church must continue to reach and teach those in need of the salvation provided by the Father through His Son Jesus Christ.

Summary

History shows us that when the church recognized the importance of teaching its membership, it flourished. During those times it failed to teach, the church declined. Though its methods have changed over the years and will continue to change, Christian education remains vital to the life of the church.

Selected Bibliography

Barclay, William, *Train Up a Child: Educational Ideals in the Ancient World*. Philadelphia: Westminster Press, 1960.

Benson, Clarence H. *A Popular History of Christian Education*. Chicago: Moody Press, 1943.

Castle, E.B. *Moral Education in Christian Times*. New York: Macmillan, 1958.

Cully, Kendig B. (ed.). *Basic Writings in Christian Education*. Philadelphia: Westminster Press, 1960.

Eavey, C.B. *History of Christian Education*. Chicago: Moody Press, 1964.

Kennedy, William B. *The Shaping of Protestant Education.* New York: Associated Press, 1964.

Lynn, Robert W. *Protestant Strategies in Education.* New York: Associated Press, 1964.

Lynn, Robert W. and Elliott Wright, *The Big Little School.* 2nd ed. Birmingham, AL: Religious Education Press, 1980.

Miller, Randolph Crump. *Education for Christian Living.* Englewood Cliffs, NJ: Prentice-Hall, 1963.

Sherrill, Lewis J. *The Rise of Christian Education.* New York: Macmillan, 1944.

---

[1]Matthew 28:19, 20

[2]1 Timothy 3:2; 2 Timothy 2:2

[3]Lewis J. Sherrill, *The Rise of Christian Education* (New York: Macmillan, 1944), p. 66.

[4]Randolph Crump Miller, *Education for Christian Living* (Englewood Cliffs, NJ: Prentice-Hall, 1963), p. 22.

[5]Sherrill, p. 20.

[6]Robert W. Lynn and Elliott Wright, *The Big Little School,* 2nd ed. (Birmingham, AL: Religious Education Press, 1980), p. 40.

[7]American Sunday School Union, *Sixth Annual Report* (1830), p. 3.

[8]Lynn and Wright, p. 165.

[9]Edward L. R. Elson, "J. Edgar Hoover—Churchman," *Presbyterian Life* (November 27, 1948), p. 5.

[10]Wesley Shrader, "Our Troubled Sunday Schools," *Life* (February 11, 1957), p. 110.

CHAPTER 4

Communicating the Word to the World

As you read, think about these questions:
—What are four major changes in the composition of the population of the United States?
—List at least two implications for the church about each population change.
—What are six social trends that affect the church in this generation?
—How does each trend affect the teaching ministry of the church?
—List at least one thing the church can do to meet the challenge of each of the six social trends.

Christian education is more than a process of simply explaining the Word of God to a waiting audience. The audience itself, and the world of which that audience is a part, affects the communication process. The Word of God penetrates the heart of man and affects a change in conduct so radical as to be called conversion. The chances of successful communication of that Word can be improved when the communicator understands those to whom he is speaking.

The forms of Christian education differ from age to age, not because the message changes, but because the social context does. Communication processes differ from social group to social group. Communication media improve. Population demographics shift. Social trends come and go. All affect the *how* or *when* of Christian education.

It is useful, then, to examine the present social setting into which the Word of God is to be communicated. This chapter will examine first the changes in demographic structure, then present current trends that are critical for a Christian educator to understand as he teaches individuals, plans, or administers programs of Christian education.

Demographic Trends

Increasing Population

From 1950 to 1985, the total world population grew from 2,524,622,000 to 4,826,328,000, an increase of over 91% in this thirty-five-year period. By the year 2000, the world population is projected to reach 6,115,514,000, an additional increase of nearly 27% in less than fifteen years. The figures are staggering for the church, whose mission it is to disciple these peoples of the world, especially when one acknowledges that only a small percentage of that population is Christian.

At the same time, population figures in the United States grew from 152,271,000 in 1950 to 234,548,000 in 1985—an increase of 54% (less than the overall world population growth, but a significant increase nevertheless). The population in the year 2000 is projected to reach 263,829,000, an additional 12.5% increase. The population of the United States represents only 4.9% of the total world population.

Changing Ethnic Composition

Further examination of United States population figures reveals a changing ethnic composition (see Table 4-1). Caucasians still are a majority in the population, though a shrinking one. Blacks represent the second largest group, followed by Asians, who have increased in percentage in recent years. American Indians are only a small fraction of the population.

These changes have urgent implications for the Christian educator. The first challenge to the thinking of churches and educators is the rapidly increasing world population—and the decreasing percentage of that population living in the United States. It presents a clarion call for cross-cultural education that cannot be ignored for another generation without serious erosion to the influence of the church worldwide.

Ethnic Background	Number	Percentage
White	226,546,000	83.15
Black	26,495,000	11.70
Asian, Islander	3,500,000	1.55
American Indian	1,420,000	.63
Other	6,758,000	2.98

Table 4-1. Ethnic Composition of U.S. Population[1]

But cross-cultural communication is not a matter for overseas missions alone. Although Asians, blacks, and other groups are yet a minority in the United States, these groups are increasing in number and as a percentage of the total population. Churches in every metropolitan center in the United States must seek ways to teach the Word of God to those who may be first generation citizens and who may not fit into the typical white, Anglo-Saxon, middle class congregation. Christians must be educated to be more concerned—not only about the world, but about those of other cultures who live or work where they do.

In terms of Christian education, the church has not reached the black community with any degree of success. The challenge confronting the church in this generation is to seek ways and means by which the Bible may reach those who have been spiritually disenfranchised.

The challenge for cross-cultural communication of the Word of God confronts the preacher, the teacher, and the missiologist alike. This challenge may require new forms of Christian education, perhaps new methods. It will certainly require a massive Christian education program at the local level to equip people both attitudinally and intellectually for the task.

Changing Age Composition

A look at the population from a different point of view reveals something else of significance—the age composition of the United States population. That too has changed dramatically (see Table 4-2). Whereas in 1900, nearly 40% of the population was eighteen and under, that had decreased to 28.1% in

Age	1980	1970	1960	1950	1940	1900
0—8	12.9	16.2	19.8	18.0	14.4	21.6
Under 1	1.6	1.7	2.3	2.1	1.5	2.5
1-5	7.1	8.6	11.2	10.5	8.1	11.9
6-8	4.3	5.9	6.3	5.4	4.8	7.1
Youth	15.2	18.0	16.1	13.2	16.2	18.8
9-11	4.9	6.2	5.8	4.6	5.1	6.6
12-14	4.8	6.1	5.5	4.4	5.5	6.2
15-17	5.5	5.8	4.7	4.2	5.6	6.0
Adult	60.6	55.9	55.1	60.6	62.5	55.3
18-24	13.3	11.7	8.7	10.5	12.6	13.6
25-44	27.7	23.6	26.2	29.9	30.1	28.0
45-64	19.6	20.6	20.3	20.2	19.8	13.7
Old Age	11.3	9.9	9.0	8.2	6.8	4.1

Table 4-2. Age Composition of U.S. Population[2]

1980. Correspondingly, the percentages of adults from eighteen to sixty-five increased from 55.3% in 1900 to 60.6% in 1980. The percentage of adults sixty-five and over increased from 4.1% in 1900 to 11.3% in 1980.

The number of children of elementary age has declined significantly in the last fifteen years.[3] This number will increase again by the year 2000 because of slightly rising birth rates.[4] Likewise the numbers of high school students have decreased since 1980 and will continue to do so until well into the 1990's.[5] The decline in children correspondingly means an increase in adults.

Every church ought to examine its age composition in light of these figures. A church that is reaching a cross section of population will have 8.7% preschoolers (birth through 5), 9.2% elementary children (grades 1-6), 10.3% youth (grades 7-12), 60.6% adults (18-65), and 19.6% older adults (over 65). Table 4-3 translates this into numbers for congregations of various sizes.

	(Size of Entire Congregation)					
Age	**50**	**100**	**200**	**300**	**400**	**500**
Preschool	5	9	17	26	34	44
Under 1	1	2	3	5	6	8
1-5	4	7	14	21	28	36
Elementary	5	9	18	28	37	46
6-8	2	4	8	13	17	22
9-11	3	5	10	15	20	24
Youth	6	10	21	31	41	52
12-14	3	5	10	14	19	24
15-17	3	5	11	17	22	28
Adult	30	61	121	182	242	313
18-24	7	13	27	40	53	67
25-44	14	28	55	83	110	139
45-64	9	20	39	59	79	107
Old Age	4	11	23	33	46	45

Table 4-3. Numbers of Various Ages in a Congregation

A congregation can compare its numbers in each age category to the numbers in the community or in the nation. It is a useful way to evaluate the effectiveness of a Bible school in reaching various age levels. It may indicate ages for which new classes should be started and the target population for evangelistic efforts.

Perhaps the biggest challenge confronting the church in the immediate future is adult education—reaching and teaching adults with the Word of God so that the necessary changes for growth into Christlikeness can occur. The church should not ignore children's and youth programming, but adult study groups must have a high priority in a congregation's planning, staffing, and resources.

The day is long past when adults simply drop their children off for Sunday school. But the day is likewise past when adults will endure any kind of teaching situation, however mediocre, simply because their children need to be in a teaching program. Adult education is critical both for evangelization of all ages and for mobilization of all believers for ministry.

Shifting Regional Population

The population of the United States has been redistributed in recent years. That shift will continue at least to the year 2000 and probably beyond. At the turn of the century, the major population centers were in the Northeast and the North Central sections of the United States. The shift is now to the South and the West. Of the nineteen fastest growing states at the present time, fifteen are west of the Mississippi River.[6] Table 4-4 illustrates the point.

Region	1980	1990	2000
Northeast	21.7	19.4	17.4
North Central	26.0	24.2	22.3
South	33.3	35.2	37.0
West	19.1	21.2	23.4

Table 4-4. Regional Composition of United States Population[7]

The implications are clear. The church must develop a concerted effort to establish new churches in the South and West if the masses are to be reached. The church must furthermore tailor teaching programs to the needs and lifestyles of those in each section of the country. It may need to change its methods to reach those who have been transplanted from one part of the country to another. But the need to teach is still very much a part of the task of the church, wherever it is located.

Social Trends

The United States is in the throes of massive change that calls for the traditional Christian message to be presented in nontraditional forms. Alvin Toffler stated, "Change is the process by which the future invades our lives, and it is important to look at it closely, not merely from the grand perspective of history, but also from the vantage point of the living, breathing individuals who experience it."[8]

Transience

Toffler proceeds to analyze the changes as he saw them in 1970. The first major change that he noted was *transience*. People move from place to place within a given geographical region with ease. It is only a bit more difficult to move from region to region.

In 1914, the average person traveled 1,640 total miles per year (1,300 of it by walking). By 1970, the average person was driving 10,000 miles per year. Many exceed this figure by several times. This ease of travel has created a demise in knowledge of geography and even an obliterated many of the previous regional differences in speech, personal preferences, and lifestyles.

A transient society uses throwaway products. Fast food and rapid transit are typical. Unfortunately, a mind-set that appreciates throwaway products may also adopt a throwaway values orientation.

Even language changes. For example, when Shakespeare wrote, there were 250,000 usable words in the English vocabulary. That had increased to 450,000 by 1970—and has continued to grow since then.

The church must aggressively pursue an audience that may have discarded Christian values as irrelevant—or relegated these values to nothing more than a Sunday religion. Yet it must carry out its mission among a better educated, more widely traveled, transient population that will adopt Christian values *only* when they are presented intelligently and with relevance.

The Family

A second change is *the family*. Family disintegration has reached epidemic proportions in American society. The divorce rate continues at high levels, although it may be reaching a plateau.

The church must examine the issue of divorce and remarriage. On the one hand, the Christian ideal of one man for one woman for a lifetime must be upheld. But on the other hand, those who have fallen short of the Christian ideal must hear a voice of grace and caring from the church as they put their lives back together. The children from these families need the special ministry that a caring church and teacher or youth leader can provide. These children can also benefit from having more couples teaching in children's and youth classes. Married couples could demonstrate the idea of a Christian family and provide a model of a Christian lifestyle by both men and women to children who may lack one such model in their experience.

The numbers of singles are increasing. Some are single temporarily, such as the young adult who may be single only until he has completed his education and become established in a job or profession. Others are single because they have never married, for whatever reason, some not of their own choice. Even more are single because of tragic circumstances such as the death of a spouse or the disintegration of a marital relationship.

Whatever the circumstances of singleness, singles need to know that they are the church too. Single people are family units, and they need to be recognized as such. They need to be recognized as whole people who have gifts to offer in the ministry of the church. Some need to experience healing; others need to accept their singleness and use it to God's glory.

Overchoice

American society presents choices of all kinds. When you go to the supermarket to buy cheese, for example, the choices are numerous: cheddar, American, mozzarella, grated, in a roll, aged, smoked. The choices are as varied when you buy something as simple as a ball point pen or as expensive as a new automobile.

Few countries in the world experience the kinds of choices available to Americans. Some foreign countries have one television channel operated by the state. Americans with cable service may have fifty or sixty choices of programming available at any one time.

The unfortunate result is overchoice—too many choices to make on too many issues. Children, particularly, are unable to make that many choices intelligently. But overchoice also creates stress, even a frenzy, among adults who are ill-equipped to make constant choices.

The church must realize that people who make choices in every other area of their lives will do so with churches as well. There seems to be a blurring of denominational loyalties. People tend to choose a church on the basis of its capability of meeting their needs and preferences just as they choose toothpaste or cheese. They can be taught to value the Word of God, of course, but their initial selection of the congregation may be on a quite different basis.

Education

The public school has experienced a decade of criticism and decline. Schools that began in America to teach people to read their Bibles have long since left that religious motivation. The schools have been called upon to solve a wide variety of social problems ranging from racial segregation to sex education. The result has been an increasing dissatisfaction with a system that had produced too many functionally illiterate graduates (perhaps as many as 34%) and declining college entrance test scores. What it all adds up to is flight from the public school to private schools.

The rise of the Christian school has been phenomenal during the same period. The Association of Christian Schools International estimates that Christian schools are beginning on the average of one per day. Other alternative forms of education, such as home schooling, have increased as well.

Education must reflect the "information" society of which we are a part. Reading and writing skills are no longer optional—they are absolutely essential. People must also be taught to think critically and effectively.

The church doesn't escape the same educational challenge. The average churchgoer may have many confused ideas about the Bible and Christianity. He too must be taught to think critically and from a biblical perspective. As John Naisbitt stated: "We must learn to balance the wonders of technology with the spiritual demands of our human nature."[9]

Lifelong Learning

Probably the most profound change in society is the emphasis upon lifelong learning. The amazing growth of community colleges demonstrates that adults of all ages can and will learn *if* the material is relevant, the schedule is convenient, the teaching style is interesting, and the climate is comfortable.

Adults are volunteer learners who face intense demands for their time. They bring a variety of experiences and interests to the learning situation. They can identify most of their needs. Yet they are reluctant to change without sufficient reason to do so. They expect to participate in the learning process. They must feel that they belong in the group of which they are a part. When these conditions are present, an adult will continue to learn throughout his life. But if those conditions are violated, he will abandon the process.

The church must, then, reexamine grouping procedures and curriculum decisions for adult education. The needs and levels of learners must be reflected. Biblical content must be presented in a way that it speaks to life needs. Fellowship must be emphasized in the effective adult class. The learner must be involved in the learning process. All of this requires a commitment to adult education: to provide quality programs and prepare quality teachers to lead in the task.

Decentralization

The trend in business organization is from centralization to decentralization, from representative democracy to participatory democracy, from hierarchies to networking. Excellent businesses involve every employee in planning and development. This involvement requires better informed employees who are prepared for decision-making.

Perhaps the biggest challenge to the church is the layman who must be equipped to participate in the ministry of all believers. In the past, Christian education has been accomplished best when volunteers were recruited, challenged, trained, and encouraged to do the work of ministry. It will continue to be so.

The church must become fully committed to the concept of mutual ministry. Once that is accomplished, the church must develop a workable, commonsense philosophy of developing people for specific ministries. Competent leaders don't just happen—they are developed.

J. Hudson Taylor once said, "God's work done in God's way never lacks God's supply." That must be the motivation for every church: continual, careful selection, first-rate training, and adequate support for youth and adults who will use their gifts to do the work of witnessing and ministering in their church and community.

All of these trends present certain challenges to Christian educators. Art Criscoe summarizes them:[10]

1. Understand what is taking place in the world of education.
2. Lead church members to participate fully in local school activities.
3. Strengthen the Christian education processes in the local church. Sunday school and discipleship training must be regarded with new seriousness.
4. Encourage and aid more Christian education in the home by parents.
5. Develop Christian education specialists who understand the philosophical issues confronting education and can articulate those clearly both to the church and to the broader educational world.

Summary

The world to which the Bible is taught has changed dramatically in a generation. It will continue to change. The church must then keep abreast of the changing demographic and social trends so it can alter some programs and design new ones. These trends must be communicated to teachers and leaders in order to enhance the presentation of the Word of God and provide direction for planning and programming.

The twentieth-century church must acknowledge the changing population trends. Its leaders must understand the trends affecting the world of which it is a part: transience, family changes, overchoice, education, lifelong learning, and decentralization. This list is not exhaustive, but it is a starting point for analysis and planning.

These changing trends may create discomfort among church members and leaders. But they are nothing more than new challenges, new opportunities to demonstrate that the Word of God is for every person regardless of age or location.

Selected Bibliography

Brown, Marion E. and Marjorie G. Prentice. *Christian Education in the Year 2000*. Valley Forge, PA: Judson Press, 1984.

Criscoe, Art. "Current Trends in Education." Paper presented to the National Association of Professors of Christian Education/National Association of Directors of Christian Education, November 23, 1983.

Knowles, Malcolm. *The Adult Learner: A Neglected Species*. 3rd ed. Houston, TX: Gulf Publishing Company, 1973.

Naisbitt, John. *Megatrends*. New York: Warner Books, 1982.

Toffler, Alvin. *Future Shock*. New York: Random House, 1970.

---

[1]Taken from Donald J. Bogue, *The Population of the United States* (New York: Free Press, 1985). Figures are rounded off and may not total exactly.

[2]Bogue, *op. cit.* Figures are rounded off and may not total exactly.

[3]The number of elementary children numbered 28,743,000 in 1980. By 1985, that number decreased to 26,451,000, a net loss of 2,292,000 children in the elementary schools of the nation.

[4]For example, the number of preschoolers increased from 5,640,000 in 1980 to 6,443,000 in 1985. By 1990, this is projected to rise to 6,910,000, then decline slightly to 6,607,000 in 2000 (still above 1985 figures).

[5]High schoolers numbered 15,218,000 in 1980 and 13,418,000 in 1985. By 1990, the figure will decline to 11,963,000, before going up to 13,959,000 in the year 2000.

[6]Bogue, *op. cit.*

[7]*Ibid.*

[8]Alvin Toffler, *Future Shock* (New York: Random House, 1970), p. 3.

[9]John Naisbitt, *Megatrends* (New York: Warner Books, 1982), p. 40.

[10]Art Criscoe, "Current Trends in Education," paper presented to the National Association of Professors of Christian Education/National Association of Directors of Christian Education, Nashville, Tennessee, November 23, 1983, p. 16.

CHAPTER 5

Developing a Philosophy of Christian Education

As you read, think about these questions:
—Why is a philosophy of Christian education essential? How does it affect the practice of Christian education?
—What are five building blocks in a philosophy of Christian education? How does each affect the practice of Christian education?
—What are at least five approaches to Christian education?

Every Christian educator must develop an approach to the task of Christian education. Taking into account the biblical material and the world to which the Word of God is to be presented, he must develop an understanding of what Christian education is and how it is to be accomplished.

The Christian educator faces a dilemma: is Christian education to be practical or theoretical? How can responsible theory be balanced with the pragmatic problems of everyday ministry? This chapter is an effort to provide answers to these fundamental questions.

Why a Philosophy of Christian Education?

Why be concerned about developing a distinctively Christian philosophy of education? Why not simply adopt the values and practices of contemporary education?

A person's behavior is guided by his deepest convictions. What he believes determines his actions.

Take the case of disciplining a child. If you hold to the Calvinistic doctrine of the total depravity of man from the time of conception, you by necessity see a child as one who must have the devil eradicated from him—the sooner, the better. The outcome of that view is a restrictive, often harsh disciplinary procedure.

On the other hand, if you are immersed in humanistic psychology and see the child as innately good, you will handle discipline differently. The outcome of this view is to grant the child freedom to make his own decisions, imposing little firm correction and few stated behavior sanctions. The child is, after all, by this view, intent to achieve his own best interests.

By contrast, if you proceed from biblical content to discipline, you see mankind as unique, made in God's image, but sinful by choice and in need of redemption. You recognize the lofty potential of a child, yet you are well aware of the self-centeredness in his nature that leads him to fall far short of his potential. Discipline in that case becomes not only corrective, but also instructive; not merely remedial, but also informative.

Take another situation. Should you conclude with Froebel and Pestalozzi, renowned educators of a bygone era, that all truth is attainable by observation, your method of teaching is to guide the learner into self-discovery of truth. You would do very little, if any, telling of the truth. If, on the other hand, you hold an Aristotelian view that logic and discussion are the source of knowledge, you will teach quite differently. Or if you conclude with John Dewey that all truth must be discovered by the learner on his own, another approach to teaching is used.

The Bible, however, suggests that truth comes from two sources: revelation from God and from natural laws (also put in motion by God). Natural laws and their use can be found through self-discovery, though none will be antithetical to revelation. Truth from revelation may be taught in many ways, but every conclusion must be measured against the Word of God. This allows you to use a variety of teaching methods depending upon the kind of information being presented and the outcomes you are seeking.

Christian education must be concerned about teaching methods, curriculum, materials, and other educational matters. But these must always rest on biblical foundations. They must always be weighed against biblical truth. A person's teaching behavior is always guided by his most deeply held convictions.

Components of a Philosophy of Christian Education

Four essential building blocks form a foundation for Christian education. These must be understood if education in the church is to be truly Christian.

God

The first building block is an understanding of the nature and person of God.

The Bible begins with the assumption that God exists and that He acts. He created. He walked with man. He judged. He is called Father, Judge, Lord, and Mighty One—all pictures of His character and activity. He initiated means by which man could be restored to his original status in relationship to Him. The biblical record is a record of God's persistent pursuit of a people to belong to Him, to do His will, and to be His companions.

God's nature becomes even clearer in the New Testament when He invaded Earth in the form of a man. Jesus Christ, God in the flesh, took on our form, our limitations, our lifestyle, to identify with us, to relate to us, to relate us back to God.[1] This Jesus, fully God but fully human, set about God's eternal business of creating a people for himself. Paul expressed this work in 2 Corinthians 5:19: "God was reconciling the world to Himself in Christ, not counting men's sins against them." He says in Romans 5:11, "We also rejoice in God through our Lord Jesus Christ, through whom we have now received reconciliation."

Jesus Christ lived, died, was raised the third day, and ascended back to the Father. Even then God did not leave those who followed Him without witness, for the Scriptures tell us that He still relates to mankind not only in the blood of Christ, by which sins are forgiven, but in the guidance of the Holy Spirit who resides in each believer.[2] God is still at work relating people to himself.

The nature of God is to relate to those He made. They may choose not to relate to Him, but He is a relating God.

How much difference does your view of God make to Christian teaching? Think of what Christian education would be if God were an aloof, uncaring God, far above His creation. Think what it would be if He were only a judgmental God who couldn't wait to punish those who disobey Him. Think how it would differ if He were a grand old Santa Claus who showered love and gifts without any call for responsibility on the part of the recipients. Think of what it would be if He were a God who gave only in return for what He got.

But God cares. He judges, but turns right around and provides the way to avoid judgment. He gives and gives and gives, yet calls for responsible management of those gifts. His purpose is to bring people into a right relationship with Him both now and for eternity. Christian education in the church must do the same.

Man

A second building block for a philosophy of Christian education is the nature of man.

Man is unique among all of God's creation. He was created with a body and physiological functions like all of the rest of the animal kingdom. But he differs from the animals, for Genesis states that he was made in God's image: an emotional, rational, moral creature with an immortal spirit. Quite unlike dogs or cats or rats or orangutans, man was made to relate to and glorify God. He is a spiritual being at home in a natural world.

Yet man was also made to choose. He asserted his independence and chose incorrectly, succumbing to sin. After the fall, man still retained those qualities (emotionality, rationality, and morality) that made him more like God than animals. Yet he is intent on having his own way. When he uses his God-given nature for good, his magnificence is beyond belief. But when he uses it for evil, his wickedness is devastating. The Bible is a record of both his good and bad behavior.

The Bible is also a witness to the fact that try as he will, man cannot escape his bent to sin apart from Jesus Christ, whom God provided for man's salvation. But in Christ, he is a new creature[3] with the possibility of Christlikeness.[4]

What difference does a view of man make to education? If man is no more than an animal, albeit an advanced one, man learns in a mechanistic way. One need only learn the rules of modifying behavior to teach. But if man thinks and reasons and feels, there is more to teaching than a mechanical list of rules.

If sin is nothing more than social evil and not a part of man's makeup, an educational view that states man's inherent goodness is an appropriate approach to teaching. The teacher need only point a person in the right direction and he will pursue it. But if man is in fact a moral creature who is bent on rebelling, humanistic psychology alone is inadequate to explain him.

If we see man as God does, as one possessing incredible Godlike potential, yet bent on his own will, we make room for teaching practices from a variety of sources. Some learning is habitual, but other learning is creative and unique.

The Christian educator does depend to some extent upon the data available from human development, psychology, personality theory, and sociology, but only when it is consistent with the biblical picture of man who is uniquely Godlike in nature, yet by nature bent to sin and in need of redemption.

Bible

The third component for a philosophy of Christian education is the Bible, God's revelation. It is the chief source for a philosophy. It is the norm for the content to be taught.

A major decision in Christian education is its source of authority. Christian education rests squarely upon the Bible. It is *the* source of information about God, not *a* source. Scientific data may well describe the way things are in this natural world, but that is not determinative of how things were before man sinned nor how they should be after a person is redeemed in Christ.

The Bible states why it is to be taught—not for its own sake, but so that people may come to faith in God through Jesus Christ. That faith should produce changes in this life,[5] but these changes fit man for final salvation.[6] Christian teaching should motivate the learner to grow in Christlikeness during his sojourn in this world, so he can be with God eternally. It should produce maturity.[7] The Scriptures, the only available source of this information, become central to the curriculum.

Your view of Scripture influences your teaching method as well. Christian education must avoid two equally insidious errors. On the one hand, we must avoid teaching the Bible as mere information without application to life. On the other hand, we must not merely teach an experience-centered approach devoid of biblical information.

Two biblical words lend insight: *ginosko* and *epiginosko* suggest knowledge and understanding, head information coupled with practical usage. According to the Bible itself, effective teaching must include both content and application, information input and life exploration, for faith involves all of a person—his reason, emotions, physical behavior, and spirit.

A biblical approach to education defines the teacher's role and function. Two words in the Bible provide insight. The Greek word *didaskolos* carries the idea of instruction, of input of information. But the word *paideo* suggests correction and teaching to change behavior. Furthermore, in Deuteronomy 6:46 and Luke 6:39, 40, the role of showing as well as telling is emphasized. All the functions of the teacher—to tell, to correct, to demonstrate—are demands not necessarily made of teachers of other subject areas.

What difference does a view of the Bible make to teaching? If the Bible is only one source among many that gives insight to God, good teaching would require examination of all available data on any given subject, then a decision made by the learner about which is correct. (The center of authority becomes clear in that case—the learner, who decides what is right.)

If the Bible is simply facts to be communicated, then memorization and rote repetition are sufficient methods of instruction. If the Bible is merely intellectually stimulating material, then teaching is merely telling.

But if the Bible is a record of God's actions intended to bring rebellious man to *faith* (a word that implies information and action), then Bible teaching requires effective transmission of information coupled with exploration for living and occasional correction demonstrated by a teacher who lives and talks a life of faith.

Church

The final building block is the church. The church is the family of God. It is made up of people who have been reconciled to God and who seek to live a life of faith. It is the body of Christ, the bride of Christ, those called out of the world. It is the focal point for Christian teaching. Its final goal is to be delivered from this natural world into God's spiritual world, there to live forever with God.

The church is the place of fellowship and support for the believer. It is a place where Christians are to bear each other's burdens. It is an outreach center to invite others to participate in a life of faith. It is made up of those who bring glory to God.[8]

What difference does a view of the church make to Christian education? If the church is merely an organization, then teaching and organization should proceed on the basis of sociological principles. But if the church is a family characterized by a specific lifestyle, then education is designed to reproduce that lifestyle in a family atmosphere of telling, correcting, showing, and discovering on one's own.

Five Approaches to Christian Education

Four major philosophical approaches to Christian education have given direction to the teaching ministry of the church at various times throughout the ages. Each begins with certain assumptions about God, man, the Bible, and the church. This chapter also presents a fifth approach—one derived from biblical material and the best from other approaches.

Traditional Theological

The traditional theological approach to Christian education has emphasized the communication of a divine message. This approach rightly emphasizes the Bible as *the* source of revelation. The goal of Christian education is salvation. The teacher's method is verbal, and he must be an accurate transmitter of the biblical information. The basic teaching techniques are catechetical, coupled with rote memorization. This approach stresses content, sometimes to the exclusion of corresponding life changes. Teaching is evaluated by the pupil's ability to repeat back the material that he has heard.

The strength of this view is that the Bible is the authority for Christian education and God is at the center of it. But the approach seems to be weak at the point of clearly linking a knowledge of biblical information with a Christlike lifestyle. Consequently, the choice of teaching methods seems too limited to achieve a truly biblical outcome for Christian education.

Social/Cultural

Disenchanted with information that could be readily reproduced in lives that were changed little, some Christian educators adopted the liberal theological views of the early twentieth century and linked them with the pragmatic approach of the progressivism of John Dewey. The result was the social/cultural view, a life-centered approach with little emphasis upon revelation. They insisted that experience was normative; the Bible became *a* resource. The goal, rather than salvation, became the reconstruction of experience, development of social skills, character education. Somewhere within students, these theorists reasoned, was good waiting to emerge if those latent capabilities were only developed. The teacher became a developer of social skills. The basic teaching techniques were problem-solving and the project method.

This approach to Christian education is strong in the sense that the stated outcomes of Christian education are changes in lifestyle. However, the authority of Scripture has been substantially weakened, resulting in a blurring of biblical goals for Christian education. The view of man is not at all biblical, leaving the method powerless to transform.

Contemporary Theological

When the social/cultural approach failed to produce the results envisioned by its founders, a contemporary theological approach emerged. Those who are proponents of this view see the Bible as essential to Christian education, yet they may speak of the Bible as being *a* source of revelation. They have furthermore insisted that revelation has an experiential quality: revelation is information, but information to be lived. The goal is salvation and discipleship. The teacher's role is to create relationships through which and in which he may transmit information to the learner. A wide variety of teaching techniques may be used.

The contemporary theological approach to Christian education is strong in the stated goals and in the function of the teacher. However, the role of the Bible is weak, since it is not clearly seen as *the* source of revelation.

Social Science

James Michael Lee, a Catholic educator, has developed what

he calls a social science view of Christian education. He assumes that religious education is the same as all other education—students learn religion like they learn any other content. The Bible is used as content, but the real insights for teaching are to be found in the social sciences. The teacher is a planner who directs the student toward specific behaviors.

The strength of this approach is its openness to information from the behavioral sciences and in seeking behavior changes in the lives of the learner. However, this view errs in drawing all teaching information from the social sciences, as important as they are to the Christian teacher. In this approach, the role of the teacher is a technician, not a model to emulate.

A Proposed Biblical Model

A view emerging from biblical principles rests upon at least six propositions:

1. God is at the center of Christian education. Teaching is intended to relate man to Him through Jesus Christ.
2. The Bible is the source of authority for Christian education. This Bible is to be taught in a way that will bring people to faith—both intellectual assent and obedience in life decisions and behaviors.
3. Man is made in God's image, but he has sinned and must be restored into a right relationship with God. The goal of Christian education becomes twofold: to bring people to salvation and to nurture them to maturity in Christ.
4. The church is that gathering of redeemed folk who are growing in Christlikeness. It should be organized to facilitate that growth and should result in glory to God.
5. The teacher is a teller, a doer, a planner, a model.
6. A wide variety of teaching methods and techniques may be used inasmuch as they support the previous five assumptions.

Summary

Successful Christian education is rooted in a sound philosophy. The message and the procedure must never work in opposing directions. Teaching takes into account relevant facts and experimental data (these are, after all, God's truth too), but these must always be interpreted by a biblical view of God, the Bible, man, and the church. Christian education is concerned with the supreme task of relating man to God. It must then rest on sound biblical principles.

Selected Bibliography

Burgess, Harold. *An Invitation to Religious Education*. Mishawaka, IN: Religious Education Press, 1975.

Cove, Mary K. and Mary Louise Mueller. *Regarding Religious Education*. Mishawaka, IN: Religious Education Press, 1977.

DeWolf, L. Harold. *Teaching Our Faith in God*. Nashville, TN: Abingdon Press, 1965.

Little, Lawrence C. *Foundation for a Philosophy of Christian Education*. Nashville, TN: Abingdon Press, 1962.

Miller, Randolph Crump. *Biblical Theology and Christian Education*. New York: Charles Scribner's Sons, 1956.

________. *The Clue to Christian Education*. New York: Charles Scribner's Sons, 1950.

________. *Education for Christian Living*. Englewood Cliffs, NJ: Prentice-Hall, Inc., 1956.

Rood, Wayne R. *Understanding Christian Education*. Nashville, TN: Abingdon Press, 1970.

---

[1]John 1:1-5, 12-18

[2]John 16:5-15; Acts 2:38; Romans 8

[3]2 Corinthians 5:17

[4]Matthew 5:48

[5]Colossians 1:9-14

[6]Ephesians 1:3-14

[7]Colossians 1:28

[8]1 Corinthians 1:2; 12:12, 27; Galatians 6:2; Ephesians 2:1-10, 19-22; 4:1-16; Revelation 21:1-7; 22:1-4

Part Two

MATERIALS AND METHODS FOR CHRISTIAN EDUCATION

Section Outline

6. The Teaching/Learning Encounter
   A. The Purpose of Bible Teaching
   B. How the Purpose Is Achieved
   C. Communicating the Word to the Learner
   D. The Role of the Christian Teacher

7. Helping Preschoolers Learn
   A. Understanding the Preschool Learner
   B. Goals for Early Childhood Education
   C. Teaching Preschoolers

8. Helping Elementary Children Learn
   A. Understanding Elementary Children
   B. Goals for Teaching Children
   C. Teaching Elementary Children

9. Helping Youth Learn
   A. Understanding the Adolescent
   B. Goals for Teaching Youth
   C. Teaching Youth

10. Helping Adults Learn
    A. Understanding Adults
    B. Goals for Teaching Adults
    C. Teaching Adults

11. Helping Exceptional Persons Learn
    A. Traditional Categories of Special Education: Aids in Defining Potential
    B. Principles in Educating the Exceptional Person

12. A Curriculum for Christian Education
    A. What Is Curriculum?
    B. Prerequisites for an Effective Curriculum
    C. Principles for an Effective Curriculum
    D. Selection of Curriculum Materials
    E. Guidelines for Evaluating Curriculum

13. Audiovisual Methods
    A. A Biblical Basis for Using Visuals
    B. Values of Audiovisual Aids
    C. Types of Audiovisuals
    D. Evaluating Audiovisual Material
    E. Organizing Audiovisual Materials

14. Helping the Family Teach
    A. The Family in the Bible
    B. Biblical Guidelines for the Family
    C. Contemporary Problems Facing the Family
    D. The Church and the Family

15. Building and Equipping for Christian Education
    A. Current Trends in Buildings
    B. Planning for Building and Equipment
    C. The Needs of Each Age Group
    D. Adaptation of Existing Space

Christian education involves a specific point of view that rests upon the biblical, historical, and psychological foundations. These foundations are crucial if Christian education is to remain *Christian*.

From foundations grows the actual practice of Christian teaching. Every congregation and teacher proceeds with some kind of method, planned or not. All select and use materials that rest upon some kind of assumptions for the practice of teaching. Those methods and materials should be in harmony with biblical principles.

The second section of this book explores principles to guide the selection and use of methods and materials. The section begins with an examination of the teaching/learning encounter as it emerges from biblical examples. The next five chapters examine various groups of learners—their characteristics, organization of their learning experiences, and possible teaching methods. The last four chapters present principles that apply to four special areas—the family, audiovisual materials, curriculum, and buildings and equipment.

CHAPTER 6

The Teaching/ Learning Encounter

As you read, think about these questions:
—What is the purpose of Bible teaching?
—What are the three components of maturity?
—What four life behaviors indicate Christlikeness?
—How may the process of maturing be described?
—What are the parts of an effective Bible lesson?
—What are the qualities of an effective Bible teacher?

"When Jesus had finished saying these things, the crowds were amazed at his teaching, because He taught as one who had authority, and not as their teachers of the law."[1] What teacher would not desire a response like that? Who wouldn't want to teach as powerfully and persuasively as Jesus?

He who teaches God's Word is in the business of communication. How can he communicate effectively? The place to begin is with the example of Jesus himself. A look at Jesus, the master teacher, reveals the purpose of Christian teaching as well as a means for accomplishing the goal.

The Purpose of Bible Teaching[2]

One of the lengthiest accounts of Jesus teaching is recorded in John 4. Jesus engaged in dialogue with a Samaritan woman.

He began by asking her a simple question, but one that was designed to achieve a goal (4:7). The woman was surprised that He would talk to her. He was, after all, a Jew and a man—Jews never talked with Samaritans, and men in that culture didn't talk with women in public. In this very act, Jesus provided a basis for all of Christian education: *all persons everywhere are to be recipients of the good news.*

The dialogue continued (4:9-15). It was genuine dialogue. Jesus, the Son of God, who had every truth of God at His disposal, chose to let this unlearned woman speak. Why did He not lecture and she listen? He is granting us further insight into the nature of Christian teaching, i.e., it is person-related.

As the dialogue developed, Jesus became more personal in His teaching (4:16-18). He was so personal, in fact, that this nameless woman was willing to argue a theological dispute that had separated Jews and Samaritans for centuries (i.e., whether true worship was to occur in Samaria or in Jerusalem), so she could avoid the uncomfortable admission that she was living with a man who wasn't her husband (4:19, 20). If she could divert Jesus' attention from self to informational and interpretational issues, she would be comfortable. But Jesus would not be diverted from His purpose. He refused to win an informational encounter and lose the person (4:21-24).

The purpose for Jesus' teaching becomes evident shortly thereafter. The woman, still speculating about information, insisted that the Messiah would explain all of the finer points of theology when finally He would come (4:25). And Jesus simply announced, "I who speak to you am he" (4:26).

The woman must have been amazed. The simplicity of His revelation was different from what she expected. Her response was to leave her waterpot, return to the village, announce Christ's presence, and invite her fellow citizens to see Him too (4:28-30).

This passage clearly demonstrates the purpose of Christian teaching. It is designed to produce the necessary life changes that will bring an individual into proper relationship with God in the first place or subsequently to lead him to maturity in Christ. It is indeed correct to observe that Jesus taught information—but always for greater purpose than mere information. The intent was always life change.

The passage also affords insight into the communication process: the teacher must value the learner for himself and then involve the learner in a discovery process that leads toward the goal of the teaching session.

Jesus' last command to His disciples provides further foundation for Christian teaching. They were to "make disciples," He instructed (Matthew 28:19). That is the work of introducing a person to Christ, a task that may be accomplished by preaching, teaching, testifying, or reasoning, according to the New Testament words used to describe the outreach of the first century church. But then He added, "teaching them to obey everything I have commanded" (Matthew 28:20).

Colossians 1:28 sums up the purpose for Bible teaching. "We proclaim Him," Paul said, "admonishing and teaching everyone with all wisdom, so that we may present everyone perfect in Christ." *Everyone. Perfect in Christ.* The audience is the world. The goal is nothing short of maturity.

In Christian teaching, the central issue is life—new life first, then a mature life in Christ. Life in Christ means to be *like* Christ. Much of education is concerned with helping people know what their teachers know. But Christian education is concerned with helping people become what their Teacher is.

An understanding of the purpose of Christian teaching is essential. Christian education is for every person, not just the saints or Americans or children or any other one group. Christian education is designed to produce maturity, a lifestyle, not merely people who can recite the Word or feel good about the Word.

How the Purpose Is Achieved

Colossians 1:9-14 provides helpful guidelines for developing maturity.[3] It is a prayer that Paul offered for the church at Colossae. It precedes the section that states that the goal for every activity, teaching included, is maturity.

Components of Maturity

Paul begins by stating that the foundation of Christian maturity, hence the beginning point for Christian teaching, is a knowledge of God's will (1:9). A knowledge of God's will begins with information from God's Word, of course. It is found in the Bible. It does not come from any secret source. Despite the mood of the times, it is fact, not feeling, that provides foundation for maturity.

Christian teaching in any era must center around the authoritative Word of God. It is the Bible that provides the content for Christian teaching. It is the Bible that undergirds procedure. It is the Bible that measures the outcomes of teaching. "All Scripture is God-breathed and is useful for teaching, rebuking, correcting and training in righteousness, so that the man of God may be thoroughly equipped for every good work," Paul stated (2 Timothy 3:16, 17). The Bible is the foundation for Christian maturity.

However, knowledge of God's will implies more than a head full of information about God. It is also a comprehension of that will of God and its application to life. Paul prayed for a knowledge of God's will for the Colossians—but with it wisdom and understanding (1:9).

Teachers often assume that mere recital of facts is an adequate outcome. We hear children recite, "Be ye kind to one another," and promptly hit each other with their blocks. We could even explain that behavior on the basis of lack of mental and emotional maturity, but that explanation is woefully inadequate when adults recite the same verse, yet crucify each other with their words!

The story is told of a lad who lived in Russia prior to the Bolshevik revolution. His village was desperately poor not only economically, but also spiritually. The Orthodox priests decided to offer rewards for the children if they would memorize Bible verses. One Bible verse memorized, one piece of candy earned. That was powerful incentive for poor children. One lad memorized more verses than any of the other children, hence more candy. Some would be tempted to hold this child up as the epitome of Bible learning. But that lad was Nikita Khrushchev! He had learned—but only words, not wisdom.

There is a substantial difference between being *smart* and *wise*. The first can be defined as an ability simply to recall facts—but wisdom is the ability to use that information in a practical fashion.

Perhaps the best example of wisdom is found in 1 Kings 3. God told Solomon he would be given whatever gift he chose. He chose wisdom, and God granted him this gift. The same chapter records how his wisdom was demonstrated. Two prostitutes came to Solomon with one baby. Each claimed the baby as her own. The wise king, who surely had a grasp of the principles we call psychology, made no effort to recite them. He simply asked for a sword in order to cut the baby in two and give half to each woman. He knew, of course, how a mother's mind works. One offered, "Please, my lord, give her the living baby. Don't kill him." Solomon knew that she was the mother. What a practical demonstration of wisdom!

But true knowledge always results in changed behavior (Colossians 1:10-12). Understanding God's revelation is always connected with right behavior. How did Jesus know that the Samaritan woman understood who He was and what it implied for her life? It was evident only when she left her waterpot, returned to the city, and testified that she had found the Christ. It is true for every Christian teacher: he knows that he has taught when his learners begin to *obey* Christ's commands.

Paul warned of the danger of those who are always learning but never acknowledging the truth (2 Timothy 3:7). He said on another occasion that if a person deliberately keeps on sinning after he has received the knowledge of truth, no sacrifice for sins is left (Hebrews 10:26). It is a reminder that the student's grasp of facts must result in behavior changes.

Jesus said the same thing when He asserted, "Not everyone who says to me, 'Lord, Lord,' will enter the kingdom of heaven, but only he who does the will of my Father who is in heaven" (Matthew 7:21).

Indicators of Maturity

The Christian lifestyle is demonstrated in four simple ways. The first is that the individual will bear fruit (Colossians 1:10). Galatians 5:22, 23 identifies that fruit: love, joy, peace, patience, kindness, goodness, faithfulness, gentleness, and self-control—all qualities of life designed to demonstrate His life to the lives of others.

Paul added that a second change in lifestyle is that one will grow in the knowledge of God (Colossians 1:10). That seems a puzzling statement at first glance: grow in knowledge so that you will grow in knowledge.

But the truth of the statement is evident in the physical realm. One must use his food intake if he is to have a healthy appetite. Overeating results in an unhealthy body, an unhealthy appetite, sometimes no real delight in food even though it is consumed in large quantities.

Some years ago I went to India to visit a mission. The trip was nearly twenty-four hours in duration with only brief stops in London, Frankfurt, Istanbul (where the ongoing passengers couldn't depart from the airplane because of security regulations), and Tehran (where everyone was confined in a small crowded area). There was little opportunity to use food for the purpose for which it was intended. Yet in that twenty-four hour period, the passengers were expected to consume dinner, breakfast, lunch, dinner, and breakfast. By the time the third meal arrived, I had no appetite for it. The previously ingested food had not yet been used for the purpose for which it was intended.

That is a picture of the Christian life. If one continues to take in facts, facts, facts, and never weave those into his lifestyle, he is satiated with facts as surely as the airplane passengers were with food. But if he takes in facts and uses them in his lifestyle, his appetite for Bible study is healthy.

The third lifestyle indicator is that the learner will gain endurance and patience (1:11). "We will no longer be infants, tossed back and forth by the waves, and blown here and there by every wind of teaching and by the cunning and craftiness of men in their deceitful scheming," Paul said. "Instead, . . . we will in all things grow up into Him who is the Head, that is, Christ" (Ephesians 4:14, 15). James said that "perseverance must finish its work so that you may be mature and complete, not lacking anything" (James 1:4).

Finally, the Christian lifestyle is a thankful, joyful one (Colossians 1:12). It is a life that praises God whatever the circumstances.

The Process of Maturing

One could say that Christian education is an enculturation process more than an academic exercise. Enculturation requires a grasp of information, to be sure, but it becomes a way of life.

I was reminded of that process a few years ago when I was in Papua, New Guinea. I was there as a board member of a mission group to spend my time with missionary families who had their children in home schooling situations. I learned what I could about Papua, New Guinea before I went: it is a third world country; people in some areas suffer from hunger and tropical disease; personal hygiene is nothing like that of Americans; women in the village wear nothing from the waist up. I *knew* it, but that didn't make any difference in the emotional responses when I arrived at the first bush assignment.

For a week, I stayed in a house with no indoor plumbing facilities. I heard lizards and rats slithering around all night. I endured mosquito bites and survived a tropical ulcer on my leg. I worshiped with beautiful Christians. But in no way did I become enculturated. It was a pleasure to set foot in Seattle when I returned to the United States. I was relieved that there were no lizards or rats in my home. I'm American in lifestyle. Though I can tell you many facts about life in Papua, New Guinea, I am not New Guinean. Nor would I be if I stayed a lifetime, though I could become as much—or perhaps even more—New Guinean than I am American.

That same understanding is critical for the Bible teacher. Christian education requires knowledge. But it also requires transformation into Christlikeness. The teacher must never confuse a recital of facts for the real thing. It is all too possible to talk about the Bible, recite the Bible, answer Bible questions, spout off Bible history, identify Bible places, even teach or preach the Bible. But that by itself does not make one mature. A person shall move not one inch toward Christlikeness until he knows the Word and *does* it.

Christian education can never be said to be complete with a mere grasp of information. It must produce the necessary lifestyle to demonstrate a walk with Christ. The function of the Christian teacher is best summed up in the words of Paul, who said, "It was [God] who gave some to be apostles, some to be prophets, some to be evangelists, and some to be pastors and teachers, to prepare God's people for works of service, so that the body of Christ may be built up until we all reach unity in the faith and in the knowledge of the Son of God and become mature, attaining to the whole measure of the fullness of Christ" (Ephesians 4:11-13).

Communicating the Word to the Learner

Communicating the Word to the pupil to achieve the biblical outcomes of teaching is the crux of Bible teaching. Effective communication involves at least three parts: imparting Bible facts, discovering how those facts can be used in life, and modeling the use of the Word in the life of the teacher.

Effective communication begins with a *goal*. Jesus had a goal when He taught the woman at the well. So must today's Bible teacher. The teacher wrestles with the biblical content long enough for it to work in his own life. But he must then focus on one truth appropriate for the needs of his class members. Then he identifies the changes of behavior he will seek in the lives of the pupils. As Lois LeBar observes, "A pupil's growth is determined not by what he hears, but what he does about what he hears."[4]

We may describe the communication process by four words: *hook, book, look,* and *took*.[5]

The teacher first decides how to gain the pupil's attention. This is the *hook*. How will he whet the pupils' appetites for biblical material?

Next the teacher will guide the pupils in a study of the Bible. This is the *book* section. Not only does the teacher determine what truth should be discovered, but also how he will involve the pupil in the process of discovering it for himself.

The next step is to examine implications for today's living that are suggested by the Bible material. This is the *look* section. Again the teacher must decide how he will guide the pupils to active exploration of life implications.

The teacher completes the learning cycle by guiding the pupil to decide how he will respond to the material he has studied. Although the teacher cannot follow each class member around in the ensuing week, he can send the Bible material and implications with the learner by providing a *took* in each lesson. He does so by eliciting a specific response that the student agrees to make as a result of the lesson.

The teacher is a resource person, a planner, a guide, a fellow learner. He designs goals and accomplishes them by building a sound lesson that begins with a need, proceeds to information, examines implications, and stimulates decision making.

The Role of the Christian Teacher

Who Is an Effective Teacher?

Researchers have tried for years to isolate the characteristics and practices of effective teachers. Their conclusions have failed to identify any particular teaching methodology or specific traits possessed only by effective teachers.

Ryans conducted a comprehensive study on the characteristics of teachers who had been rated "good" or "poor" by trained observers. The observers evaluated twenty-two dimensions of classroom behavior. Despite the expected individuality in personal traits, Ryans found certain traits common among the teachers who were rated "good:" they tended to see the good side of other people; they enjoyed social relationships, including those with their pupils; they possessed superior verbal intelligence and a strong interest in reading; they tended to let the pupil learn for himself rather than directing his learning; and they were well-adjusted emotionally.

Arthur Combs summarizes the evidence from studies about effective teachers in this way:

> As we have seen, research on the competencies had been unable to isolate any common trait or practice of good teachers. But the unanimous failure in itself demonstrates an important fact: a good teacher is primarily a unique personality.... *A good teacher is first and foremost a person* and this fact is the most important and determining thing about him. He has competence, to be sure, but not a common set of competencies like everyone else.[6]

Like Combs, Morse and Wingo conclude that the teacher is the key to good teaching: "The characteristics which are important to good teaching involve the ability to relate to and work with pupils and the ability to organize the learning experiences in some systematic manner."[7] Jesus had demonstrated that long before researchers began their exploration.

Qualities of the Effective Teacher

What qualities are part of that unique personality that makes an effective teacher? The following acrostic suggests some of the necessary qualities.

T—*Teachability.* An effective teacher is willing to learn. He seeks new information, tries new methods, and continues to grow in his personal spiritual life.

E—*Example.* An effective teacher, especially in Christian education, must be a worthy example of what he is teaching. He is fully aware of the truth of Jesus' statement, "Can one blind man be guide to another? Will they not both fall into the ditch? A pupil is not superior to his teacher; but everyone, when his training is complete, will reach his teacher's level."[8] The teacher models the process of Christian growth. He can say with Paul, "You know yourselves how you ought to copy our example."[9]

A—*Attitude.* An effective teacher is positive. He believes in his pupils. He believes that he is doing God's work. He really wants to teach.

C—*Commitment.* An effective teacher is committed first to the Lord Jesus Christ, to His Word, the Bible, and to the ministry of sharing Jesus with people. He is committed even in the face of difficulties that he will most certainly encounter.

H—*sense of Humor.* An effective teacher possesses a healthy sense of humor. Although he need not be an extremely witty person, he appreciates the humor of his students and circumstances.

E—*Enthusiasm.* An effective teacher has a zest for living, a joy in the Christian life, and the enthusiasm to share his joy with the individuals who make up his class.

R—*good Relationships with people.* An effective teacher understands that his goal is to help individuals to know the Lord. Therefore, he loves people and builds personal relationships with them. He is interested in people and is sensitive to their needs. He never forgets that his message is to people and for people. In short, he knows that:

> For truth to have its transforming impact on the human personality, love is utterly essential! It is truth that is communicated in the context of a close and loving relationship that will be used by God to remold and renew the believer's personality toward God.[10]

Responsibilities of the Teacher

What are the responsibilities of an effective Christian teacher? The Bible explicitly states those duties.

1. *Study God's Word carefully and consistently.* "Try hard to show yourself worthy of God's approval, as a labourer who need not be ashamed; be straightforward in your proclamation of the truth."[11] The reason is evident—that pupils will be introduced to Jesus Christ. The curriculum is the Word of God, brought alive by a growing, developing Christian teacher.

2. *Be willing to do whatever is necessary to be an effective teacher.* "Take your share of hardship, like a good soldier of Christ Jesus. A soldier on active service will not let himself be involved in civilian affairs; he must be wholly at his commanding officer's disposal. Again, no athlete can win a prize unless he has kept the rules."[12] No teacher worth his call attempts to get by with as little as possible.

3. *Be an example.* "In everything set them an example by doing what is good. In your teaching show integrity, seriousness and soundness of speech that cannot be condemned."[13] The effective teacher's words and behavior are in harmony.

4. *Be prepared.* "Hold the Lord Christ in reverence in your hearts. Be always ready with your defence whenever you are called to account for the hope that is in you, but make that defence with modesty and respect."[14]

5. *Know your pupils.* Take the time to get to know each person in your class, so that you can teach him what he really needs to know.

6. *Teach with purpose and for a decision.* Bible teaching is more than mere impartation of facts. In the New Testament, teaching is always the presentation of information in a way that requires people to make a decision about it. Jesus called for a response from the learner; an effective teacher does the same.

Summary

The purpose of Bible teaching is to bring change into the life of the learner until he has reached maturity in Christ—a lifelong task. This maturity is achieved when a person has a knowledge of God's Word, with understanding, that results in changed behavior: bearing fruit, growing in knowledge, becoming stronger in endurance and patience, and being thankful.

To be effective, Bible teaching proceeds according to a design: a goal, an attention getter, Bible exploration, life exploration, and decision making.

The effective teacher is someone who models Christlikeness, provides needed information, relates to the learners, and plans for active pupil involvement in the learning process.

Projects

1. Observe a Bible teacher in action. How well does the teacher demonstrate the qualities of an effective teacher? How well does he follow the plan for communicating the Word of God effectively?
2. Using the material in this chapter, evaluate your own potential as a teacher of God's Word. Cite areas of strength. Where do you need to improve?

Selected Bibliography

Brown, Lowell. *Sunday School Standards*. Glendale, CA: Gospel Light, 1981.

LeBar, Lois. *Education That Is Christian*. Westwood, NJ: Revell, 1958.

Richards, Lawrence O. *A Theology of Christian Education*. Grand Rapids, MI: Zondervan Publishing House, 1975.

_______. *Creative Bible Teaching*. Chicago: Moody Press, 1970.

---

[1]Matthew 7:28, 29

[2]Since this section specifically presents a biblical account of teaching, the Scripture references will remain in the text. Otherwise, Scripture references will be footnoted as all other references are.

[3]*Ibid.*

[4]Lois LeBar, *Education That Is Christian* (Westwood, NJ: Revell, 1958), p. 136.

[5]Lawrence O. Richards, *Creative Bible Teaching* (Chicago: Moody Press, 1970), pp. 108-112.

[6]Arthur Combs, *The Professional Education of Teachers* (Boston, MA: Allyn and Bacon, 1965), pp. 6, 8.

[7]William C. Morse and G. Max Wingo, *Psychology and Learning* (Chicago: Scott-Foresman, 1962), p. 9.

[8]Luke 6:39, *NEB*

[9]2 Thessalonians 3:7, *NEB*

[10]Lawrence O. Richards, *A Theology of Christian Education* (Grand Rapids, MI: Zondervan Publishing House, 1975), p. 45.

[11]2 Timothy 2:15, *NEB*

[12]2 Timothy 2:3-6, *NEB*

[13]Titus 2:7, 8

[14]1 Peter 3:15, *NEB*

CHAPTER 7

Helping Preschoolers Learn

As you read, think about these questions:
—What are the most important characteristics of a preschooler for a teacher to understand?
—How do the characteristics of the preschooler affect the way his teacher teaches?
—How should a preschool teaching session be organized?
—What are at least five methods used to teach preschoolers?

Todd is five years old. He was born only a short time ago, a helpless little fellow who could neither remember nor respond beyond his basic needs. But five years have passed quickly. He is now a sturdy, at times independent, learning personality. He has learned an immense amount in language, attitudes, skills, and facts during these five years—more than he will learn in any comparable period of time during the rest of his lifetime.

How has Todd developed? How do the principles and facts of his development contribute to the determination of teaching goals and methods for him?

Understanding the Preschool Learner

Physical Development

The preschool years are years of almost continual physical

growth and change. Small and helpless as he is, the newborn infant possesses that which is essential for him to grow and develop physically. It is his God-made nature to grow and mature, even if the rate is slow. Each individual has his own rate and pattern of development.

Physical growth is initially rapid. During the first year an infant will triple his weight. By the time he is two, a child is approximately one-half of his eventual adult height. From the age of two until six, a child grows approximately nine inches and gains an average of five pounds per year.

Motor development accounts for significant physical growth during the preschool years. During the two or three years following the rapid physical growth of the first eighteen months, the dominant physical change is large muscle development. The pattern of development proceeds from large muscles to small muscles. Small muscle development will not be finished during the preschool years, however.

A child first learns to grasp objects and to follow them with his eyes. He rolls over and lifts his head. He learns to walk perhaps as early as nine or ten months of age, nearly always by fifteen to eighteen months old. Then he explores by touching and handling objects. His preschool years are spent in adding, then refining, a variety of physical skills: jumping, skipping, running, and manipulating. A major achievement is toilet training, which is dependent upon adequate muscle development so that the child can control urination and elimination.

The latter part of the preschool years shows a shift to small muscle development, although that continues into the elementary school years. Small muscle development allows for the handling of pencils and scissors, for example, and eventually increased visual acuity.

Because of his rapid growth and continuing development of motor skills, activity is a chief characteristic of a preschooler. He cannot be expected to sit still for long periods of time without a change of focus to keep his attention. He likes to move and learns through activity when it is planned and guided. His attention span is roughly one minute per year of age.

The preschool teacher should take into account these principles to better accommodate a preschool child physically:

1. Use equipment geared to the child's size. The child's feet should touch the floor when he sits in a chair. If that isn't

possible, it is more effective to have the children sit on the floor rather than in chairs.

2. Avoid small muscle activities such as intricate coloring and cutting. Use large crayons and pencils.

3. Change activities often in order to maintain attention.

4. Use visual aids to keep attention during times when the children are sitting still and listening.

Intellectual Development

A child is more than a physical being. He can express himself with language even when very young. His intellectual nature distinguishes him as a member of humanity. How does it develop?

Intellectual development is affected both by heredity and environment. It once was thought that intelligence was entirely attributable to genetic inheritance. Although intelligence does depend to a large extent upon genes, early care and early intellectual and language stimulation are major factors as well. Some research suggests that those environmental factors may mean as many as fifty to seventy-five points on later intelligence scales.

What is measured as intelligence in Western culture is dependent largely upon language development. Acquiring language is perhaps one of the most important learning tasks of the preschool years. When a child can finally speak and express himself, he becomes more than a bundle of physical needs. He has the tools to express thought and develop measurable intelligence.

Language development follows an orderly pattern, not only in Western culture, but in other parts of the world as well. Babies begin the journey toward language by cooing and crying during their first five months. These seemingly meaningless sounds are essential for future language development. Then at about six months, the infant begins to babble. Various sounds are distinguishable, but nothing is yet understandable. Finally, when the baby is about ten months old, he begins to imitate sounds. By the time he reaches a year, he is finally able to say two or three words.

Five factors contribute to language development. The first is *grammatical structure,* which is well developed by six and fully adult by the middle elementary years. At age one, a child uses one word sentences. By the time he reaches eighteen months, he uses two word sentences. He begins to use three-word sentences by the time he is two. Finally, by the time he is four, he is capable of composing full, complex sentences. Children usually use nouns first, then add interjections, verbs, adjectives, pronouns, and adverbs in that order.

A second factor is *pronunciation*. Many children experience difficulty with *st, str, dr, fl,* and *th* sounds, sometimes due to hearing problems. Usually patient teaching and careful pronunciation will overcome such problems. Speech models are particularly important for a child to learn to pronounce words correctly.

Stuttering may also occur during the preschool years, often because the child thinks more rapidly than he is able to express himself. A child usually outgrows this problem unless undue pressure and attention is directed toward it. It also helps to encourage the child to slow down when he speaks.

A third factor in language development is *vocabulary*. It develops slowly during the child's first eighteen months, although he will recognize many more words than he says. By the time a child is two, he has a working vocabulary of about 272 words. His vocabulary increases to 846 words by age three, 1,540 by age four, 2,072 by age five, and 2,562 by age six—rapid growth indeed.

The fourth factor in language development is *rate of speaking*. The fifth is *communication style*, which is a combination of the other four factors. Both depend upon the models to which a child is exposed.

Language development is a complex process that affects a child's ability to express himself and his thoughts. He is born with the innate qualities from which language develops. How well it develops depends upon his language models, how much language stimulation he receives, the amount of reinforcement given to him, and his own rate of development.

Intellectual growth occurs in an orderly sequence, just as language does. Jean Piaget, a Swiss geneticist turned psychologist, studied intellectual development in children and youth. He concluded that there are definite stages of thought through which a child progresses.

Before the age of two, a child is preoccupied with sensory experiences and motor activities. Piaget called this the *sensori-*

motor stage. During this period, a child does not usually develop new ways of dealing with unique situations, but resorts to responses that worked in similar earlier situations.

The remainder of the preschool years is spent in what Piaget called the *preoperational* stage. While the sensorimotor child is restricted to direct interactions with his environment, the preoperational child can manipulate symbols (like words) that represent the environment. This is closely related to vocabulary development.

Although language symbols are used, the period from two to seven differs from later periods. One difference is concreteness. An adult can analyze and synthesize information, but a preschooler cannot. His thinking is limited to objects actually present or those he has experienced directly.

Preschool thought is also marked by *irreversibility.* Reversible thought is the basis for logical thinking. For example:

$$3 + 5 = 8 \text{ and } 8 - 5 = 3$$

or

All men and all women = all adults
and
All adults except all women = all men

In each case, one thinks his way from one place to another and then back again. A preschooler cannot do that. Ask a four-year-old boy, "Do you have a brother?"

He answers, "Yes."

"What is his name?"

"Shawn."

"Does Shawn have a brother?"

The reply is, "No." He is not ready for logical thinking.

Preschoolers also center their attention on one detail of an event and do not shift attention to other aspects. Show a preschooler two clay balls of equal size and ask, "Are they the same size?" and he will say that they are. Then, right before his eyes, roll one ball into a sausage shape. He will insist that one is now bigger than the other. That happens because he centers on only one detail. (If he centers on height, he will think the round ball is larger. If he centers on length, he will believe the sausage to be larger.)

This information about the intellectual development of preschoolers has some important implications for Bible teachers:

1. Choose concrete words to communicate to preschoolers.
2. Center on one theme or concept for a Bible lesson. Avoid too many details in stories or pictures.
3. Use a wide variety of sensory experiences in teaching—visuals to look at and objects to feel, smell, and taste—as well as listening.
4. Avoid detailed, logical explanations.
5. Use visual aids to illustrate and reinforce words and ideas.
6. Inasmuch as possible, find ways for children to experience the Bible truth by doing.

Psychosocial Development

A preschooler is a physical being and a thinking, intelligent individual. But he is more than that. He is also a feeling personality.

A newborn infant is limited in his range of emotional response. He expresses distress (mostly vocally) and delight. When a baby is distressed, he is very, very distressed and lets it be known in no uncertain terms. But when he is happy, he is all smiles and gurgles and cooing. Before many months, perhaps by five or six months, he experiences and expresses anger. By the time he reaches his ninth month, he experiences anxiety with strangers. Fear appears between twelve and eighteen months of age. Those fears are nearly always of tangible objects or circumstances: large animals, new places, and new people, for example.

At best, emotional responses of young children are unstable. They react strongly to frustrating or rewarding experiences. It is an arduous journey from the first appearance of emotional responses to the ability to control emotional behavior.

A second facet of psychosocial development is *socialization*, or the ability to live in a social setting. A child brings into the world his unique genetic inheritance, which affects his social development as surely as it does physical and intellectual growth. But living in society is also a matter of learning. Parents serve as key persons, although teachers and other care givers also contribute to social learning.

Play behavior provides a fascinating view of social development. Before eighteen months, children react to each other only as objects, not as playmates. Between eighteen and thirty-six months, true social interest emerges, but children still do not play *with* each other; they engage in parallel play. But from three years on, peers become increasingly important. Play progresses from associative play with no organization at age three to self-organized, cooperative play at four. Such progress assumes adequate social interaction with peers.

"Play" is a child's word. Adults play to escape the routines of life, but children play to imitate life. They are great pretenders who use ideas, information, and behavior from "real life" in their play. By so doing they develop and reinforce their ideas.

Development of self is another facet of psychosocial behavior. Self-concept is an individual's awareness of his own characteristics and attributes. It begins to emerge by age two or three. Closely akin is self-esteem—the value a child puts on himself. Self-esteem emerges before kindergarten.

Identity is the next step in the development of self. Identity may be defined as awareness of group membership and the expectations, privileges, restraints, and responsibilities that accompany membership in the group. The foundations are laid during the preschool years when a child learns acceptable social behavior.

Self is developed most adequately when certain factors are present. One is parental acceptance of the child, which is demonstrated by affection and a comfortable family life. A second is discipline—clear rules consistently and firmly enforced. Physical abnormalities and maturation rate also contribute to development of the self.

Another aspect of psychosocial behavior is sexual development. Sex-related behavior appears first at ages three to five. Sex interest and sex play are common among preschoolers. They are curious about the differences between boys and girls.

Although children must be taught modesty and proper sexual behavior, their interactions with adults about sex should be based on honesty and acceptance. Healthy psychosocial development depends in large part upon models of self-acceptance and observation of physical affection between parents. A loving father (or a surrogate) is particularly important for a child to see and imitate in order to learn appropriate male and female behavior.

This information about psychosocial development has the following implications for the teacher of preschoolers.

1. Be prepared for fluctuations in emotional response.
2. Be prepared to repeat rules for behavior and to correct misbehavior over and over again. Self-directed social behavior does not emerge overnight.
3. Use guided play experiences to teach.
4. Praise the child for what he does well. A good rule is to say something good about every child during every class session. Be sure that praise is genuine and about items the child can control. For example, say, "You did a good job of picking up the blocks. That is very helpful," rather than responding to the same incident with, "You are the best little girl." Such a response will allow her to repeat acceptable actions and to change unacceptable ones.
5. Establish clear boundaries for behavior in the classroom. Enforce them consistently and firmly.

Moral and Spiritual Development

Man is moral because he is spiritual, rational, and able to choose. What is moral-spiritual development? Cornelius Jaarsma offers an insightful explanation:

> It is nothing less than development of the whole person in all dimensions of personality such that consecration of the spirit to the service of God and moral righteousness find expression in the fulness of life.... Moral-spiritual values of the Christian flow from a restored relationship to God in faith and a humble obedience to His will as He makes it known in His Word.[1]

Moral behavior includes two facets. The first is development of intention and conscience (which is internal), and the second is adherence to social norms and responsibilities. Indicators of moral behavior are (1) resistance of temptation, (2) guilt, (3) independence of action from external sanctions, and (4) confession and assumption of responsibility for actions. Not all of these are fully developed during the preschool years.

Conscience begins to emerge during the preschool years. Loving home conditions are vitally important for healthy conscience development. Parental warmth plus firmly enforced rules tend to produce well-behaved children who are able to accept responsibility for their behavior and who internalize behavior expectations. A warm, loving father is especially important for conscience development for both boys and girls.

A young child is growing morally. His morality is determined largely by the rules laid down by others (usually his parents). He judges things and events as either black or white. At first he behaves properly because of fear of punishment; later he behaves properly in order to please. Not before the middle of his elementary school years does he consistently behave properly because of his own decision.

At the same time, the preschooler can be taught to love Jesus and to want to please a loving God. His attitudes toward God will reflect the concrete relationship he experiences with his own father (or surrogate). The major area of spiritual growth is the shaping of attitudes toward God, the Bible, and the church.

A teacher of young children should take into account the following principles:

1. Work with simple spiritual concepts related to the experiences of the child.
2. Build basic attitudes toward God, Jesus, the church, the world, the Bible, the family, and self.
3. Recognize that your warmth and caring may teach as much as the Bible facts you share.

Goals for Early Childhood Education

The basic goal for all Bible teaching is summed up in Colossians 1:28: "We proclaim him, admonishing and teaching everyone with all wisdom, so that we may present everyone perfect in Christ." Or as Paul put it to the Ephesians, we teach ". . . until we all reach unity in the faith and in the knowledge of the Son of God and become mature, attaining to the whole measure of the fullness of Christ."[2] The foundations are laid in the preschool years by using the Bible effectively and creating a loving community in which children may be nurtured.

Much preschool Bible teaching time is spent in laying foundations. Basic Bible stories are presented to build a love for the Bible and an acquaintance with God, Jesus, and those who loved Him. Conversion will not come for some time yet, but ideas and attitudes begin to sprout in the early years.

Bible material must be presented in a loving environment in order to build basic attitudes. Attitudes and values and faith are modeled and reinforced by teachers who care and by a church community that lives the faith.

The goals for preschoolers can be summarized in this way:

1. Each child will be familiar with the powerful, yet loving nature of God and Jesus.
2. Each child will associate God, Jesus, the natural world, and the Bible with the love of people around him.
3. Each child will have basic knowledge of God, Jesus, the natural world, and the Bible.
4. Each child will know that he is important because he is made by God.
5. Each child will want to respond to God appropriately.

Teaching Preschoolers

Arranging Teaching Time

Teaching time should be flexible for preschoolers. The purpose is to provide satisfying learning experiences from the time the first child arrives until he departs for home. It is preferable to develop the Sunday school and church times into one time block for this age level. One set of curriculum material can then be used to teach one concept per Sunday.

Figure 7-1 shows a teaching schedule for preschoolers. It includes a design for a department in which two or more teachers share together, as well as a plan for one teacher who conducts a class all alone.

The key to arranging teaching time is to provide for frequent change of activities.

Choosing Methods

Preschoolers learn primarily through their environment and through the people in that environment. Earlier discussion of the characteristics of preschoolers suggested that children learn from guided play experiences that use ample sensory experiences. Preschool Bible lessons may be built around several kinds of activities.

Block building may be used during Activity Time or Choos-

Segment	One or More Teachers	One Teacher	Time
	Sunday School Time		
Learning Activities	Children select activities from several options; a teacher is at each center	Teacher plans several activities; all do each at the same time	2's/3's 35-40 min 4's/5's 25-30 min
Together	All children together for music and special features		10-15 min
Bible Story	Children in small groups, each group having one teacher; pupil's book	Story; pupil's book	2's/3's 10-15 min 4's/5's 15-20 min
	TRANSITION—5 minutes		
	Church Time		
Choosing	Choose from activities used in Sunday school; include one new activity all do at the same time	Repeat activities used in Sunday school; include one new activity	2's/3's 30-35 min 4's/5's 25-30 min
Together	Retell story, music, finger plays, snack, rest		20-25 min
Story	Life-related story, review Bible story		10-15 min

Figure 7-1. Sunday Morning Teaching Schedule, Preschool Department

ing Time. Use large cardboard blocks for toddlers, even 2's and 3's, but if possible, provide wood blocks for 4's and 5's. A creative teacher will be able to use conversation and questions to stimulate children to build many Bible-related items with blocks.

Nature objects are effective for either Activity Time or Choosing Time. This center may include nature books, planting, nature walks, caring for animals, and slides and pictures of nature objects and scenes.

Books are also best used for Activity Time and Choosing Time, although they are often useful for Together Time as well. Collect a variety of books, but on any given Sunday, put out only the books relating to the Bible concept for the day.

Puzzles are best used for Activity Time and Choosing Time. A variety of puzzles should be collected, but just as with books, put out only the puzzles relating to the theme for the day.

Home living activities may be planned for Activity Time and Choosing Time. This center allows the child to practice Bible concepts in everyday situations like those at home. Home living materials may be made or bought.

Art activities may be used during Activity Time and Choosing Time. Painting, finger painting, working with clay, cutting and pasting, drawing, coloring, and making simple crafts are all useful art activities.

Storytelling may be used at any time, but it is the central method for Bible Story Time, Together Time, and Story Time.

Music may be used throughout the session. It is most often used during Together Time. Rhythm instruments may be introduced as well as singing. Records and tapes are also helpful.

Pictures illustrate concepts mentioned at any point in the day's activities. They are especially useful as an aid to storytelling. Pictures include felt pictures, standup figures, flannelgraph figures, dioramas, or filmstrips. Use them often.

Guided conversation is used with the active methods suggested for Activity Time and Choosing Time. While the children do the activity, the teacher can ask questions and make statements that will link the activity with the Bible.

Four criteria should be applied to the selection of methods for any given Bible lesson:

1. Will this method present, reinforce, or otherwise relate to today's Bible concept?

2. Is this activity one my class enjoys and is capable of doing?

3. Do I have access to the necessary materials for this method?

4. Is there someone available to guide this activity?

Making the Lesson Plan

A lesson plan is a map for the teacher. It includes the central focus of the lesson, the expected learning outcomes, the methods used to achieve the outcomes, and the amount of time to be devoted to each part of the lesson.

The following lesson plan demonstrates the arrangement of a teaching session for preschoolers. It is a session designed to be used by one teacher with a group of children. However, the activities selected could be readily used in a classroom with two or more teachers.

Title: God Made Everything
Scripture: Genesis 1
Central Truth: God made everything in our world.

Objectives: At the end of the session, the pupil will be able to: 1) name things God made and 2) express thanks to God for what He has made.

Activity Time (30 minutes)

1. Picture center (children select pictures of their favorite foods), 5 minutes

Conversation Ideas: Who made that food? Are you glad that God made that food? What other foods did God make?

2. Book center (children may choose one book from *How God Gives Us Peanut Butter* and *How God Gives Us Bread),* 10 minutes

3. Food center (children make peanut butter sandwiches and eat them), 10 minutes

Conversation Ideas: Who made bread? Who made peanut butter? Let's thank God for bread and peanut butter.

4. Nature center (children examine a tulip), 5 minutes

Conversation Ideas: Who made a tulip? I'm thankful God made tulips. Let's thank God for making tulips.

Together Time (10 minutes)

1. Sing "Who Made the World?"—children will substitute items for several verses

Bible Story Time (20 minutes)

1. Tell the Bible story (use flannelgraph figures), 8 minutes
2. Plant radish seeds in styrofoam cups with potting soil, 12 minutes

Conversation Ideas: Who made radishes? I'm thankful God lets me help Him with all the things He has made. Can you take your seeds home and water them? When they grow, remember to tell God thank you for all that He has made.

3. Close with a prayer.

Summary

Teaching Todd the preschooler is challenging, fun, and rewarding when you remember Todd's physical, intellectual, emotional, and spiritual capabilities and then plan to meet them. Set your goals, arrange your schedule, and select the best ways to stimulate him to learn. Lay Bible foundations and shape attitudes for those later days when he will make the decision to live his life with Jesus Christ.

Projects

1. Observe a preschool child. How is he like the description in this textbook? How is he different?
2. Talk to someone who works in a preschool department. How is the Bible teaching time arranged? Why? What teaching methods are used?
3. Plan a Bible lesson for preschoolers using Luke 2:8-20 as the text. Use the lesson plan form illustrated above.

Selected Bibliography

Aldridge, Betty. *You Can Teach Preschoolers Successfully.* Cincinnati, OH: Standard Publishing, 1983.

Cully, Iris V. *Christian Child Development*. San Francisco, CA: Harper and Row Publishers, 1979.

Harrell, Donna and Wesley Haystead. *Creative Bible Learning for Young Children*. Glendale, CA: Gospel Light, 1977.

Joy, Donald. *Bonding*. Waco, TX: Word, Inc., 1985.

Klein, Karen. *Bible Learning Activities: Ages 2-5*. Ventura, CA: Gospel Light, 1982.

Phillips, John, Jr. *The Origins of Intellect: Piaget's Theory*. San Francisco, CA: W.H. Freeman and Co., 1969.

Price, Max. *Understanding Today's Children*. Nashville, TN: Convention Press, 1982.

Richards, Lawrence O. *A Theology of Children's Ministry*. Grand Rapids, MI: Zondervan Publishing House, 1983.

Santrock, John. *Life Span Development*. 2nd ed. Dubuque, IA: William C. Brown Co., Publishers, 1986.

---

[1]Cornelius Jaarsma, *Human Development: Learning and Teaching* (Grand Rapids, MI: Wm. B. Eerdmans Publishing Co., 1961), p. 155.

[2]Ephesians 4:13

CHAPTER 8

Helping Elementary Children Learn

As you read, think about these questions:
—What are the chief characteristics of elementary learners?
—How do these characteristics affect how they learn?
—What are the goals for teaching elementary children?
—How should teaching time for children be organized?
—What are at least ten methods for teaching children?

Jeffrey is six years old. He only faintly resembles what he was as an infant six years ago, but he will hardly be the same child six years from now. At six, he is in the first grade, ready to begin formal education and immense changes. The foundations were laid during his preschool days, but now the superstructure begins to emerge. Jeffrey continues to grow physically, and expands and refines the social, emotional, intellectual, and spiritual areas of his life.

Jeffrey is about to experience significant changes during these coming six years. His teachers will do well to understand and respond to those changes.

Understanding Elementary Children

Physical Development

Growth rate slows during the elementary years, perhaps as a

prelude to the rapid physical development that will occur during adolescence. Changes in height and weight are steady but slow. Coordination improves dramatically, and so does motor development, which approaches adult standards by the end of elementary school.

Perhaps the most dramatic physical transition occurs late in elementary years when prepubertal changes begin. This is especially important for girls who not only undergo prepubertal changes, but are likely to experience the onset of puberty itself. Girls will likely experience a growth spurt during the late elementary years, probably outgrowing the boys. Many girls will also begin their menstrual cycles.

The onset of puberty has definite social implications. Early-maturing girls, especially tall ones, may well experience some self-esteem problems related to their size. The teacher must be attuned to the child's need for personal affirmation.

A high premium is assigned to motor skills at this age level. This too has profound social implications. Children are selected or passed over for most childhood games on the basis of physical skills and coordination. The child with well-developed skills has an advantage in social relationships, the means by which self-concept is built.

At any stage along the way, the most accurate description of elementary children could be "Active!" These youngsters can concentrate on a task for a significant amount of time *if* they are actively involved in it. With their tendency to overdo, they need enforced periods of relaxation or quiet involvement.

Eyes do not fully mature before eight years for most children. Therefore, primary-age children often have difficulty focusing on small print or objects.

The alert teacher will observe physical characteristics by heeding the following principles:

1. Alternate active with quiet times, but at all times, keep the child actively involved in learning.
2. Be alert for concern among early-maturing girls and late-maturing boys. Give them personal affirmation so they can learn to accept themselves.
3. Use large lettering for primaries so that children may read easily.
4. Give each child recognition and affirmation—not just those who are popular among their peers.

Intellectual Development

Perhaps the most significant achievement of the elementary years is learning to read. The foundations were laid in the preschool days, when the child acquired language. Now language can be used not only for oral communication, but for visual communication as well. Successful reading depends upon five environmental factors as well as innate capabilities:

1. Rich language environment.
2. Significant adults who read a great deal.
3. Attainment of concrete operations intellectual level (see later in this section).
4. Interaction with adults interested in reading.
5. Appropriate social and emotional development.

Elementary age children are curious about nearly everything. During the primary years especially, curiosity and interest may shift from one thing to the next. But by fifth and sixth grades specific interests begin to emerge.

Distinct sex differences can be found in specific abilities and overall academic achievement. For example, girls generally are superior in verbal fluency, spelling, reading, mathematical computation, and overall grades. On the other hand, boys excel in mathematical reasoning and spatial manipulation. These differences may be due to the fact that girls are more intent on pleasing others while boys tend to spend their time doing things that interest them. Males generally achieve at a higher level than females later in life.

A child enters elementary school still thinking in a preoperational manner (as described in the previous chapter). Somewhere near age seven, he begins to enter the concrete operations period, which will extend to the end of his elementary years. His thinking begins to develop in several areas.

1. *Conservation of number.* During the preoperational period, even after a child can make one-to-one correspondence between symbols and what they represent, he may be fooled if one set of objects (vases, for example) is placed in a line and the other set (flowers) in a cluster. He will perceive the sets to be no longer equal. However, once he reaches a concrete operations stage, he cannot be fooled.

2. *Conservation of weight, size, and volume.* The preschooler sees two balls as equal if they are shaped alike, but when the shapes change before his eyes, he will say that they

are of different sizes. At about seven, a child will agree that the quantity of the two balls is the same, but will deny that weight is. Later, at about nine years, he will agree that weight is the same, but not volume. Finally, by age eleven, he will say that volume is the same too.

3. *Numbering in a series.* A preoperational child finds it impossible to match one set of objects to another set of different objects while at the same time arranging them in order of size. He can arrange objects in order of size, but when he does, he ignores number. He can count, but when he does, he ignores differences in size. The child at a concrete operations level can do both. We can summarize by saying that the elementary child can begin to reverse thought and also to decenter. (Both concepts were explained in the last chapter.)

The mental activities of a child have moved from sensory experiences (at birth), to perceptions, to intellectual operations. This progression makes it possible for him to understand cause-and-effect relationships, scientific information, and mathematical computation and reasoning. The bases for logical reasoning are established.

Differences in cognitive style also become apparent. "Cognitive style" refers to ways of thinking and responding. Impulsive thinkers are concerned about quickness, while reflective thinkers are more concerned about correctness of answers than speed in answering. Children also differ in distractibility, ability to memorize, and ability to solve problems.

Recent research indicates that there may exist seven types of intelligence: linguistic, musical, logico-mathematical, spatial, bodily-kinesthetic, personal knowledge, and knowledge of others.[1] This research suggests that children learn best via experiences that capitalize upon their kind of intelligence. Hardly anyone shines in all seven areas, so it is important to appreciate those a child does have rather than lament those he does not possess.

A teacher of elementary children should take intellectual characteristics into account by observing the following principles.

1. Be alert to individual differences in rate and style of learning.
2. Stimulate natural curiosity. Relate learning to the child's interests.

3. Avoid abstract logical reasoning, especially before fifth or sixth grade.
4. Provide a variety of instructional activities and styles in order to appeal to the variety of skills, abilities, and interests in the class.

Psychosocial Development

In elementary school, one's peers are powerfully important. Feelings of competence and a sense of worth depend upon foundations laid in the family, but those foundations of self-concept are tested against the reactions of a social group. A child relates to peers not as a subordinate as he does with adults, but on equal status. To some degree, the quality of those relationships determines his ego strength and behavior. "All the boys do it," is a logical argument for almost any elementary-age boy.

As the children reach nine, ten, and eleven, they assert increasing independence. Their newfound independence is evidenced by wandering afield without permission, by less communication with adults, and sometimes by carelessness in appearance. Until then, however, a child is usually eager to please adults.

Boys are more aggressive than girls. When a group of boys are together, plenty of wrestling, shoving, and punching can be reasonably expected. Both boys and girls are highly competitive. There is usually a certain amount of competitiveness between boys and girls.

Elementary-age children become selective in their choice of friends. They have a best friend and sometimes an "enemy" as well. Friendships are generally with someone of the same sex.

Prejudicial attitudes begin to emerge. These reflect the opinions of older behavior models.

Sexual interest is also prevalent, especially among girls, many of whom reach puberty before they finish elementary school. Children's interactions with adults about sex need to be based on honesty, truth, and openness. Correct terminology should be used. A child's healthy psychosexual development depends upon having an adult who models self-acceptance and who expresses physical affection. The model is usually provided by parents or parental substitutes.

Perhaps the most crucial condition for healthy psychosocial

development during this period is the existence of appropriate behavior expectations coupled with firm, consistent enforcement of them. Parents and teachers must not abdicate their leadership and authority before the child is ready for excessive independence.

Observance of these characteristics will make teaching elementary age children a satisfying experience. Take into account the following principles:

1. Be alert to the need of each child for affirmation. Be generous with praise—but offer praise for specific behaviors that the child can choose to control.
2. Arrange your teaching time in such a way as to permit each child to choose the activities he will participate in. This principle will be developed further later in this chapter.
3. Capitalize upon competitiveness, but make it competition in which everyone can be a winner. Set it up so that the child competes against himself.
4. Be honest and open with children.
5. Set and enforce reasonable behavior standards.

Moral and Spiritual Development

A child's conscience continues to develop during the elementary years. As it was during the preschool years, models are most important—especially warm, nurturing fathers or father substitutes. The primary child has yet to internalize behavior sanctions—he still determines morality by parental rules and the threat of punishment. But as the elementary years draw to a close, the youngster begins to behave appropriately most of the time because he chooses to. Much of his moral behavior is related to psychosocial maturity as well as to direct moral instruction.

The older child begins to make moral judgments in more than black and white terms. He still is not intellectually capable of abstract reasoning and complex logical thinking, but he begins to see moral decisions in their context. He can assume the other person's point of view, which allows him to consider possible alternatives for action.

A child is sensitive to spiritual teaching, especially when it is presented by caring adults whose lives reflect the teachings they are giving. He is ready for Bible teaching if it is presented in concrete, life-related terms.

Many elementary children make salvation decisions, usually based upon a desire to please Jesus more than from a deep sense of sin. They can define sin, but in terms of specific behaviors rather than as a state of rebellion toward God. Such an understanding is an adequate beginning point for the Christian life, especially if they are led to the next stage of understanding as adolescents.

The teacher of elementary children should observe these principles:

1. Teach him to trust God and His Word.
2. Use concrete biblical experiences to support Bible concepts.
3. Practice what you teach.

Goals for Teaching Children

Goal setting is essential. Teachers must know what they want to accomplish when they teach children. At least three objectives determine the kind of teaching given to elementary children.

The most basic goal is to teach Bible facts. By the time a child completes his elementary years, he should know basic people and events of the Bible, be able to name and find the books of the Bible, be able to find Bible references, and be able to name and describe the divisions of the Bible. Primaries will continue to work with the simple concepts of the preschool years, adding some detail, but Middlers and Juniors can work with chronological information.

A second goal is to continue to build attitudes toward God, Jesus, the Bible, the church, and self. Although teaching must emphasize Bible facts, it goes beyond mere presentation of information. It must be related to the feelings and behaviors of children in day-to-day living. That is how faith is built.

Third, the foundations should be laid for conversion, which may not occur until the early adolescent period. Facts and attitudes contribute to conversion, but sin, forgiveness, and obedience must also be stressed—not as a way to manipulate children to make decisions they are not yet ready to make, but in order to provide a biblical basis for salvation decisions whenever they do occur. The children who do become Christians also need guidance in Christian living—information, practice, and encouragement.

Teaching Elementary Children

Arranging Teaching Time

The Sunday school for children should allow the children to make choices and provide for normally active children to participate in the learning process. Children's departments operate on the same overall schedule as the rest of the Sunday school. The time block should be arranged to permit children to learn most effectively.

Small Groups, 15-20 minutes:

Each child chooses a planned introductory activity such as a puzzle, game, or art when he arrives. The activity is related to the teaching aims for the day.

Entire Class Group, 30-35 minutes:

The Bible materials are presented and life application is made. Activities completed during the small-group time may be displayed or reported as they relate to the lesson presentation.

Entire Department, 10-15 minutes:

All classes within a department share together with music, prayer, and presentation of class activities.

Adjustments to this schedule may be made for either a greater or lesser time allotment.

Choosing Methods

The teacher of children may choose from seven basic categories of teaching methods.

Art. Children enjoy art activities and learn by expressing themselves artistically. What they create visualizes the Bible material for themselves and others in the class. Art methods are especially appropriate for children who find it difficult to express themselves verbally. Here are some easily used art activities:

Making cartoons. This can be used well both to illustrate Bible accounts and to show how to apply Bible truth.

Charts. Children may make charts to show themes from a Bible account.

Dioramas. Children may make three-dimensional scenes to illustrate a Bible account or show how to apply a Bible truth.

Maps. Older children may use these to locate Bible places.

Murals. Children may make a series of pictures to illustrate a Bible account.

Mobiles. Children may make symbols to be hung in a mobile to illustrate a Bible account or show how to apply a Bible truth.

Making filmstrips and slides. Children make their own filmstrips on blank filmstrip material or 3″ x 5″ write-on slides to illustrate a Bible account.

Posters. Children make these to illustrate a Bible account or show how to apply the Bible truth.

Time lines. These may be made to reinforce chronological studies.

Drama. Creative dramatics allows children to reinforce concepts and facts while also experiencing the feelings of those with whom they identify in the drama. A variety of dramatic activities are possible.

Interview. Children may do imaginary interviews with Bible people.

Monologue. A child may present instructions from a Bible person.

Pantomime. Children may act out the Bible account.

Puppet plays. Children may make various kinds of puppets and present the Bible account with the puppet they have made.

Role playing. Older children can act out life situations and show how to apply the Bible truth.

Written Communication. Written activities are appealing to many children. They are effective for reporting and recording information, reflecting feelings, and expressing ideas and feelings.

Diary writing. Children may make imaginary entries into the diaries of Bible characters.

Letter writing. Children may write letters to or from Bible characters.

Newspaper writing. Children may write Bible accounts into newspaper stories.

Poems. These may be written to apply a Bible truth.

Story writing. These may be written to apply a Bible truth.

Word games and puzzles. Hidden words, acrostics, crossword puzzles, and others may be used.

Oral Communication. Communication probably shall always include oral forms—teacher-to-pupil, pupil-to-teacher, and pupil-to-pupil. Every Bible lesson will depend upon some oral communication forms: discussion, question-and-answer, and storytelling.

Games. Children explore their world through games. Games are effective ways to present and review information and to teach Bible verses. Use the list below or make up your own.

Bible Verse Games	*Facts Games*	*Review Games*
Connect the Words	Flash cards	Add-a-Word
Match Picture to Idea	Matching	Fill in Blank
Match the Halves	Password	Matching
Put in Order	Spinner	Bible Baseball,
Match the Words	TV Formats	Hockey, Football,
		Basketball

Music. Children enjoy and respond to music. Music is used for worship experiences, but musical activities are also valuable to teach or reinforce facts or concepts and to express response to biblical material. Children can *choose songs* to illustrate a Bible concept, *create original songs* to relate a Bible account or to tell how to apply a Bible truth, *illustrate songs* that relate to the Bible truth for the day, and *listen to music* that relates to the Bible truth for the day.

Research. Research and report methods work well with children, especially if the type of research is varied. Children can *go on field trips, find answers to questions from Bible texts,* and *make reports.*

Writing the Lesson Plan

A good lesson plan for children identifies the central Bible truth to be communicated, the expected learning outcomes, and the methods by which the outcomes will be achieved. This example of a lesson plan will provide guidance.

Title: Overcoming Temptation
Age: Grades 5-6
Scripture: Luke 4:1-12
Central Truth: Jesus' example can help us resist temptation.
Objectives: At the end of the session, the pupils will be able to: 1) name the temptations Jesus faced, 2) tell how He overcame them, and 3) make a plan for resisting temptation themselves.

Bible Readiness (20 minutes)

Children may choose one of these three activities to do.

1. Read the Bible text, then make a mural to illustrate it.
2. Play "Temptation Game," a spinner game found in the visual packet.
3. Answer questions from the Bible text (found in the pupil's book).

Group Bible Study (25 minutes)

1. Mural group presents the Bible story.
2. Group who found answers to questions lead the rest of the class in answering the questions in their pupil books.
3. Teacher fills in needed details that were missed by either group.
4. Report from game group on what happened when they gave in to temptation.
5. How can we resist temptation? Children talk about ways, then develop their own plan by completing the activity in the pupil's book.

Department Time (10 minutes)

Led by department leader

Summary

The world of an elementary child is an expanding, fascinating one. Teaching Jeffrey is a matter of first understanding his physical, intellectual, psychosocial, and spiritual capabilities and then designing lessons to communicate with him. It is challenging and worthwhile to see children grow in faith and response toward God.

Projects

1. Observe two elementary-age children, a second grader and a fifth grader. How are they like each other? How are they different from each other? How do they match the description made in this chapter? How do they differ from it?
2. Interview a worker in a children's department. How is the teaching time arranged? Why? What methods has the teacher used?
3. Plan a Bible lesson for children using John 20:1-18 as the text. Design it as the sample lesson plan did above.

Selected Bibliography

Bolton, Barbara and Charles Smith. *Creative Bible Learning for Children, Grades 1-6*. Glendale, CA: Gospel Light, 1977.

Bolton, Barbara. *How to Do Bible Learning Activities: Children Grades 1-6*. Volume 1. Glendale, CA: Gospel Light, 1982.

Bolton, Barbara. *How to Do Bible Learning Activities: Children Grades 1-6*. Volume 2. Glendale, CA: Gospel Light, 1984.

Elkind, David. *The Hurried Child*. Reading, MA: Addison-Wesley Publishing Company, 1981.

Phillips, John, Jr. *The Origins of Intellect: Piaget's Theory*. San Francisco, CA: W.H. Freeman and Co., 1969.

Price, Max. *Understanding Today's Children*. Nashville, TN: Convention Press, 1982.

Richards, Lawrence O. *A Theology of Children's Ministry*. Grand Rapids, MI: Zondervan Publishing House, 1983.

Santrock, John. *Life Span Development*. 2nd ed. Dubuque, IA: William C. Brown Co., Publishers, 1986.

Shelly, Judith Allen. *The Spiritual Needs of Children*. Downers Grove, IL: Inter-Varsity Press, 1982.

Sias, Twila. *You Can Teach Children Successfully*. Cincinnati, OH: Standard Publishing, 1983.

---

[1]Howard Gardner, *Frames of Mind* (New York: Basic Books, 1983).

CHAPTER 9

Helping Youth Learn

As you read, think about these questions:
—What are the chief characteristics of youth?
—How do the characteristics of youth affect how the teacher teaches?
—What are the goals for teaching youth?
—How is the teaching time for youth to be arranged?
—What are at least ten different methods of teaching youth?

Henrietta Mears, long-time Director of Christian Education at First Presbyterian Church in Hollywood, California, herself an exceptional teacher of youth, used to say, "No one loves junior highs except their mothers—and even they wonder on occasion!" More than a few who have tried their hands at teaching junior highs and senior highs would agree.

Teaching youth is, at best, demanding. It calls for committed teachers who try to understand teenagers and who communicate the Word creatively, speaking to the needs of teens. But teaching youth, when it is done well, is rewarding for both now and the future.

Understanding the Adolescent

Physical Development

Dozens of definitions of adolescence have been offered. None seems to be adequate by itself, for adolescence is a complex interaction of physical, emotional, intellectual, and cultural factors that affect the entire personality. Adolescents are individuals, each developing at his own rate. Besides that, adolescence, as we know it, is not a universal phenomenon.

Adolescence, whenever it begins and ends, and in whatever culture it occurs, involves significant physical changes called puberty. Most girls will experience the onset of puberty sometime before they become teenagers, a fact that affects self-image. On the other hand, boys may not experience puberty until eighth or ninth grade, fully two years later than girls on the average. For boys who mature even later than the average, self-image is negatively affected.

A predictable sequence of physical changes occurs for both boys and girls. Both begin with a change in hormone balance. But the age at which puberty occurs is unpredictable. The following list shows the sequence of changes:

Girls	**Boys**
Change in hormone balance	Change in hormone balance
Rapid skeletal growth	Rapid skeletal growth
Breast development	Enlargement of genitals
Appearance of straight pubic hair	Appearance of straight pubic hair
Maximum growth spurt	Voice cracks
Appearance of kinky pubic hair	First wet dream
Onset of menstruation	Appearance of kinky pubic hair
Appearance of underarm hair	Maximum growth spurt
	Appearance of downy facial hair
	Appearance of chest and underarm hair
	Final voice changes
	Appearance of coarse facial hair

The average age for puberty for girls is eleven to twelve, fourteen for boys. The physical process will usually be completed by the end of high school, although some boys add height after their high school graduation.

Both boys and girls may expect a growth spurt. Girls usually experience theirs earlier than do boys. It is not as extreme for them as for boys, who sometimes add six inches and twenty-five pounds in a single year. Rapid growth produces awkwardness—and that carries with it profound social implications.

Sexual characteristics, both primary and secondary, are predominant among the physical changes of adolescence. The changes bring about new, intense feelings, which teenagers must learn to identify and handle. The onslaught of these feelings, and how the adolescent handles them, has significant social implications. For example, research indicates that the male sex drive peaks at age seventeen or eighteen—before most men have a socially acceptable means of sexual expression.

Acne is a frequent result of hormone changes. For appearance-conscious teens, it is devastating.

Much of a teen's sense of worth centers around physical characteristics and appearance. He cannot change them (except possibly for skin conditions), so he needs to learn to accept himself as he is. To do so is to take a giant step toward maturity.

The alert Christian teacher observes the following principles to take into account physical characteristics of youth:

1. Avoid calling attention to awkwardness or unusual physical characteristics.
2. Get acquainted with each pupil individually.
3. Deal with sexual matters honestly and without embarrassment. Hold forth a Christian view of sexuality.
4. Provide grooming and hygienic information on an individual basis for those who need it.

Intellectual Development

According to the Swiss psychologist, Jean Piaget, the teen makes the transition from the concrete intellectual operations of childhood to formal, abstract, logical thought. It is no small transformation, for it permits him to think creatively, to test hypotheses, to build and follow logical arguments. The process begins in the late elementary or early junior high years and is usually completed by age fifteen.

Because teens can understand cause and effect and can begin to reason abstractly, they can also begin to plan a long-range course of action. Yet teens are people of the "here and now" Their actions are much more likely to be dictated by the feelings and pressure of the present than by the hopes of the future. Still, they do possess the capacity for future planning.

Three teaching principles should be observed by a teacher of teens:

1. Challenge teens with biblical material that goes beyond mere restatement of factual material learned during childhood. Deal with the meanings of the Bible and how biblical material fits into God's overall plan for man.

2. Later teen years are ideal times to deal with doctrinal material.

3. Whatever the nature of the biblical material, whether factual or doctrinal, be clear and specific in making life applications.

Psychosocial Development

Psychosocial development is probably the most crucial transition of the teen years. Physical changes inevitably happen, but emotional and social changes are not nearly so routine. Somehow a teenager must make the culturally-expected changes from childhood to adulthood. It does not happen without a certain amount of personal struggle.

Teen years are a time of starting a search for personal identity. The crucial questions are, "Who am I? Where am I going? Why am I here?" Healthy family relationships permit the answers to be found more easily than they would be otherwise.

Identity seeking is done in a variety of ways. Some experience what may be called identity confusion, which is characterized by little trust of others, difficulty with interpersonal relationships, and experimentation with socially inappropriate behavior such as drug usage, misuse of sex, and/or delinquent behavior.

Others seems to declare a moratorium in the process of finding identity. They choose to experiment and to toy around with extreme behaviors. Their behaviors, short of delinquency, tend to resemble those of confused identity.

Some choose identity foreclosure. They experience little, if any, crisis. They simply adopt the attitudes and behaviors of adults with few, if any, questions asked.

Another group of teens choose the route of achievement.

Their behavior is relatively mature and flexible. They experience good interpersonal relationships and tend to be leaders.

Whichever route to identity is chosen, an adolescent must see himself as an individual, apart from his parents. This need for independence, important as it is, is probably the source of more parent-teen conflicts than any other source. Teens often assert themselves merely to test independence, especially when parents are reluctant to grant it or when they grant more than youth need at that time. Teens need a degree of freedom, but at the same time they need solid parental standards to bounce against.

Not the least of the psychosocial struggles is the adoption of appropriate sex roles. Healthy family models and relationships are of great value at this point. Teens tend to adopt the roles they have observed, if what they have seen is positive and if there has been open discussion of sex roles and functions.

Teens must also learn to accept their own physiques. This task is accomplished far better in the presence of loving, supportive adults.

Peer pressure is intense during the teen years. Everybody needs somebody to belong to, and for a teen it is usually his peers. Cliques tend to shape many teenage standards: dress, hair, sexual behavior, political opinions. An intense loyalty exists among clique members. They fiercely defend each other to adults or to those outside their social set. Not all peer pressure is negative, of course, especially if the social set holds high standards.

Moods are unpredictable among teens. Much of their moodiness is due to physical factors, but their need to solve the question of identity is also a factor.

Adolescents spend considerable time falling in and out of love. Early adolescents often have crushes on teachers and counselors. In later adolescent years, crushes occur with teens of the opposite sex. Teenage love is intense and all-absorbing. It also creates jealousy, felt every bit as intensely as love.

Dating begins during adolescence. It is a valuable experience, because it helps a teen to relate to the opposite sex, learn sex roles, and achieve a degree of emotional independence. The lack of this dating experience can have a distinct negative effect on self-image.

While peers do exert powerful pressure on teens, so do parents—for grades, achievement, college, a "proper" career choice, acceptable friends. Those pressures are generally handled well by teenagers who experience healthy family relationships. Yet incidences of suicide have increased almost to epidemic proportions in recent years among teens who are identity-confused or in moratorium.

A youth worker cannot ignore the psychosocial characteristics of those he teaches. To do so is to invite failure. Careful observance of the following principles will give a boost toward success:

1. Involve teens in planning for Bible material to be covered, group activities, and expected group behaviors.
2. Hold forth high expectations and standards for your teens. Challenge them. But be sensitive to those youth who are struggling with self-image and perceptions of failure.
3. Build the confidence of teens by giving them opportunity to perform tasks and by praising them for genuine effort and achievement.
4. Be prepared for unpredictability in moods and behavior. Do not berate teens for moodiness and erratic behavior. Lead by example.
5. Recognize the importance of peers. Do not try to undermine group loyalty, but work with each teen to encourage him to make his own decisions. Give him support when he must stand against his peers.

Moral and Spiritual Development

During adolescence, one establishes his own value system. No longer will parents' values and religion be adequate without personal examination and decision. Given the teen's independent nature and search for identity, the quest for a personal value system follows naturally.

Doubts emerge during these years. A teenager, armed only with the facts and faith of childhood, confronts scientific and philosophical material of all kinds—much of which ignores or denies the truth of the Bible. He handles the new material either by reexamining and reconfirming his faith or by abandoning it. His reevaluation will proceed far more positively if he finds a supportive atmosphere of faith in which to express his doubts and to seek answers.

Although many adolescents reject their childhood faith, evidence indicates that spiritual questions are not set aside. However, teens seem to have little reverence for what the older generation considers sacred, at least until they reach the same conclusions on their own. While an adult reasons logically, a teen, although capable of such reasoning, frequently draws his conclusions on the basis not only of fact, but of peer concerns and personal feelings that have not yet been tested out by fact or experience.

Merton Strommen did a comprehensive study of the values of 2,952 youth. He found marked differences between boys and girls. More girls than boys aspire to religious goals, social service, and reflection. Boys, however, were more likely to follow through on their aspirations.

Strommen further discovered a lack of relationship between religious knowledge and values. However, teens are challenged by a religious experience that calls for commitment and loyalty. They respond to Bible study that moves from the mere presentation of facts to the integration of biblical material with daily behavior. They respond when they are forced to think for themselves, as they are led face to face with Christ.

Strommen draws four conclusions that the Christian teacher of youth would do well to heed:[1]

1. The vitality of a youth ministry varies in direct proportion to the degree of sensitivity and concern that adults hold toward their youth.
2. Adults hold an image of youth that tends to increase the chasm between the two and make communication increasingly difficult.
3. Youth need the dynamic faith that indoctrination alone cannot give. They require Bible facts coupled with life application presented in an atmosphere that permits questioning and discussion.
4. Youth are reachable by and for the church.

Goals for Teaching Youth

Teachers of youth need a clear sense of direction for their efforts. Three basic goals give needed guidance.

The first goal is to provide for spiritual growth. Growth is made on the basis of Bible information that is more than a mere retelling of stories as they were presented during childhood. The first step is discovery of facts and principles from God's Word, and the second step is exploring how those facts and principles apply to life situations. The final step is to practice using the principles and to share the results. This first goal deals with the thinking, feeling, and doing processes, all of which are essential for spiritual transformation.

The second goal is to activate youth for service. This goal is logically linked to the first. A study of God's Word, as outlined above, results in motivation for service. The teacher provides guidance in choosing and carrying out acts of service.

The third goal is to challenge youth to make decisions on the basis of Bible principles. Moral and ethical conduct, choice of vocation, use of leisure time, and dating behavior are all decisions that should be affected by commitment to Jesus Christ. Every teacher should make it his goal to bring teens to make those decisions in light of God's Word.

Three goals—spiritual growth, service, decision-making—give a clear sense of direction to the teacher of teens. They are attainable and desirable.

Teaching Youth

Arranging the Teaching Time

A variety of patterns may be used to organize the time block assigned to the youth department. On rare occasions it may be desirable to have the entire department together for the total teaching time. Such an arrangement would be appropriate for guest speakers and films.

At other times, the entire department could gather for a brief assembly time and then divide into small permanent class units. Or they could meet in permanent class units followed by a departmental assembly. The normal pattern, however, is for each small permanent class group to spend the Sunday school time together. The teacher must then plan and use the time block to the greatest advantage.

A Bible teaching session should be built in this way. The teacher focuses on a life-related theme from the Bible material for the day, formulates appropriate objectives, and plans the various parts of the lesson to accomplish the objectives.

The diagram below pictures suggested time allotments within three possible time blocks.

Lesson Section	**60 min.**	**45 min.**	**30 min.**
Attention Step	10	5	5
Bible Study	25	20	15
Application	20	15	5
Conclusion and Decision	5	5	5

Time allotments may be altered, depending upon the subject matter and objectives.

Whatever pattern is chosen and whatever the time available, the entire session should be developed to focus on the objectives for the day. Films, lectures, music, and any other large-group activities should be chosen because they contribute to the lesson objectives.

Choosing Methods

Methods for communicating God's Word to teens are predicated upon four assumptions:

1. The Holy Spirit is the chief agent of Christian nurture. Our purpose is to provide the context in which He can work.
2. The whole Bible is the source of truth.
3. The teacher communicates nonverbally, with body language and example, as much as he does with what he says.
4. The learner learns best when he is actively involved in the learning process.[2]

A wide range of activities are available to stimulate and inspire youth.

Lecture. This is essentially one-way communication. It is best used to present information in limited time segments. It is the most efficient method for large groups. But lecture can be varied to involve the learners. Try some of these techniques: *films, interviews, listening teams, symposiums,* and *panels*.

Discussion. This is deliberate conversation among two or more people. It explores issues and answers and attempts to solve problems. Discussion does not always just happen; it must be planned and stimulated. Techniques such as these can be used to help initiate good discussions: *agree-disagree statements, buzz groups, case studies, debates,* and *question-and-answer.*

Written communication. Another means by which youth may be involved is to have them write out their ideas. These activities are especially good for clarifying feelings and stimulating thinking. Possibilities are: *letters* to or from a Bible person or for application, *diary entries or memo writing* for youth to commit himself to what he will do as a result of the lesson, *modern parables* or *newspaper stories* to report what happened in Bible accounts, *paraphrases* of Bible material, *writing poetry* in response to a Bible truth, *writing prayers, self-evaluation forms,* or *stories* to demonstrate a Bible truth, *a TV script* to report Bible facts and feelings, and *word puzzles.*

Drama. Many youth like to dramatize roles, either biblical or present-day. These activities encourage the learner to identify with the feelings of an individual and to gain insight and understanding of actions. Try *formal dramas, pantomimes* of Bible accounts, *role plays* to apply Bible truths, and *skits.*

Art. Any pictorial or graphic expression of Bible material or concepts can be classified as art. Art activities are especially good to visualize and reinforce truth. Possible activities are: *advertisement brochures* to relate a concept or application of Bible truth, *banners, book covers, bumper stickers, campaign badges, collages, graffiti posters, maps, mobiles, murals,* and *rebuses.*

Music. Music activities are helpful in presenting Bible truth and for expressing thoughts and responses to that truth. Some activities are: *concept and song match, hymn paraphrase, musical commercial, singing,* and *writing a song.*

Research. Any activity that involves a learner in consulting resources may be called Bible research. It provides opportunity for a learner to discover Bible truth for himself. Possible activities are: *book reports, research reports, field trips, time lines,* and *finding answers to specific questions.*

A teacher must choose from the multitude of methods available to communicate God's Word. What determines his choice of the means by which he will communicate? Six factors serve as criteria:

1. Aim of the lesson.
2. Size of the group.
3. Size of the room.
4. Resources and supplies available.
5. Abilities and interests of students.
6. Time available.

Writing a Lesson Plan

Like the teacher of all other age levels, the teacher of youth must determine a central focus for his lesson, state desired learning outcomes, and then choose the methods by which to accomplish the objectives. He should then write out the plan as the example below.

Title: All New?
Scripture: 2 Corinthians 5:1-21
Central Truth: When a person becomes a Christian, he begins to change in every way.
Objectives: At the conclusion of this session, the pupils will be able to: 1) list at least five ways that the Christian changes, 2) tell how each change in the text would affect his family and school, and 3) select one of the changes that he will work to demonstrate this week.

Attention (10 minutes)

1. Each person will write at least one response on the graffiti poster on the wall which says, "A Christian is . . ."
2. Review the responses. Let students tell why they wrote what they did.
3. Point out that Christians are different.

Bible Study (25 minutes)

1. Read 2 Corinthians 5:1-21.
2. Have class members work in pairs. They are to read the text and list the ways that a person changes when he becomes a Christian.

3. Have reports from the groups. Add changes that they did not identify. List these on the chalkboard.

4. Call attention to 2 Corinthians 5:17—one who becomes a Christian changes so much that he is called a new creature.

Application (20 minutes)

1. Divide the class into groups of four or five. One will answer this question: "If I am new in Christ, how will this be demonstrated in my personal life?" Another group will answer: "If I am new in Christ, how will this be demonstrated in my home?" A third group will answer: "If I am new in Christ, how will this be demonstrated at school?"

2. Ask for reports from groups and discuss their responses.

Conclusion and Decision (5 minutes)

1. Summarize the teaching of 2 Corinthians 5:1-21.

2. Have each person write a memo to himself telling how he will demonstrate his newness in Christ this week.

3. Close with prayer.

Summary

A visit to the world of adolescents will assist the potential Bible teacher. As with any other age level, teaching adolescents requires an understanding of their physical, intellectual, emotional, social, and spiritual characteristics. Once that understanding is reached, a lesson can be planned to communicate to them. The challenge is demanding, but the rewards are abundant.

Projects

1. Observe a junior high student and a junior in high school. How are they like each other? Different? How do they match the descriptions outlined in this chapter? How do they differ?
2. Think back to the youth classes in your home church. How is the teaching time arranged? How many different teaching methods are used? How could the classes be improved?
3. Plan a Bible lesson for youth using Luke 15:11-32 as the Bible basis. Use the form illustrated above.

Selected Bibliography

Adams, James F. *Understanding Adolescence: Current Developments in Adolescent Psychology.* Boston, MA: Allyn and Bacon, 1980.

Narramore, Bruce. *Adolescence Is Not An Illness.* Old Tappan, NJ: Fleming H. Revell, 1980.

Reed, Bobbie and Rex E. Johnson. *Bible Learning Activities: Grades 7-12.* Glendale, CA: Gospel Light, 1977.

Reiswig, Roy. *You Can Teach Teens Successfully.* Cincinnati, OH: Standard Publishing, 1983.

Roadcup, David (ed.). *Ministering to Youth.* Cincinnati, OH: Standard Publishing, 1980.

Roadcup, David (ed.). *Methods for Youth Ministry.* Cincinnati, OH: Standard Publishing, 1986.

Santrock, John. *Life Span Development.* 2nd ed. Dubuque, IA: William C. Brown Co., Publishers, 1986.

Strommen, Merton P. and Irene. *Five Cries of Parents.* San Francisco, CA: Harper and Row, Publishers, 1985.

Warren, Michael (ed.). *Youth Ministry: A Book of Readings.* New York: Paulist Press, 1977.

Wyckoff, D. Campbell and Don Richter (ed.). *Religious Education Ministry with Youth.* Birmingham, AL: Religious Education Press, 1982.

Zaffore, Kathleen. *Teens Can Make a Difference.* Cincinnati, OH: Standard Publishing, 1987.

---

[1]From *Profiles of Church Youth* by Merton P. Strommen. © 1963 Concordia Publishing House. Used by permission.

[2]Edward D. Seely, *Teaching Early Adolescents Creatively* (Philadelphia, PA: Westminster Press, 1971), p. 11.

CHAPTER 10

Helping Adults Learn

As you read, think about these questions:
What are the major characteristics of each level of adulthood?
—How do these characteristics affect what a teacher does to teach?
—What are the goals for teaching adults?
—How should the teaching time for adults be arranged?
—What are at least ten methods for teaching adults?

Adult—adults—adulthood. Those words are used often, but they are difficult to define.

An adult can be defined in physiological terms—sexual maturity, for example. But that hardly seems to be an adequate definition. (Consider all of the teenage pregnancies—are all of those girls adults?) The definition can also be made by intellectual measures, or financial independence, or legal age, or work, or marriage, or willingness to assume personal responsibility. Each of these measures by itself is inadequate: each is an important facet of adulthood, but each, when taken alone, excludes some whom we judge to be adults.

In some cultures, adulthood is marked by an initiatory rite; an individual moves directly from childhood to adulthood. In Western culture, this is not the case. Instead, an individual experiences a lengthy adolescence that finally blurs into adulthood. As a result, there is little agreement about a precise time or definition for the beginning of adulthood. When does adulthood begin? Age eighteen is a logical lower limit, because of the significant marker events that occur at that time: a person reaches legal age, graduates from high school, and attains some degree of independence.

Even if the beginning of adulthood can be defined, further definition is necessary. The adult years cover three-fourths or more of the average person's life span. Adulthood is not just a succession of years of dull uniformity. The adult years are characterized by changes just as significant as those in childhood and adolescence.

Most psychologists divide adulthood into at least three distinct periods: young adulthood, middle adulthood, and older adulthood. The dividing lines between these periods are just as difficult to define as the lower limit of adulthood. One cannot be dogmatic about the ages assigned to each period, but for the discussion in this chapter, the following definitions will be assumed: young adulthood extends from eighteen to thirty-nine, middle adulthood from thirty-nine to sixty-four, and older adulthood from sixty-five until death.

Understanding Adults

Everything that happens to a person affects him in some way—graduation, childbirth, getting a job, going to college. These concrete experiences are called *marker events,* and much of life can be evaluated on the basis of them. But not everything that happens to an individual can be defined or explained by external marker events, for much change comes from within. These internal stages are called *developmental stages.*

An adult's life includes both internal and external changes. Sometimes an adult attributes internal changes to external events—that is, he believes that internal changes would have been eased or avoided altogether if he had experienced different marker events. However, adults will experience predictable developmental stages whatever the marker events. Far from causing developmental stages, marker events are often affected by developmental stages.

What are the expected developments at each stage of adulthood?

Young Adults

Young adulthood has been characterized by some as pulling up roots and formulating a personal self-definition not totally dependent upon one's relationships with his parents. Two major tasks confront the young adult on his way to achieving self-definition. One is the completion of identity formation, a task begun during adolescence, and the second is competency in what he does. The young adult may choose from a variety of lifestyles, but whatever his choice, he must come to a clear image of himself as an adult and a feeling of being competent in an adult world.

A variety of marker events accompanies the internal development stages. A significant one is selecting a marriage partner—or learning to live as a single adult. Choice of partner and the process of learning to live with him reveal much about a person's self-identity and feelings of competence. Success or failure of the marriage contributes to feelings of competence. Women, especially, tend to derive identity and competency from the marriage relationship itself.

Closely akin to marriage is managing a home and family. Young adults must decide if and when they will have a family, where they will live, and how to manage money. All of these decisions contribute to self-identity and personal competency.

A third event is the beginning of a vocation. To a degree, that is a reflection of personal identity, but it is a key to the search for competency as well. Vocation is especially important for men who must be the breadwinners for a family (career women experience the same needs).

Each of these three marker events require reevaluation during the thirties, when one must modify his expectations for his marriage and job. The seventh year of marriage is critical because of the readjustments demanded. The same is true of the seventh to tenth years in a vocation. The individual must reexamine and recommit himself to the marriage and/or job. If he does not, the marriage fails or a job change is negotiated. Either outcome affects identity and competency. Eventually the thirties take on a more orderly and rational lifestyle.

Middle Adults

Middle adults are caught in the squeeze between two generations. It is not an easy dilemma to resolve. Much of the middle adult's developmental work is wrapped up with those two generations.

The squeeze comes from parents on the one side. Although parents are more and more peripheral to the middle adult's day-to-day routine, he eventually must come to grips with parental aging and the decisions it demands. In the person of aging parents, he is also brought face-to-face with his own mortality.

On the other hand, middle adults are confronted with the reality that their children are less and less involved in family life. Children grow to be adolescents and adults, and they pull up roots and strike out on their own. Unless middle adults have a clear sense of the squeeze in which they find themselves, they often resort to excessive control of children in an effort to maintain a sense of safety and immortality.

Physiological changes are clear signals to middle adults that they are not immortal after all. Gray hairs, hard-to-lose extra pounds, tiring more easily, menopause—all are reminders that the body is aging and will one day die. Friends die of heart attacks and cancer, another personalization of death, a fact to be dealt with either positively or negatively.

Marriage requires renegotiation. Children leave home, and partners are left to deal directly with each other. It is another critical time for a marriage, calling for patience and sharing.

The adult of thirty to fifty faces a distortion of time: *whatever is to be done must be done now.* How he handles this is determined by his view of himself.

A middle adult comes to terms with age in one of three ways.

1. The middle-aged kid tries to relive adolescence and free himself from responsibility.

2. The protector of the status quo grows old before his time with rigid attitudes and lifestyle.

3. The well-adjusted person seeks to achieve renewal—realizing physical and vocational limitations and accepting them without undue regret, coming to terms with age and enjoying it, redefining attitudes toward money, finding a sense of meaning in life, accepting death, and approving self.

Usually the middle adult will handle much of his developmental work by age fifty or so, and his pattern will then follow him through the remainder of his life. If he chooses the middle-aged kid route, he will likely move from one self-defeating pattern to another. If he protects the status quo, he becomes old and set in his ways. But if he chooses and achieves renewal, he lives the final decade or so of the middle years with zest, growing toward old age with the feeling that he has done well in life. He grows into older adulthood gracefully.

Older Adults

Older adulthood has sometimes been called a "period of decline," but it could just as easily be viewed as a time of delight and enjoyment. Which way it is viewed (and lived) by the older adult depends largely upon how well he made the adjustments of middle adulthood. Assuming that one did cope well with the reality of mortality, older adulthood becomes a time for living.

Even so, there are new adjustments to be made, many of them associated with external circumstances—decreasing strength and vitality, wrinkled skin, aches and pains. Physical response slows, medical needs arise, and eyesight and hearing begin to fail. The older adult must learn to handle these changes without loss of self-esteem.

Retirement brings with it another set of adjustments, some economic and others psychological. Retirement results in reduced income, which alters lifestyle and, sometimes, living arrangements. Retirement creates idle time that must be handled responsibly and creatively if older adulthood is to remain lively and satisfying. Retirement also relays a message to the retiree: Am I any longer worth anything? Who needs me now? Reassessment of meaning is essential.

Loss of a spouse might have occurred earlier than age sixty-five, but it will occur in older adulthood if it has not already. Not only will the older adult lose his spouse, but he will lose other loved ones and friends. He must deal with grief and loneliness. Loss of spouse may also result in economic and residential readjustments.

Older adults must learn to meet civic, social, and spiritual obligations. They can grow old isolated from the rest of society, or they can blossom and contribute the wisdom of their years to those around them.

Older adults, then, have their own growth process. How well they experience this process is determined to a large extent in middle adulthood, but their maturity is demonstrated in the final set of adjustments before they "step over Jordan" to meet the Lord.

Single Adults

More than seven million single adults live in America, a sizeable segment of the adult population, far too many to be ignored. A single adult is any unmarried adult; having been widowed, divorced, separated, or never-married.

The previous description of adults at each level of development applies to single adults too. But because of their singleness, single adults find some of those needs intensified.

Never-marrieds experience need for intimacy and companionship. They must learn to accept singleness so that they can create healthy relationships with others in order to meet companionship needs. They experience sexual temptations and the temptation to avoid responsibilities to others. They must also resolve the tension between dependence and independence.

Divorced and separated singles experience the same needs as never-marrieds, but also the need to forgive oneself and one's mate for the failure in the marriage. They have difficulty making reentry into society and the church as a single. They often experience financial and family stresses, especially when children are involved. Both men and women require readjustment in personal support systems (many men may need to learn how to do the laundry, keep house, and cook, while women may know little about caring for the car or the property).

Widows and widowers experience most of what never-marrieds and the divorced do, but they must also deal with grief and loneliness. Their self-concept requires readjustment from being an extension of their partner back to being single.

Extra attention to the unique needs of single adults will help them use their singleness for ministry rather than misery.

Distinctives of the Adult Learner

The adult learner is far more than a child to whom grownup stories are told. He is more than an adolescent with doubts and yearnings for independence. He is an individual seeking maturity while beset by complex pressures. He cannot be expected to respond if he is treated as a child or adolescent.

The teacher of adults must understand the basic distinctives that mark the adult learner:

1. He is a unique person with his own individual history and present needs. Every learner at every age is unique, but not in the same sense as an adult. Although ten-year-olds differ in some ways, they are very much alike in others. But it is almost impossible to make any generalized statement about a forty-year-old (or any other adult, for that matter). There is no physical uniformity, no likeness of thinking style, no uniform procedure in making emotional adjustments.
2. He learns as a total person, not just intellectually (except for those characterized as learning-oriented or task-oriented). His developmental work—the way he handles his internal changes—will affect his perceptions and reactions.
3. He brings valuable experience, definite ideas, and well-formulated attitudes to the learning situation. These affect the learning situation.
4. He learns best when he is an active participant. Yet involvement is voluntary; careful planning by the teacher is required to motivate him to participate.
5. He learns through interaction with others and identification with groups. Once he trusts and values people and groups, he is open to accepting their attitudes and values, which he begins to emulate.
6. He learns by association with a teacher who models a particular lifestyle. He imitates the lifestyle and seeks the information the teacher has to offer.
7. He has not learned until he translates learning into personal behavior.

Goals for Teaching Adults

Three basic goals give direction to teachers of adults. The first is to provide sound biblical instruction, which means more than a weekly mini-sermon. Using group participation methods, the teacher will guide students to explore God's Word systematically to find its message for today. The lesson will involve reviewing Bible facts and exploring the meaning of the biblical material for the lives of the students.

But adult Bible teaching requires more than a mini-college approach. It does not merely present academic material, but explores how that material is usable in daily life. A second goal, then, is the application of biblical material to contemporary life. Good Bible teaching confronts the learner, and demands that he decide how to use Bible material in real-life situations. This goal forces the teacher to deal with attitudes as well as with data.

The third goal for adult Bible teaching is to equip adults for service. Service and outreach should be practical outcomes of effective teaching. Once a person learns God's Word and understands its demands on his life, he will want to become involved in ministry to others. A good adult teacher will be alert for opportunities to minister to others and will challenge his pupils to take advantage of those opportunities.

Teaching Adults

Arranging the Teaching Time

A Sunday school session for adults should be structured carefully. Everything that happens must contribute to the goal for the day.

A four-step structure for adults is shown in Figure 10-1.[1]

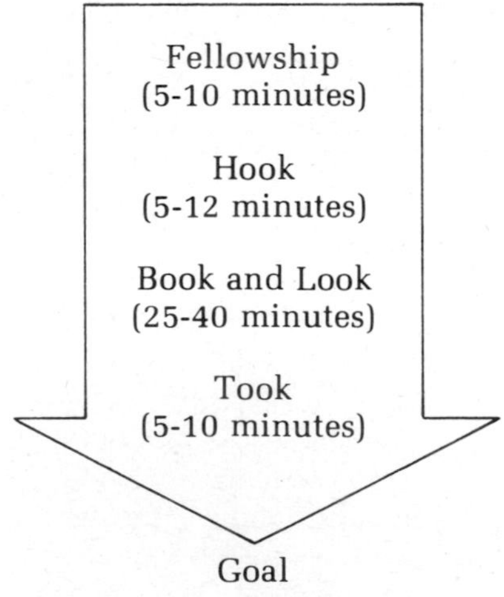

Figure 10-1. Structure for an adult Bible lesson.

Fellowship activities should be planned to direct people to share with one another. Although serving coffee and donuts can help toward this end, other definite sharing experiences should be planned.

The Hook is critical, for it should be designed to stimulate interest. It serves to whet the appetite of the pupils.

The Book and Look sections direct the adult learner to an exploration of God's Word and its meaning for life. The wise teacher utilizes a variety of methods to involve the learner in the process of discovery.

The Took section involves the learner in deciding how he will use the biblical material in his life. These decisions may be shared with others unless they are too personal to share.

Choosing Methods

A wide variety of teaching methods and techniques are at the disposal of the teacher of adults. Perhaps those mentioned here will stimulate the teacher's imagination.

Discussion. Most adults like to be involved in a class session. However, good discussion requires planning and stimulation. Some possible ways to accomplish this are: *agree-disagree statements, brainstorming, buzz groups, case studies, completion of statements, panels, picture responses, question-and-answer, word association, neighbor nudges,* and *listening teams.*

Writing. Adults respond well to writing that summarizes Bible material or reflects upon it. Several techniques are possible: *word acrostics,* using a key word from the lesson; *graffiti posters; letter writing; keeping a log, diary, or journal; writing a memo; writing news stories or headlines; outlining; taking notes; paraphrasing* a text; *writing poetry; writing prayers; making up puzzles or scrambled verses or statements.*

Art. Some adults enjoy expressing Bible truth and application through art forms. Choose from this list: *banners, bulletin boards, bumper stickers, cartoon strips, charts, collages or friezes, mobiles, slides,* and *symbolic shapes.*

Drama. Another method is drama, in which the learner portrays the biblical material and/or application of it. *Panto-*

mimes, role plays, skits, and *TV news programs* are possibilities.

Music. Adults respond well to musical activities to express Bible facts or applications. Consider these possibilities: *writing a song or commercial jingle, hymn/Scripture comparison, hymn paraphrase,* and *hymn/song response.*

Oral communication. This is a basic form for teaching adults. Possibilities for involving class members include: *assignments, lecture, memorization,* and *reports.*

Writing the Lesson Plan

The teacher of adults, like every other age level, must develop a focus for the session, define learning outcomes, and put the session together. Then he should write his lesson plan. Use the one below as a guide.

Title: How to Deal With Sin in the Body
Scripture: 1 Corinthians 5:1-11
Central Truth: The church is responsible for dealing with sin within the body.
Objectives: At the end of the session, the pupils will be able to: 1) define the circumstances when sin within the body should be dealt with, 2) explain the procedure for dealing with sin, and 3) identify a case within the congregation about which he is concerned and decide how to deal with it.

Hook (10 minutes)

1. Assign pupils to groups of six when they arrive. Give each group one of the following situations to discuss.

a) A teenager in this congregation is reported to be involved in using drugs recreationally. You are not certain how widespread this knowledge is. What is your responsibility?

b) The church secretary is involved in an extramarital affair. You know this to be a fact. Yet it seems not to be common knowledge within the congregation. What is your responsibility?

c) A man who has been nominated to be a deacon has a reputation as being dishonest in his business dealings with your employer. What is your responsibility?

d) Your Sunday school teacher has been seen downtown drunk. What is your responsibility?

2. Report of decisions by the groups.

3. Make the transition to the Bible study by stating that Paul gives us directives for how to deal with sin within the church.

Book (25 minutes)

1. Read 1 Corinthians 5:1-11 aloud.

2. Each student is to find the answers to the following questions:

a) What sin within the church occasioned Paul's directive to the Corinthians?

b) Why should the church deal with sin within its midst?

c) What sins is the church to deal with?

d) Summarize Paul's teaching about dealing with sin in the body.

3. Lead a discussion using the answers to the questions.

Look (20 minutes)

1. Is Paul's advice to disfellowship a person from the church the first step in dealing with sin? Why?

2. Let's suggest a procedure that an individual should use to deal with sin in the church. We will assume that the last resort is to disfellowship the person.

3. Have each group reexamine its original problem. Now they are to suggest how they will deal with the situation.

Took (5 minutes)

1. Explain that so far as you know there are no such situations in this body. But point out that there may be situations that only one person knows about.

Ask each person to think of a person about whom he is concerned. What should be his procedure?

2. Each person will write a memo committing himself to carry out his decision.

3. Pray for strength to do what has been decided.

Summary

Adults experience developmental adjustments just as learners of any other age. An effective Bible teacher will take careful note of the special needs at each level of adulthood. Wise is the Bible teacher who heeds the guidelines for teaching adults. His efforts will be blessed!

Projects

1. Interview three adults, one at each level of adulthood. Find out what they perceive their needs to be. Ask them to react to the textbook description. Find out what appeals to them in an adult Bible class.
2. How are the adult classes in your home church taught? Compare those classes with the guidelines described in this chapter.
3. Plan a Bible lesson for adults using Ephesians 4:17—5:7 as your text. Use the lesson plan above as a pattern.

Selected Bibliography

Conway, Jim. *Men in Mid-Life Crisis*. Elgin, IL: David C. Cook Publishing Company, 1978.

Conway, Jim and Sally. *Women in Mid-Life Crisis*. Wheaton, IL: Tyndale House Publishers, 1983.

Fowler, James and Sam Keen. *Life Maps*. Waco, TX: Word, Inc. 1978.

Knowles, Malcolm S. *The Adult Learner*. Houston, TX: Gulf Publishing Company, 1973.

Marlowe, Monroe and Bobbie Reed. *Creative Bible Learning for Adults* Glendale, CA: Gospel Light, 1977.

Peterson, Gilbert A. (ed.). *The Christian Education of Adults*. Chicago: Moody Press, 1984.

Reed, Bobbie. *Single on Sunday*. St. Louis, MO: Concordia Publishing House, 1979.

Sell, Charles M. *Transition: the Stages of Adult Life*. Chicago: Moody Press, 1985.

Sheehy, Gail. *Passages*. New York: Dutton, 1976.

You Can Teach Adults Successfully. Cincinnati, OH: Standard Publishing, 1983.

Wilbert, Warren. *Teaching Christian Adults*. Grand Rapids, MI: Baker Book House, 1981.

Wood, Britton. *Single Adults Want To Be the Church Too*. Nashville, TN: Broadman Press, 1977.

---

[1]Monroe Marlowe and Bobbie Reed, *Creative Bible Learning for Adults* (Glendale, CA: Gospel Light, 1977).

CHAPTER 11

Helping Exceptional Persons Learn

As you read, think about these questions:
—What is the difference between *being* value and *doing* value?
—What are the traditional areas of special education?
—What barriers hinder the development of potential in exceptional persons?
—What general principles can be derived to help discover and develop potential in exceptional persons?

This chapter deals with an educational ministry too often neglected by the local church: the Christian education of the exceptional person. The reasons for this neglect include feelings of fear, lack of confidence in the ability to organize and conduct programs, and the pragmatic questioning of the expenditure of resources for individuals "who are never going to learn, anyway." The aim of this chapter is (1) to replace fear with understanding, (2) to encourage the pursuit of competence in methods and techniques for educating the exceptional person, and (3) to answer the questioning of pragmatists with a different perspective—one that encourages every human being to measure his own spiritual growth and development not in comparison to others, but in relation to his own potential for thinking, feeling, and acting.

The perspective for the Christian education of exceptional persons rests on the distinction between value based on *being* and value based on *doing*. *Being* value is the value that every person has because man is a special creation, made in the image of God. David, in the eighth Psalm, gives us insight into *being* value. Mankind stands just below the angels and above the rest of creation. The majesty of His creation makes us stand in awe of the value God has bestowed upon us.

Every person has *being* value, regardless of his circumstance. It is not assigned by man. Others may choose to acknowledge it or to ignore it, but its existence and extent is not determined by others. It is God-given. *Being* value also carries with it the capacity for value based on *doing*. Psalm 8:6 points out that a part of human nature is the capacity for extending control over the environment. Man has the capacity for achievement, that is, the potential for value based on doing.

Doing value differs from *being* value in some important ways. First, while each person has *being* value simply because he is created in the image of God, *doing* value must be acquired or earned. It is the extent to which an individual develops the potential he has. Secondly, while *being* value is absolute and universal, possessed to the same degree by everyone, *doing* value is relative. People differ in the amount and in the nature of their potential. *Doing* value is not based on potential itself; it is based on the extent to which one develops whatever potential he has.

If we had some way of measuring human value, we could say with certainty that in terms of *being* value each person's worth is the same. In terms of *doing* value each person could possibly be worth the same as any other person; that is, each person could measure up to one hundred percent of his potential. Individual differences in *doing* value are not due to differences in potential, but to differences in the extent to which each person achieves his potential.

The distinction between *being* value and *doing* value provides the foundation for the education of exceptional persons and for their Christian education in particular. If we understand and accept these two kinds of value, we can no longer ask, "Is he worth it?" Each person is worth it from two perspectives. He is worth it because he has *being* value, the same as any other person. But especially important for Christian educators, he is worth it because he has the same possibility for *doing* value as anyone else: one hundred percent of his potential, whatever that may be. The exceptional person is also entitled to the same opportunity for developing that value as anyone else. The challenge that the exceptional person presents to Christian educators is not only to help them develop potential that is obvious, but to uncover potential that may be hidden behind handicaps.

Traditional Categories of Special Education: Aids in Defining Potential

Traditional categories of special education can be thought of as labels that identify limitations, or they can be thought of as information that gives insight into potential. The Christian educator should adopt the "potential" perspective, for it requires him to search actively for possibilities for *doing* value. The "limitations" perspective focuses on non-possibilities.

The categories that will be discussed in this section are disorders in hearing, vision, motor abilities, and behavior, as well as mental retardation. A description of each category will be given, along with a discussion of the major barriers to developing potential and the ways to overcome these barriers.

Hearing Disorders

A major concern in working with the hearing impaired is language development. Most individuals learn to understand concepts through hearing and learn how to express ideas through hearing others do so. The extent to which impaired hearing affects understanding and communicating is an important educational consideration. It is influenced by three factors: the degree of hearing loss, the age at which the loss occurred, and the type of defect. The degree of loss determines the extent to which sounds, especially speech sounds, are heard. The age at which the loss occurred is important because a loss suffered after age two has a much less severe effect on the development of speech and language. The type of defect is important because it determines the way in which the loss can be compensated for.

Degree of loss. The exact extent of a hearing loss is measured in decibels (dbs) on a device called an audiometer. Five levels of hearing loss have been defined, each having a more marked effect on understanding speech and, consequently, on language development. The person with a slight loss (26-40 db) may have difficulty hearing faint or distant speech. The person with a mild loss (41-55 db) can understand face-to-face conversation, but may miss as much as fifty percent of a class discussion. The person with a marked loss (56-70 db) can hear conversation only if it is very loud. He has difficulty in group discussions and probably will have difficulty in understanding some concepts. The person with a severe loss (71-90 db) may hear loud voices about one foot from the ear. He is likely to have marked defects in speech and language. The person with an extreme loss (91 db or more) may hear some loud sounds, but is more aware of vibrations than tonal patterns. He relies on vision more than hearing for communication.

The hearing impaired individual is classified as deaf or partially hearing, depending on the extent to which the sense of hearing is functional for learning language. If he can use hearing for learning language, he is partially hearing. If not, he is deaf.

Age at Onset of Loss. For the person classified as deaf, the age when the hearing loss occurs is an important factor in learning language. Losses occurring before 18-24 months of age have a much more profound impact than losses that occur later in life. The deaf individual who suffers impaired hearing before the age of 18-24 months is referred to as "congenitally deaf." The individual who loses his hearing after that age is called "adventitiously deafened."

Type of Defect Resulting in Loss. The type of defect resulting in impaired hearing affects the extent to which the loss can be compensated for. There are three types of defects: conductive, sensory-neural, and central or perceptual. A conductive loss is one resulting from a defect of the outer or middle ear that interferes with the transmission of sound vibrations to the inner ear. A sensory-neural loss is one resulting from a defect of the inner ear that interferes with the reception of sound impulses at the nerve endings located there. A central or perceptual loss is one resulting from a defect of the auditory nerve pathways from the inner ear to the brain.

Conductive losses affect the intensity or loudness of the sound heard. They can, to a certain extent, be compensated for by amplifying sound and using an alternate route for transmitting the vibrations. This is the function of a hearing aid. Sensory-neural or central losses affect the frequency or tone of the sound heard. A person with a sensory-neural or perceptual loss cannot hear certain sounds or ranges of sound. These cannot be restored, although hearing aids are often used to magnify those sounds that can be heard.

The Communication Barrier. For the hearing-impaired person, the main barrier preventing the development of potential is a communication barrier. Not only is there a problem with speech as a mode of understanding and communicating, but often the development of language is delayed, so that even when alternate modes of communication (such as signing or finger spelling) are used, some ideas may not be understood.

Developing the ability to understand and communicate is the key to developing the potential of the hearing-impaired person. The three basic types of communication training for the deaf are oral, manual, and total communication. The goal of oral communication is that the individual be able to communicate with the broad community, not just with other hearing-impaired people. The emphasis is on speech reading and voice training. The learning process is a slow one.

The goal of the manual method is that the individual be able to understand and communicate as early as possible. Finger spelling and signing provide the mode of communicating and understanding. This method is learned much more rapidly than the oral method, but it restricts communication to those who know finger spelling and signing. This excludes most of the hearing community and creates another kind of isolation.

Total communication is an attempt to combine the benefits of the oral and manual methods. Its goal is that the individual use all of his resources to be able to understand and communicate as early as possible to as broad a community as possible. The child is encouraged from a very early age (parent-child programs may begin at birth) to use his voice and any residual hearing. He is also taught to understand and express himself through finger spelling, signing, and even natural gestures. The child trained in total communication should be able to use speech reading and vocalization to communicate with the hearing community, and still have the advantage of early language development. He will then be able to interact with both the hearing and with the deaf world.

Because in any given community he may find individuals with manual, oral, or total communication training, the Christian educator must be prepared to adapt to any of these methods in order to overcome the communication barrier.

Vision Disorders

There are two classification systems for visual disorders; legal and educational. An individual is declared legally blind if central visual acuity is 20/200 or less in the better eye with best correction. The term 20/200 indicates that the individual can distinguish at 20 feet what the normal eye sees at 200 feet. An individual is declared to be legally partially sighted if his acuity in the better eye with best correction is better than 20/200 but less than 20/70.

The educational classification system is based on the individual's ability to use his vision for educational purposes. An individual is educationally blind if he must rely on Braille rather than print for reading. He is partially sighted if he can read print given sufficient magnification or other special conditions. The distinction between the legal and educational classifications is important. Individuals with the same acuity (that is, the same legal status) may use their vision with differing degrees of effectiveness. An individual may be legally blind while educationally he is partially sighted, because he has learned to make good use of the vision he has.

Types of Visual Disorders. Visual disorders may be grouped into four types: disorders of the receptive structures, refractive disorders, defects in muscle functioning, and disorders due to some other interference in the visual system.

Disorders in receptive structures affect the retina or the optic nerve. The retina is the nerve structure that receives the visual image. Retrolental fibroplasia, a condition once common among premature infants, and detached retina are among the disorders that can affect it. The optic nerve connects the retina to the brain. Deterioration of the optic nerve and severed optic nerve are among the conditions that can affect it.

Refractive disorders are probably the best known. These disorders interfere with the focusing of light on the retina that is essential to proper vision. They include myopia (nearsightedness), hyperopia (farsightedness), and astigmatism, an irregularity in the curvature of the lens or of the eyeball itself.

Muscle disorders interfere with the coordinated movement of the eyes. Among these disorders are "lazy eye," crossed eyes, the quick, jerky movement of the eyes, and double or multiple vision.

Disorders due to interference in the visual system include glaucoma, the build up of interocular fluids, and cataracts, the development of an opaque film on the lens.

The Experience Barrier. The major barrier to the development of potential in the visually impaired person is one of limited kinds of experience. Things that are learned visually by most of us must be learned through some other mode by the visually impaired person.

Lowenfeld suggests five basic principles by which the best use of other means for gaining experience can be made.

1. Individualization. Educational programs should be geared to the needs of each child.
2. Concreteness. As much as possible, the child should have direct experience with the things he is to learn. Knowledge should be gained through using real objects and events where possible and scale models or simulated events when necessary.
3. Unified instruction. Instruction should be integrated into a total life experience.
4. Additional stimulation. Incorporate as much stimulation of the sense of hearing, smell, taste, touch, and movement as possible.
5. Self-activity. The student should be encouraged to do most activities himself.

These principles are also appropriate for the partially sighted, although use of concreteness should be extended to include visual media adapted for their use. Additional stimulation should strongly encourage the child to use his vision as much as possible.

Disorders in Motor Abilities

The common features relating the disorders in this category is that they all in some way impair movement. A set of terms—the "plegias"—are used to describe the number and location of limbs affected by a motor disorder. These terms are defined as follows:

Monoplegia: one limb is affected
Hemiplegia: one side of the body is affected

Triplegia: three limbs are affected
Quadriplegia: all four limbs are affected
Diplegia: four limbs are affected, more involvement in the legs
Bilateral hemiplegia: four limbs are affected; more involvement in the arms

Although these terms are often used in connection with paralysis, they do not describe the nature of the disorder itself. They merely refer to the location of the affected area.

Two categories of motor disorders will be discussed.

Cerebral Palsy. Cerebral palsy is a general term that includes five major types of motor disorders caused by brain damage:

1. Spasticity, the most common type, is characterized by a lack of coordination between muscle pairs that control voluntary movement. Purposeful movements are jerky and uncoordinated. Affected limbs may be drawn inward toward the body when the individual is at rest.

2. Athetosis, the second most common type, is characterized by involuntary movement, especially when the individual attempts deliberate, purposeful action. Throat and diaphragm muscles are often affected, so speech problems frequently accompany this condition.

3. Ataxia is the result of damage to the portion of the brain that controls balance. It is characterized by staggering, off-balance movement.

4. Tremor is characterized by small rhythmic involuntary movement of the affected limb or limbs.

5. Rigidity, as the name suggests, is characterized by a resistance to movement.

The brain injury that results in cerebral palsy can occur anytime before, during, or after birth. Prenatal infections or absence of oxygen may have been factors for those born with cerebral palsy. Injury, poisoning, high fever, or other factors can cause cerebral palsy at any time during the life span.

Since cerebral palsy is the result of brain damage, other conditions attributable to brain damage may accompany it. These include disorders of speech, hearing, and vision, and mental retardation.

Other Motor Disorders. Two other motor disorders are common enough to warrant a brief discussion. Spina bifida is a congenital condition characterized by a failure of the spine to close, leaving the spinal cord exposed at some point. It is often accompanied by hydrocephaly (increased cerebrospinal fluid in the skull) and in severe cases can lead to paralysis and loss of bladder and bowel control. Muscular dystrophy is a progressive disease affecting children and young adults in which muscle tissue is replaced by fatty tissue. The result is the gradual loss of voluntary muscle control. At present there is no known treatment that will reverse the progress of the disease.

Physical Barriers. The most obvious barriers to the development of potential for those with motor disorders are physical barriers. Stairs, narrow aisles, narrow halls and doorways, sanctuaries and rooms that cannot easily accommodate a wheelchair, and even certain procedures for passing Communion or receiving an offering can inhibit the participation of individuals with motor disorders. Many physical barriers can be removed without costly structural changes. Consultation with an occupational or physical therapist (most hospitals have them on staff) might prove beneficial in learning some simple modifications that can help remove these barriers.

Behavior Disorders

Kirk defines a behavior disorder as a deviation from age-appropriate behavior that significantly interferes with either the child's own growth and development or with the lives of others or both. Behavior disorders may be divided into two types, social maladjustment and emotional disturbance.

Social maladjustment is disruptive behavior that is unacceptable to society and violates cultural norms. It includes chronic disobedience, disruptiveness, defiance, and lack of cooperation.

Emotional disturbance refers to personal distress suffered by the individual. With some types of emotional disturbance, the individual does not withdraw from reality even though his distress may be intense. Among these types are chronic anxiety, a general uneasiness about the future not related to any specific cause and not focused on any specific object or event. Also included in this group are phobias (intense, irrational fears), obsessions (preoccupation with the same thought), and compulsions (repetitive, "driven" behavior).

Sometimes the emotional disturbance is such that the individual withdraws from reality. Such conditions include infantile autism (the individual fails to develop emotional relationships with others), regression (the individual reverts to a less mature level of behavior), and schizophrenia (characterized by severe withdrawal and the presence of conflicting impulses, thoughts, and ideas).

The "Self" Barrier. The main barrier inhibiting the behavior-disordered child's development of potential is himself. Sometimes the individual unconsciously sets up barriers that inhibit his own development. (This fact does not contradict our "possibilities" orientation, nor does it suggest that society, family, or other individuals are not contributors to the problem.)

The first step in removing this barrier is to recognize that inappropriate behavior obscures but does not destroy potential. Such behavior should not be overlooked, but dealt with as a barrier that hides potential. The second step is to maintain consistent, realistic expectations. These can be determined by working closely with the individual's parents and the professionals involved. Procedures for holding the individual to these expectations should also be developed. Such expectations provide consistency for the child and lend much-needed support to his parents.

The Mentally Retarded

The American Association of Mental Deficiency has defined mental retardation as follows: "Mental retardation refers to sub-average intellectual functioning which originates during the developmental period and is associated with impairment in adaptive behavior." In general, mentally retarded individuals are identified by their uniformly low performance on tests of ability and achievement. They seem sub-average in almost all areas of development—intellectual, social, emotional, and often physical.

Levels of Mental Retardation. The three levels of mental retardation are: the educable mentally retarded (EMR), the trainable mentally retarded (TMR), and the profoundly retarded.

The educable mentally retarded individual is one whose development is one-half to three-fourths the rate of the normal individual. He typically achieves a score between 50 and 75 on a mental ability test (a normal IQ score equals 100). Educational programs for the EMR include the basic academics, vocational training, and independent living skills.

The trainable mentally retarded individual is one whose rate of development is one-third to one-half that of the normal individual. He typically scores between 25 and 50 on general mental ability tests. Educational programs emphasize self-care and general safety skills, but happily there is a trend away from assuming that academic skills are totally beyond the TMR child's capabilities. Although TMR individuals are likely to require some kind of direct supervision over their entire life span, they may be expected to contribute both economically and socially to the well-being of the community.

The profoundly retarded individual is likely to score below 25 on tests of general mental ability. Educational programs emphasize sensory stimulation and the development of basic skills such as sitting, walking, self-feeding, and toileting. Usually the profoundly retarded individual requires direct care over his entire life span.

Causes of Mental Retardation. In most instances of mental retardation the cause is unknown. The known causes can be categorized as prenatal (before birth), perinatal (during the birth process), and postnatal (during the developmental years).

Prenatal causes of mental retardation include genetic ones such as Down's syndrome, drugs and toxic substances, incompatibility in the Rh blood factor, and maternal malnutrition. Some maternal illnesses can lead to retardation in the unborn infant. One such illness is rubella, or three-day measles. Rubella, if contracted by the mother during the first three months of pregnancy, can result not only in retardation in the infant but also in hearing and vision difficulties, absence or malformation of limbs, or severe heart disorders.

Perinatal causes of mental retardation include prolonged labor, other difficulty that interferes with the oxygen supply to the infant, or any physical trauma leading to brain injury.

Postnatal causes include physical trauma or interference with the oxygen supply to the brain. Toxic substances and malnutrition are other causes of postnatal mental retardation.

So far we have dealt with only organic causes of mental retardation. Environmental factors also have a strong influence on the extent to which an individual is able to use his inherent mental abilities. The extent to which environment affects intelligence is still being debated. However, it is fairly safe to say that many instances of mental retardation, especially at the

EMR level, are directly related to a non-stimulating environment during the developmental years.

The Complexity Barrier. A primary barrier to developing potential for the mentally retarded might be called a complexity barrier. Many of the actions, events, concepts, and thought processes that we think of as single, simple entities are actually made up of several related entities. The normal individual is able to deal with this complexity. The greater the degree of retardation, the less a mentally retarded individual is able to handle it.

Task and concept analysis is an important tool in teaching the retarded. Here, to whatever extent is necessary, the teacher breaks down each task or concept into its components and their relationships. Tasks or concepts are then taught as a series of related events rather than a single event. Breaking down the complexity barrier is a key to uncovering and activating potential in the mentally retarded person.

Principles in Educating the Exceptional Person

In addition to the barriers associated with each category of exceptionality, general factors also obscure potential for the exceptional person. These general factors give rise to a set of principles of Christian education that can help the teacher discover and help develop the potential of the exceptional person.

The first obscuring factor is that of limited or different experience. We have already discussed the problem of limited experience in visual disorders and mental retardation. Individuals in most other areas of exceptionality have also had limited or atypical experiences. Those with motor impairments as well as the visually impaired often lack the freedom to move and explore that others have. Those with sensory impairments miss out on experiences perceived through their impaired senses. Those with problems requiring hospitalization, institutionalization, or special schooling encounter a whole set of atypical experiences. Potential may be obscured in individuals with limited or different experiences.

A second obscuring factor is delayed development. Development is measured by certain milestones. Mobility milestones include sitting, crawling, and walking. Communication milestones include imitating sounds, speaking, and writing. Cognitive milestones include generalizing, categorizing, and dealing with abstractions. Delay in reaching these milestones can be an early indicator of mental or physical problems, but delay does not necessarily mean that the potential for their achievement is nonexistent. It may indicate that development must take a different course.

A third obscuring factor is unique expression. We often think of the hearing-impaired person when we think of unique modes of expression, but anyone's potential can be obscured when we fail to allow for unique modes of expression. We often associate the potential for kindness, for example, with the ability to "do something" for others. But we have come to define a certain range of possibilities for "doing something." We must redefine that range of possibilities when considering exceptional persons.

The leaders of a Sunday morning class for exceptional persons were skeptical when Bob, a man with the use of only one arm, claimed he could play the guitar—until he played several songs one Sunday morning. How did Bob do it? A friend of his, a man rather low in general mental ability, but with a good sense of rhythm, did the strumming while Bob fingered the chords. Bob's range of possibilities might have been restricted had not someone shown him this unique way of demonstrating them.

A fourth obscuring factor is unique ability. The exceptional individual often has unique qualities or abilities or has developed certain qualities to a greater extent than others. Failure to recognize and use these abilities can limit the development of potential. For example, those with severely impaired vision are often able to use their senses of hearing, touch, and smell to a greater extent. The severely hearing-impaired can detect very subtle changes in facial expression to distinguish speech sounds. But the exceptional person may possess other unique abilities that are just as significant: a highly developed quality of patience, a profound sense of gratitude, an uncommon willingness to accept others as they are. These qualities are unique in today's world and can serve as a foundation for developing potential in those exceptional persons in whom they are found.

From these four factors, we can derive a set of principles that can guide us in uncovering and developing potential in the exceptional person. These principles can help us contribute to the confirmation of *being* value and the development of *doing* value in exceptional persons:

1. Build on unique experiences and expand limited experiences in a direction that will encourage the discovery of new possibilities.
2. Act on the possibility that skills and concepts that have not naturally developed may be explicitly taught.
3. Search for unique ways for the individual to demonstrate his abilities or express his understanding.
4. Search for unique abilities and qualities and build on these for further growth and development.

Summary

Every person made by God is valued by Him regardless of that person's functional ability, or lack of it, in society. The thesis of this chapter has been that every person, even those severely handicapped and functionally dependent upon others, deserves opportunity to hear the message of God's love. To communicate that message requires an understanding of types of disorders and how to meet them. It requires a commitment to confirm *being* value and to develop *doing* value.

Projects

1. Visit a center for exceptional persons such as a special classroom, shelter care home, or sheltered workshop. If possible, arrange to participate in some social activity with the students or residents. Your goal: to discover possibilities and potential you have not been aware of.
2. On a sheet of paper list the four primary external barriers that hinder the development of potential in exceptional persons (communication, visual experience, physical barriers, and complexity). Under each heading list specific characteristics of your local church—the building itself and the services held in it on a typical Sunday—that contribute to these barriers. Suggest ways these barriers could be eliminated or modified.
3. Select one of the categories of exceptionality. Prepare a lesson (perhaps using one of the parables). Show how you have taken into

account that category's primary barriers to developing potential, the general factors obscuring potential, and the general principles for educating the exceptional derived from these factors.

Selected Bibliography

Bogardus, LaDonna. *Christian Education of Retarded Persons.* Nashville, TN: Abingdon Press, 1969.

Kirk, S. A. *Educating Exceptional Children.* Boston: Houghton-Mifflin Co., 1972.

Lowenfeld, B. *Psychological Considerations: The Visually Handicapped Child at School.* New York: John Day, 1973.

Smith, R. M., and J. Neisworth. *The Exceptional Child: A Functional Approach.* New York: McGraw-Hill, 1975.

CHAPTER 12

A Curriculum for Christian Education

As you read, think about these questions:
—Define *curriculum*.
—What are three prerequisites for curriculum for Christian education?
—What are four principles for curriculum planning? Define each.
—What criteria should be used to evaluate curriculum materials?
—Who should select curriculum materials for a congregation?

What Is Curriculum?

The word *curriculum* is used in a variety of ways, as the following statements illustrate. Look for the key word or phrase in each:

1. "Our curriculum prepares leaders for the church. Look at the courses we offer for adults."
2. "We buy our curriculum from X Publishing Company."
3. "Our curriculum prepares people for responsible membership in the church. Each department uses content that builds upon the previous department. It includes a class about how to become a Christian and another on discovering gifts for ministry. Every class offered in our church must relate to the objective of becoming a disciple."

Review the definitions. In the first example, curriculum equals classes. In the second, it becomes materials. The last example includes classes and materials, but it is more comprehensive. It assumes a goal, classes, and materials as well as a design to fit all of these experiences together to achieve the goal.

The word curriculum literally means "race course" or "race track." It may be used to include everything that happens in the educational setting, but that definition is much too broad for our use in the church. A minister, Christian educator, or superintendent can neither foresee nor control everything that happens educationally to those in the church. However, they can plan and implement some experiences that affect the life of the learner.

Curriculum may be defined in this way: "A curriculum is a plan by which the teaching/learning process may be systematically undertaken."[1] This definition assumes that the following conditions be met:

1. Curriculum is planned.
2. It is planned with specific goals in mind.
3. It is designed—it begins at point A and proceeds in an orderly fashion to point B.
4. Its content is selected in order to achieve specific goals.
5. It uses materials designed to achieve these goals.
6. It requires the presence and influence of a teacher.
7. Its methods are chosen so as to achieve the goals.

Curriculum: goals, plan, design, materials, teachers, methods. A good curriculum doesn't just happen. It requires understanding and application of basic principles.

Prerequisites for an Effective Curriculum

Based on the Bible

The most important question about a curriculum for Christian education is what will be taught. For Christian education to be genuinely Christian, the curriculum must be based upon the Word of God. That does not mean that extra-biblical content cannot be used, but it does demand that any extra-biblical material be used in harmony with the purpose and message of the Bible. The Bible is the textbook for Christian education. It controls the curriculum.

To say that the curriculum is Bible-based is to imply more than mere transmission of facts. Memorization of information or recital by rote, as beneficial as both may be to provide a basis for knowledge, are inadequate by themselves. The word *knowledge*, as it is used in the Bible, assumes that information is always coupled with behavior.

A Bible-based curriculum accepts the inspiration of the Bible and uses the Word itself to guide what is taught. It keeps Christ and the pupil's response to Him in clear focus. It teaches the Bible from the perspective of faith and calls for a definite response from the learner.

Related to Pupil Needs

An effective curriculum also meets the needs of the pupil. It takes the learner into account: how old he is, what he already knows, what his capabilities are, and how he learns best. A curriculum for preschoolers would be quite different than one for adults if not in sections of Scripture covered, then certainly in goals and methods.

To plan an effective curriculum, the planner must answer some basic questions about each age level:

1. What of the Bible can be understood by this age group?
2. What of the Bible is most important for this group of learners?
3. How do these learners learn most effectively?
4. What shall we teach to them? In what order? How?

Characteristics of the various age groups are detailed in Chapters 7—11.

Utilizes Sound Teaching Principles

An effective curriculum is based on sound teaching/learning principles. Learning is most effective when the lesson and the material used are related to the learner's experience. Learning is most efficient when the pupil learns by actively participating. The basic principles of effective learning are developed in further detail in Chapter 6.

Principles for an Effective Curriculum

D. Campbell Wyckoff outlines four principles for constructing an effective curriculum. These four principles serve as the outline for this section.

Principle of Context

Where does Christian education take place? The principle of context takes into account where people are when they are confronted with the Word of God.

The first place for many to be introduced to the Word of God is the home. Children observe the ways parents demonstrate their faith. They absorb attitudes toward God, Jesus Christ, and the church. Although the home may teach specific Bible information, its chief function is to transmit attitudes, responses, values, and lifestyle.

Christian education also occurs in one-to-one situations. Two friends discuss the Bible over lunch. A caller explains salvation to a non-Christian in his home. A mother answers her child's questions. All of these are Christian education.

But the local congregation is also responsible for Christian education. Two centuries ago, formal Christian education happened in a public school in which a preacher was the teacher. But the public school has long since ceased providing Christian education. Therefore, the church has developed a variety of formal teaching programs to fill the gap. Sunday school, children's church, youth groups, Vacation Bible School, and weekday classes are examples of such programs.

A congregation that takes seriously its commitment to Bible teaching will acknowledge and observe the principle of context. Although it cannot control what happens within the walls of each home, it can provide information, materials, and programs to support and strengthen parents. Neither can a congregation plan and control every one-to-one contact made by its members. But just as with the family, the church can provide materials, information, and programs to equip the individual for fruitful one-to-one contacts.

Despite these limitations, a congregation can plan and design the formal learning experiences that occur within its corporate life. The principle of context demands that curriculum not be left to chance. Curriculum must be chosen according to a plan for each teaching program, and then those programs must be coordinated with each other. The plan should take into account what is taught in Sunday school and how that subject matter is complemented or supplemented by what is taught in youth meetings, Vacation Bible School, children's church, and midweek classes.

Month	Sunday School	Graded Worship
Sept.	Going to God's House (4 weeks)	We Talk With God We Worship God We Work With God We Obey God
Oct.	Going to God's House (1) Giving for God's House (4)	We Love Our Parents We Love Our Friends We Tell Others About God's Love We Send God's Helpers Far Away We Help at God's House
Nov.	Thanking God for His House (4)	We Thank God—Homes We Thank God—Food We Thank God—Water We Thank God—Care
Dec.	The Baby Jesus (4)	God Sent His Son Jesus Was Born People Visit Baby Jesus God Watches Over Jesus
Jan.	The Baby Jesus (2) The Boy Jesus (3)	Jesus Is God's Son Jesus Is Kind Jesus Helps People Jesus Forgives Jesus Loves Everyone
Feb.	The Boy Jesus (1) The Man Jesus (3)	Jesus Teaches About God Jesus Teaches to Pray Jesus Teaches Us to Love God's House Jesus' Disciples Help Him Do God's Work

Figure 12-1. Curriculum for 2's and 3's, September–February

For example, a curriculum for preschoolers might use the same theme (perhaps even the same content) for Sunday school, children's church, and youth meetings, because this age level benefits more from repetition of concepts than it does from a large volume of information. Figure 12-1 illustrates such a curriculum.

At the youth level, a Bible book study for Sunday school and topical studies for youth meetings may be planned. To assure coordination, the topical studies could be developed from themes from the book being studied in Sunday school. Or supplementary topics, not covered elsewhere in the youth curriculum, could be chosen.

A family enrichment calendar can also help to coordinate the different parts of the curriculum. The calendar would suggest family activities designed to complement and reinforce the biblical material used in the church's formal teaching programs.

However it is implemented, the principle of context demands that a curriculum take into account all agencies of teaching, not just the Sunday school.

Principle of Scope

The principle of scope refers to the choice of what content to include for each age level. An effective curriculum will seek to acquaint the pupil with God's will. The curriculum planner must decide what specific portions of the Bible are understandable to and teachable for a particular age group. A well-planned curriculum must also plan in what order biblical portions will be studied—not only in a given year, but from age level to age level.

W. Kent Gilbert, in *The Functional Objectives for Christian Education*, explores what subject matter is appropriate for each age level. He divides biblical content into six categories—God, Bible, church, fellow man, world, and self—and suggests content and goals for each category and each age group. This resource provides valuable assistance for the curriculum planner.

The principle of scope is taken into account by each publishing company as it plans a total curriculum for babies through adults. A congregation must be especially careful to take this principle into account when curriculum materials from several different sources are used. The principle also helps to avoid overlap from one teaching program to the next.

The principle of scope requires that at least three other decisions be made:

1. How much time will be given to various portions of Scripture? An effective curriculum should not teach entirely from the Old Testament or from the New Testament. Some balance must be maintained.

2. In what order will the Bible content be studied? This needs to be planned so that the Bible will make sense to the learner.

3. What needs are evident in the lives of the learners? Content should be life-related.

The principle of scope, then, refers to what is studied and in what order it is pursued.

Principle of Process

The principle of process refers to the way in which content is communicated. It deals with the question of teaching methods. A curriculum cannot be considered complete until thought is given to the most effective method for teaching specific age levels.

The teacher is the key to effective communication of the Bible. First of all, he is a model of the power of God's transforming grace. He demonstrates what he teaches with his own life if he teaches well. He also plans for a certain classroom atmosphere as well as lesson structure and presentation.

Curriculum materials are designed to help the teacher with process. Curriculum writers assist by suggesting ways to set up the classroom, build the lesson, and present the content. Materials are resources for the teacher; they are never substitutes for his personal example and creativity.

Principle of Design

The principle of design refers to the manner in which learning experiences are woven together. A variety of designs is possible. Four are most common.

1. *Uniform.* Everyone in the church studies the same Bible content at the same time. The advantage is that everyone in the family studies the same subject, and the content can later serve as the basis for family worship and discussion. However, some content is too difficult for some age levels (for example, Romans or Leviticus for preschoolers and early elementary chil-

dren). At the same time, the content most appropriate for preschoolers may not best meet the needs of teenagers. Few publishers continue to pursue this design.

2. *Cycle graded, or group graded.* In this design, a cycle of lessons is designed for particular age levels, usually a two-, three-, four-, or six-year cycle. For example, there may be a four-year cycle of lessons for preschoolers. All preschoolers deal with the same material on the same Sunday. Over a four-year period, the entire cycle will be covered. A different cycle is then used for elementary children, another for youth, and another for adults. This way, the content that is most appropriate for each age level and learning ability can be chosen. On the other hand, group grading eliminates the advantage of a common theme for family worship and discussion. Several publishers follow this pattern.

3. *Closely graded.* The lessons are graded year-by-year for each age level. It is an attempt to plan Bible curriculum much as public school curriculum is planned. Fifth-grade classwork builds upon fourth-grade skills that rest upon third-grade content. Such a design focuses upon the needs of a narrow age level, but in this advantage also lies it main weakness. Not all people begin their Christian education at the same age level, or progress at the same rate. Few publishers use this approach, not because it is undesirable, but because it is expensive.

4. *Electives.* In an elective system, each person chooses his own course of study from a list of studies available each quarter. Sometimes a class selects its own study topic (another type of elective). This system is commonly used for adults and sometimes for senior highs.

The curriculum planner must decide which approach he will use.

Selection of Curriculum Materials

Who Selects Materials?

Every church must settle the issue of who is to select curriculum content and materials: the teachers, the learners, or someone else?

The teacher could make the choice. He is the key to effective communication of biblical material. He should teach what he feels comfortable sharing. However, such an arrangement permits little coordination among teachers, classes, and other teaching agencies. Nor does it provide a needed check and balance system to assure that biblically sound materials are chosen.

A case can also be made for allowing the learner to select his own curriculum. Curriculum must be need-related, and the pupil should know his needs better than anyone else. His interest would be increased if he were to select his own course of study. The biggest danger to this approach is that sometimes real needs are not felt. The average learner also has a tendency not to push himself into new areas of content, attitudes, and behaviors, unless he is guided or motivated to do so.

How should content and materials be selected? The overseers of a congregation are the likely candidates for the job. One task of an overseer is to model the Christian lifestyle.[2] A second task, as a shepherd of the people, is to feed the flock and to protect it.[3] The overseers may (and probably should) seek the counsel of teachers, parents, learners, educational planners, and developmental psychologists. They may commission the minister or Christian education director or other qualified persons to design the curriculum. But the final approval of content and resources should be left to the overseers, whose job it is to feed and protect the flock of God.

How Are Materials Chosen?

The final selection of materials must be founded upon criteria that takes into account both content and methodology. The following form was developed and used by Standard Publishing Company in a recent curriculum evaluation project. It can serve as a guide for your evaluation of materials.

Guidelines for Evaluating Curriculum

Use the following questions to guide your evaluation. Feel free to add other comments as well. Circle the scale number that best indicates the extent to which each statement describes the material you are evaluating.

1 = Poor, 2 = Fair, 3 = Average, 4 = Good, 5 = Excellent, 6 = Superior

Appropriateness

1. How appropriate for the age level is the choice of Bible stories or passages? 1 2 3 4 5 6
2. How appropriate for the age level is the choice of Bible version(s)? 1 2 3 4 5 6
3. To what extent are the Scriptures chosen for memorization appropriate? 1 2 3 4 5 6
4. To what extent are the activities, lectures, learning centers, and other elements of the lesson plans appropriate to the developmental needs of the age group? 1 2 3 4 5 6
5. To what extent are the lesson applications appropriate? 1 2 3 4 5 6
6. To what extent are the lesson objectives appropriate for the age level? 1 2 3 4 5 6
7. How appropriate for the age level is the wording of the quarterly and lesson titles? 1 2 3 4 5 6
8. To what extent are the materials appropriate for ethnic minorities? 1 2 3 4 5 6
9. How appropriate are the visuals for the age level? 1 2 3 4 5 6
10. How appropriate is the take-home paper to the age level? 1 2 3 4 5 6

Comments:

Bible Content

1. To what extent are the materials biblically based? 1 2 3 4 5 6
2. To what extent are appropriate interpretations and applications made of biblical material? 1 2 3 4 5 6
3. To what degree are the objectives and content of the lessons based solidly on the Scriptures? 1 2 3 4 5 6
4. To what extent is an appropriate evangelistic emphasis found? 1 2 3 4 5 6
5. To what extent do the materials help the learner to know what it means to be a part of the church? 1 2 3 4 5 6
6. When the Scripture being studied is subject to different interpretations by conservative scholars, how consistently and satisfactorily are these alternative interpretations presented? 1 2 3 4 5 6

7. To what extent is the teacher helped to understand the Scriptures? 1 2 3 4 5 6

Comments:

Teachability

1. To what extent are the recommendations for supplementary helps adequate? 1 2 3 4 5 6
2. To what extent are the lesson objectives clearly stated? 1 2 3 4 5 6
3. To what extent are the verbal illustrations clear and appropriate for the age level? 1 2 3 4 5 6
4. To what extent are the definitions clear and appropriate for the age level? 1 2 3 4 5 6
5. How would you rate the degree of learner involvement in the lesson process? 1 2 3 4 5 6
6. To what degree is adequate explanation included in this material to tell teachers how to use it? 1 2 3 4 5 6
7. How adequate are the introductions provided for each unit of lessons within a quarter? 1 2 3 4 5 6
8. To what degree are teachers given adequate help in developing a satisfactory room arrangement? 1 2 3 4 5 6
9. How satisfactorily are teachers alerted to special materials that will be needed in a lesson? 1 2 3 4 5 6
10. How satisfactorily are teachers alerted to special advance preparations that need to be made? 1 2 3 4 5 6
11. To what extent is there an apparent outline of main points that are summarized and reinforced? 1 2 3 4 5 6
12. To what degree do the activities suggested lead to the accomplishment of the lesson objectives? 1 2 3 4 5 6
13. How adequate is the variety of learning activities used? 1 2 3 4 5 6
14. How well is the teacher's book correlated with the student's book? 1 2 3 4 5 6
15. To what extent are the materials adaptable to classes with only a few students? 1 2 3 4 5 6
16. To what extent are the materials adaptable for large classes? 1 2 3 4 5 6
17. Is adequate help given to adjust for exceptionally short or exceptionally long class periods? 1 2 3 4 5 6

18. How appropriate are the vocabulary and reading levels of the pupil materials for the age level? 1 2 3 4 5 6
19. To what extent are the pupils encouraged to use their Bibles? 1 2 3 4 5 6
20. To what extent are provisions made for "more advanced" and "less advanced" pupils? 1 2 3 4 5 6
21. To what extent do the visuals help to accomplish the objectives for each lesson? 1 2 3 4 5 6
22. How effective are the visuals? 1 2 3 4 5 6
23. To what extent does the take-home paper teach biblical concepts and principles? 1 2 3 4 5 6
24. To what extent are students led to carry out the concepts and principles? 1 2 3 4 5 6
25. How successful are the materials in leading pupils beyond just parroting right answers? 1 2 3 4 5 6

Comments:

Appearance

1. How attractive is the outside appearance of the books? 1 2 3 4 5 6
2. How attractive is the inside appearance of the books? 1 2 3 4 5 6
3. How attractive are the art and photographs? 1 2 3 4 5 6
4. To what extent do the materials appear to be up-to-date? 1 2 3 4 5 6
5. How attractive are the visuals? 1 2 3 4 5 6
6. How attractive is the take-home paper? 1 2 3 4 5 6

Comments:

Overall Evaluation

1. Major strengths of these materials:

2. Major weaknesses of these materials:

Summary

Curriculum is a plan by which the teaching/learning process may be systematically undertaken. An effective curriculum must be based on the Bible, be related to the pupil's needs, and utilize sound teaching principles. Four principles guide the curriculum—context, scope, process, and design. Selection of curriculum materials is the responsibility of the overseers of the church.

Projects

1. Interview an elder from your congregation. Find out what content and materials are used for each age group in the church, and why they are used. Determine who makes the final decisions about curriculum.
2. Evaluate two samples of curriculum materials for one age group. Use the criteria above. Decide which sample best illustrates the principles outlined in this chapter. According to which design is it organized?

Selected Bibliography

Colson, Howard P., and Raymond M. Rigdon. *Understanding Your Church's Curriculum*. Nashville, TN: Broadman Press, 1981.

Cully, Iris. *Planning and Selecting Curriculum for Christian Education*. Valley Forge, PA: Judson Press, 1983.

Miller, Randolph Crump. *Biblical Theology and Christian Education*. New York: Charles Scribner's Sons, 1956.

________ . *The Clue to Christian Education*. New York: Charles Scribner's Sons, 1950.

Tanner, Daniel and Laurel. *Curriculum Development: Theory into Practice*. 2nd ed. New York: Macmillan, 1980.

Taylor, Peter A. and Doris M. Cowley. *Readings in Curriculum Development*. Dubuque, IA: William C. Brown Company, Publishers, 1972.

Sources of Curriculum

Augsburg Publishing House
426 S. 5th St., Box 1209
Minneapolis, MN 55440

Concordia Publishing House
3558 S. Jefferson
St. Louis, MO 63118

David C. Cook Publishing Co.
850 N. Grove
Elgin, IL 60120

Gospel Light
2300 Knoll Ave.
Ventura, CA 93003

Scripture Press
1825 College Ave.,
Wheaton, IL 60187

Standard Publishing Co.
8121 Hamilton Ave.
Cincinnati, OH 45231

The Westminster Press
925 Chestnut St.,
Philadelphia, PA 19107

---

[1]*Theory and Design of Christian Education Curriculum,* by D. Campbell Wyckoff. Copyright © MCMLXI by W.L. Jenkins. p. 17. Used by permission of The Westminster Press.

[2]1 Timothy 3:1-7

[3]Acts 20:28

CHAPTER 13

Audiovisual Methods

As you read, think about these questions:
—What were at least six ways in which visuals were used in the Bible?
—Name at least two examples of each type of visual discussed in this chapter.
—What criteria guide selection of visuals for a given lesson?
—What equipment and materials should be included in an audiovisual center?

"A picture is worth a thousand words," states an old axiom. Visual aids communicate in a way not possible with words alone. A wise teacher uses everything at his disposal to communicate the truth of God's Word. Audiovisuals, used with the methods outlined in the previous chapters, are valuable communication tools.

A Biblical Basis for Using Visuals

Old Testament Visuals

God used visual media to communicate with His people. He spoke, and His message is recorded in the Bible. But He did more than speak. He used a variety of visuals to reinforce His message, as can be seen in His dealings with the people of Israel during the exodus and wilderness wanderings.

God led Israel from bondage in Egypt. Israel had been fully persuaded to leave Egypt, largely because of a visual demonstration of God's power through the plagues and by the work of the death angel,[1] but once the people had made their way out to the Red Sea, doubts arose. Egypt had supplied their needs and had fed and sustained them. But now with the Egyptians in hot pursuit, how were they to survive? Where was God now?

God chose to answer with a visual—a miracle of intervention. Exodus 14 records how God divided the Red Sea so that the Israelites crossed on dry land. When the Egyptians pursued them across the sea bed, the waters rushed over them, sending them to their deaths. To the Israelites it was a dramatic sign of God's power and presence with them.

Years later, when the Israelites were once again ready to cross a body of water (this time the Jordan River) to begin conquest of the promised land, God confirmed Joshua's leadership and reassured them of His presence when He parted the waters of the Jordan.[2] Again He reinforced His words with visual symbols to develop trust in Israelite hearts.

Not only did God use the visual medium of miracles, but He also placed other more enduring visual aids in the midst of Israel. For example, He ordained the Nazarite vow as a visual reminder of Israel's unique purpose and function in the world. The Nazarite vow was taken voluntarily for a fixed period ranging from thirty days to life. During the time the vow was in effect, the Nazarite was to abstain from wine, grapes, and intoxicating beverages. He could not cut his hair or approach a dead body. The meaning of the vow, established by God, was to renounce the world and become set apart to God. The men and women who took the vow were visual reminders to the rest of Israel that national separation to God was a must if Israel was to fulfill her destiny in the world.[3]

Tassels were another type of visual. Numbers 15:37-40 records God's instructions for the Israelites to put tassels on the corners of their garments as a reminder of the commandments of God and the importance of obeying them. The visual made it difficult for them to forget their obligations.

Feasts were another aid to memory. Of the Passover Feast, God instructed, "This is a day you are to commemorate; . . . When your children ask you, 'What does this ceremony mean to you?' then tell them, 'It is the Passover sacrifice to the Lord, who passed over the houses of the Israelites in Egypt and spared our homes when he struck down the Egyptians.'"[4]

Feasts were vivid reminders to Israelite adults of God's power and care. Those same feasts stimulated children to ask questions, providing excellent opportunities for teaching about God's care.

The tabernacle served as a visual, a clear declaration to Israel that "God is in our midst." It stood as silent testimony that God walked with Israel.[5]

Old Testament examples abound: God presented His message to His people using visual media. He wanted them to know beyond any doubt who He was and how they could walk with Him.

Jesus' Use of Visuals

Careful analysis of the Gospels reveals Jesus' liberal use of visual media to illustrate and reinforce His God-given message. "Look at the birds of the air," He directed, surely pointing to birds flying overhead, when He wanted to emphasize the futility of anxiety. "See how the lilies of the field grow," He added to reinforce the same concept.[6]

Jesus' parables abound with everyday pictures, vividly painted to communicate abstract truth. "A farmer went out to sow his seed," He began as He illustrated possible responses to the proclamation of God's Word.[7] Sowers and seed were commonplace, something understood by all who were listening to Him. Another time He began, "The kingdom of heaven is like a man who sowed good seed in his field,"[8] and taught them the reality of good and evil existing side by side in the world until the judgment. In parable after parable He developed an understanding of the nature of the kingdom of God.

Jesus pictured the Father's love in another set of parables. "What do you think?" He asked. "If a man owns a hundred sheep, and one of them wanders away, will he not leave the ninety-nine on the hills and go to look for the one that wandered off?"[9] Acquainted as they were with shepherds and sheep, His listeners immediately pictured a wayward lamb being hunted by a good shepherd, and they caught a glimpse of God. He illustrated the same truth by telling a story of a woman searching relentlessly for a lost coin and of a father waiting patiently for a rebellious son.[10]

The Lord's Supper was begun by Jesus as visual reminder to people of every age of His suffering for sin. "Take and eat; this is my body," Jesus instructed as He gave the Passover bread to the disciples. "Drink from it, all of you. This is my blood of the covenant, which is poured out for many for the forgiveness of sins," He said as He took the Passover cup.[11] To this day the Communion pictures the suffering and death of Jesus to all who believe.

Anyone intent on spending time reading the Gospels can find many more examples of Jesus' use of visuals. The visuals mentioned are only a few examples of His abundant use of illustrations to communicate abstract ideas.

The Visual of Baptism

Besides the Lord's Supper, baptism is the most expressive visual presented in the New Testament. The immersion of a penitent believer in water pictures far more than just a body dipped beneath water. Paul explains the significance of baptism in Romans 6:4-7:

> We were therefore buried with him through baptism into death in order that, just as Christ was raised from the dead through the glory of the Father, we too may live a new life.
>
> If we have been united with him in his death, we will certainly also be united with him in his resurrection. For we know that our old self was crucified with him so that the body of sin might be rendered powerless, that we should no longer be slaves to sin—because anyone who has died has been freed from sin.

A baptism pictures death and resurrection. The candidate enters the water. As he is plunged beneath the water, he stops breathing. At that moment, the observer pictures Jesus' death, and the one being baptized is identified with that death. But then the person being baptized reappears from beneath the water, a vivid reminder that Jesus emerged from the tomb triumphant over sin and death. The baptized person is clearly identified as a new person, having died to sin and put on Christ.

Baptism, like the Lord's Supper, is an expressive visual, reminding those who participate of Jesus' death, burial, and resurrection. The picture is worth a thousand words!

Values of Audiovisual Aids

Overcome Barriers to Learning

The language barrier is formidable at every age level, but especially so for children who lack experiences and who cannot yet think abstractly. A teacher must be able to present abstract biblical material in a visual medium understandable to the learner—this is no small task.

Children (adults too, for that matter) can easily memorize words without learning their meaning, or learning incorrect meanings. The results would be humorous if they were not so serious. Gene Getz lists several illustrations that demonstrate the misunderstandings that often occur:

"Gladly, the cross-eyed bear"
"Jesus wants me for a sun bean"
"Don't forget to play"
"When the sins go marching in"
"Sweet peas, the gift of God's love"
"There's not a friend like the lonely Jesus"[12]

Audiovisuals help to overcome the language barrier because they clarify words and meanings.

Make Learning Interesting

Audiovisuals make learning interesting because they provide an appeal to more than one sense. Speech appeals only to the auditory sense, but when visuals supplement the spoken words, an appeal is made to the sense of sight as well.

Audiovisuals also provide the basis for discussion, another way to stimulate interest. They stimulate questions, provide the foundation for problem solving, and present new information, all of which can be talked about in preparation for additional learning. Not all visuals need be commercially prepared. Pupils can make visuals themselves, as part of a learning activity. They participate in learning by visualizing the material to be learned—a process that helps hold their interest.

Make Learning Permanent

Helping pupils to remember is a supreme challenge to any teacher. It is a major problem for the Bible teacher, who usually experiences an interval of seven days between class meetings.

One reason that information is forgotten is that it is not related to life experience. Visuals help the student remember by tying the two together.

Visuals also provide meaningful associations that assist memory. People remember what is important to them and what they understand clearly.

Types of Audiovisuals

The chart on the next page illustrates the process of learning and the importance of visual experiences in the absence of direct experience.[13]

Figure 13-1 is a helpful reminder that direct, purposeful experiences are the most effective kind of learning experience. A full range of sensory experience contributes information and understanding to learning experiences.

Not all learning can be direct, however. In many cases, direct experience is not an efficient, or even possible, way to learn something. One could resort to verbal symbols, but verbal symbols alone provide little linking between new information and previous experience. The cone of experience is helpful for the teacher to recall the audiovisual experiences available to link verbal symbols with direct experiences.

Simulated Experiences

A simulated experience is a representation of real life. It simplifies a real-life experience and allows the pupil to participate in it with the added benefit of the guidance of a teacher. Simulation, case studies, models, and mockups are useful visuals to provide simulated experience.

Dramatized Experiences

Dramatization permits the pupil to see, hear, and feel ideas and experiences. Plays, skits, and role plays are valuable visual tools.

Demonstrations

A demonstration is a visualized explanation. Visual symbols are usually incorporated in the presentation of a demonstration. Demonstrations are often used to prepare for direct experience.

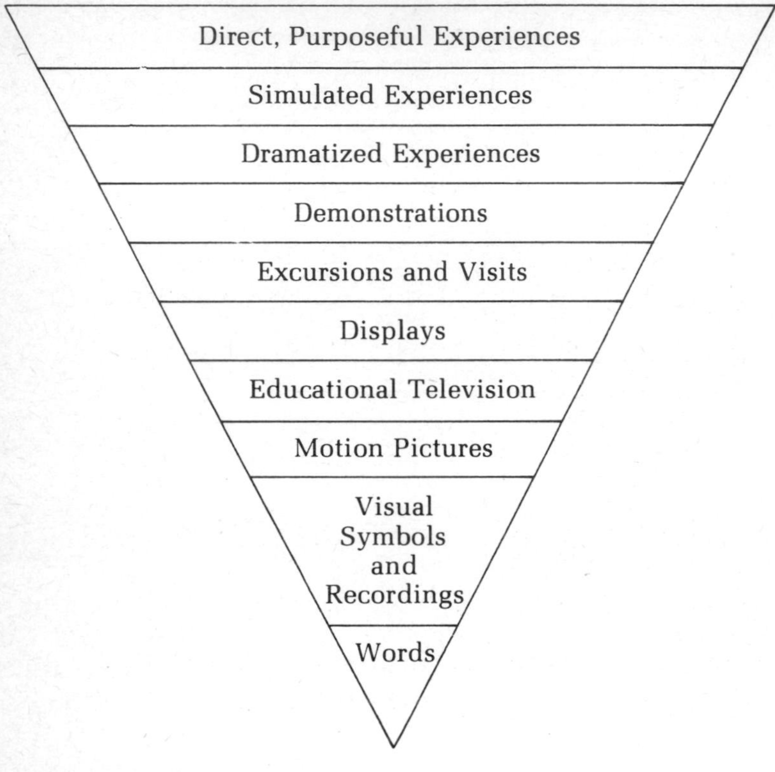

Figure 13-1. Comparative effectiveness of different kinds of learning experiences

Excursions and Visits

Study trips permit pupils to observe people and objects in their natural environment. Coupled with later discussion, field trips are a valuable tool.

Displays

Displays are to be observed, not manipulated or handled at any length. Both ready-made and homemade exhibits illustrate concepts, ideas, and information.

Television and Motion Pictures

Films compress both time and space and bring them to the

classroom. They omit unnecessary material and concentrate on important points. They reconstruct experiences and involve the pupils imaginatively.

Visual Symbols and Recordings

Still pictures, recordings, and radio provide visual and auditory experiences far from direct experience, but considerably better than verbal symbols alone. Filmstrips, slides, overhead transparencies, flannelgraph figures, standup figures, dioramas, tapes, records, cartoons, stick figures, flat pictures, and photographs are types of still pictures and recordings useful for the classroom.

Words

Verbal symbols, or words, contain no visual clues to their meaning. Used with every other experience on the cone, they too are essential for learning.

Evaluating Audiovisual Material

From the plethora of material available, both ready-made and homemade, a teacher must choose visual materials for a given lesson or unit. The following criteria will help determine the suitability of any visual.

1. Does the visual give a true picture of the idea it represents?
2. Does it contribute meaningful content to the topic?
3. Is it appropriate for the age, intelligence, and experience of the learners?
4. Is the physical condition of the visual satisfactory?
5. Will the visual stimulate thinking?
6. Is it worth the time, expense, and effort involved?[14]

Organizing Audiovisual Materials

Audiovisual Center

A local church should accumulate, preserve, and organize a wide variety of visual tools. Visual aids and equipment should be available to everyone. A well-organized audiovisual center can make this possible.

The Christian education committee or other governing body may appoint a coordinator for the center. It is the coordinator's job to organize and distribute materials. All materials should be kept in a centralized place so that files may be maintained and distribution monitored.

Items to provide in the center include:

Books and Pamphlets	Objects
Charts	Photographs
Drawings	Posters
Films	Records
Filmstrips	Slides
Flannelboard figures	Supplies for bulletin boards, etc.
Flat pictures	Tapes
Graphs	Teaching kits
Maps	Transparencies
Models	

These should be organized so that they can be easily located. Many of these items can be bought separately, but many could be added from used visual packets at the end of each Sunday-school quarter and after Vacation Bible School.

A good audiovisual center will also include equipment as follows:

Bulletin boards (portable)	Overhead projector
Chalkboards (portable)	Projection screen
Film splicers	Record players
Filmstrip projector	16mm projector
Flannelboards	Slide projector
Individual filmstrip viewers	Tape recorders and players

Adequate storage space for all equipment and materials is also essential.

Personal Files

An individual should also organize his personal storehouse of audiovisual materials into files if he wishes to preserve them for use again and again. At the beginning, a file folder for each type of item may be adequate. Eventually those will need to be subdivided.

The following outline might be helpful for subdividing pictures:[15]

Old Testament	*New Testament*	*Modern Scenes*
Creation	John the Baptist	Animals
Cain and Abel	Jesus	Going to church
Abraham	birth	Helping
Isaac	childhood	Missions
Jacob	temptation	Nature
Joseph	with children	Praying
Moses	teaching	Bible
Joshua	miracles	Sharing
Samuel	parables	Singing
Ruth	passion week	Worship
David	resurrection	Flowers
Kings	others	Buildings
Daniel	Apostles	Churches
Other prophets	Peter	People
	John	Historical events
	Stephen	Sports
	Paul	Travel
	others	

Any subheading could be further divided as necessary.

Summary

Audiovisuals are valuable tools to make learning interesting and permanent. Not at all a modern invention, God used visuals effectively in the Old Testament. Jesus demonstrated and validated their use during His ministry. A wide variety of visual media is available for organization and use by Bible teachers who want to vitalize their teaching.

Project

Using the lesson plans you prepared for teaching preschoolers, elementary children, youth, and adults, plan at least three visuals you could use for each lesson. Tell why you chose the visuals you did.

Selected Bibliography

Brown, James B., Richard B. Lewis, and Fred F. Harderoad. *Instruction: Materials and Methods*. 2nd ed. New York: McGraw-Hill, 1964.

Dale, Edgar. *Audio-Visual Methods in Teaching*. 3rd ed. New York: Dryden Press, 1969.

Getz, Gene A. *Audio-Visual Media in Christian Education*. Chicago: Moody Press, 1972.

---

[1]Exodus 7—12

[2]Joshua 3:8-10, 14-16

[3]See Numbers 6:1-21; Judges 13:7; 1 Samuel 1:11; and Luke 1:15.

[4]Exodus 12:14, 26, 27

[5]See Exodus 25:8; 33:7-11; 40:38; Numbers 9:15; 10:33-35; 1 Samuel 4:3-11; and 1 Kings 8:27.

[6]Matthew 6:26, 28

[7]Matthew 13:3-9

[8]Matthew 13:24-30; see also Matthew 13:31-33

[9]Matthew 18:12-14; see also Luke 15:4-7

[10]Luke 15:8-32

[11]see Matthew 26:26-29; Luke 22:15-20; and 1 Corinthians 10:16.

[12]AUDIO-VISUAL MEDIA IN CHRISTIAN EDUCATION by Gene A. Getz. Copyright 1972, Moody Press, Moody Bible Institute of Chicago. pp. 26, 27. Used by permission.

[13]Edgar Dale, *Audio-Visual Methods in Teaching*, 3rd ed. (New York: Dryden Press, 1969), pp. 107-135.

[14]*Ibid.*, pp. 173-79.

[15]Getz, *op. cit.*, pp. 123-25.

CHAPTER 14

Helping the Family Teach

As you read, think about these questions:
—What is the purpose of the family?
—What are the biblical functions of parents?
—What problems face the contemporary family?
—How can the church help the modern family to fulfill its biblical function?

God made the family. At the dawn of creation, before God expressed final satisfaction with the world He had fashioned, He created woman to go with man. "It is not good for the man to be alone. I will provide a partner for him,"[1] God said, and He made woman from the side of man. "For this reason a man will leave his father and mother and be united to his wife, and they will become one flesh."[2] Marriage and the home were a reality.

The Family in the Bible

God's intentions for the family were clearly stated in the Bible. Eve was to be a partner with Adam, and both Adam and Eve were to provide companionship for the Lord God.[3] They were to rule over Eden and they were free to subdue creation to serve their needs.[4] They were also instructed to be fruitful and populate the earth, sanctifying the sexual union that was theirs. The creation of the family unit was the crowning point of creation, and the remainder of God's creation was placed under their care and keeping.

Man's noble purpose was tainted, however, when he succumbed to sin. The purpose of the home remained the same, and man still retained his God-given responsibility for creation. But the reality of sin severed man's perfect relationship with God, and introduced mistrust and tension between man and his partner. Sexual union was still a part of God's plan for the home, but children born to that union would be brought forth in pain. Marriage was still sanctified by God, but henceforth there would be disharmony and tension between man and woman that could be resolved only when they reached full maturity in Jesus Christ.

Guidelines for the family are set forth in the Old Testament, but not until the era of the New Covenant did the family rediscover its full potential. Gene Getz, in his book, *The Measure of a Family,* asserts that the Christian home in the New Testament was almost synonymous with the church. This, he suggests, is why the New Testament says relatively little about the family unit. What was written to the church was also written to individual families. The family is the church in miniature, according to Getz. The truly Christian family will demonstrate the marks of a mature church.

Biblical Guidelines for the Family

Both the Old Testament and the New Testament seem to assume that under normal circumstances a home will be blessed with children. Therefore, other than the creation passage in Genesis, the laws for personal sexual conduct in Leviticus, and the treatise on marriage as a picture of the church in Ephesians, specific instructions for the family center in the business of childrearing.

Teach With Words

Parents were instructed to teach their children. God commanded that parents were to verbally instruct their children in the faith:

> O my people, hear my teaching;
> listen to the words of my mouth.
> I will open my mouth in parables,
> I will utter things hidden from of old—
> things we have heard and known,
> things our fathers have told us.
> We will not hide them from their children;
> we will tell the next generation
> the praiseworthy deeds of the Lord,
> his power, and the wonders he has done.
> He decreed statutes for Jacob
> and established the law in Israel,
> which he commanded our forefathers
> to teach their children,
> so the next generation would know them,
> even the children yet to be born,
> and they in turn would tell their children.
> Then they would put their trust in God
> and would not forget his deeds
> but would keep his commands.
> They would not be like their forefathers—
> a stubborn and rebellious generation,
> whose hearts were not loyal to God,
> whose spirits were not faithful to him.[5]

Paul restates the principle: "You fathers, again, must not goad your children to resentment, but give them the instruction, and the correction, which belong to a Christian upbringing."[6]

Teach by Example

God knew that children would watch their parents prepare for worship. Deuteronomy 6:4-9 identifies parents' responsibility to communicate faith by example:

> Hear, O Israel: The Lord our God, the Lord is one. Love the Lord your God with all your heart and with all your soul and with all your strength. These commandments that I give you today are to be upon your hearts. Impress them on your children. Talk about them when you sit at home and when you walk along the road, when you lie down and when you get up. Tie them as symbols on your hands and bind them on your foreheads. Write them on the doorframes of your houses and on your gates.

Parents teach by the way they themselves observe the Word of God. Under normal conditions, children become much like what their parents are, largely by copying their parents' model. Children critically eye parents' behavior patterns and decide if their behavior is consistent with their words. They observe parents' responses to joy and disaster. Then they usually begin to respond to situations much as their parents do.

Teaching by example is as much informal as it is formal. Family devotions, holiday traditions, mealtime prayers, bedtime prayers, and family conversation provide the atmosphere in which faith is communicated—if words and actions agree.

Discipline

Parents are also instructed to discipline their children. Proverbs records the positive results of effective discipline and the negative results of poor discipline.

> Rod and reprimand impart wisdom,
> but a boy who runs wild brings shame on his mother.
>
> A father who spares the rod hates his son,
> but one who loves him keeps him in order.
>
> Correct your son, and he will be a comfort to you
> and bring you delights of every kind.
>
> Start a boy on the right road,
> and even in old age he will not leave it.[7]

Discipline is more than mere correction. It also requires parents to direct a child's behavior into appropriate channels in an effort to lead him to healthy self-discipline. Paul's advice to the Ephesian parents applies here too: "You fathers, again, must not goad your children to resentment, but give them the instruction, and the correction, which belong to a Christian upbringing."[8] Discipline is to be administered directly, positively, and in a spirit of love. "Fathers, do not exasperate your children, for fear they grow disheartened,"[9] Paul further instructed.

Effective discipline is administered with a child's age level, capabilities, and emotional response in mind. Rules should be appropriate for the child's age, not demanding more than he can produce. Discipline preserves the dignity of the child by protecting him from nagging and ridicule, yet, at the same time, consistently insists upon clearly defined behavior standards.

Firm authoritative discipline (as opposed to a permissive or authoritarian style) results in well-socialized, emotionally secure children who grow up to be responsible adults with healthy self-esteem and the capacity to love and care for others. Children who are disciplined feel worthwhile and loved.

Contemporary Problems Facing the Family

The contemporary family is confronted with strains and stresses from all sides. Families have changed dramatically in the past four decades. Many of those changes have created grave threats to family solidarity.

One major change has been a shift from a partnership with fixed roles to a partnership with fluid roles. Before World War II, family patterns were clearly defined. Fathers were breadwinners, and sons usually followed in the vocational footsteps. Mothers were homemakers, and daughters were expected to follow their example. But such fixed roles no longer apply. In many cases, both parents work. A wide range of vocational possibilities exist for both boys and girls.

A second change, resulting from a highly mobile society, is the shift from an extended family to a nuclear family unit. Prior to the past four decades, when most people married they settled near their parents. Families included grandparents, cousins, aunts, and uncles as well as parents. Holidays and Sundays brought together the whole clan. Children grew up with the security of knowing who they were in relation to their family heritage. Parents enjoyed the advantage of knowing that the values and lifestyle they taught their children were reinforced by the larger clan. But most families no longer enjoy this luxury. In this day of high mobilization, families see the extended clan no more than once a year, leaving parents alone with their childrearing responsibilities and leaving children without benefit of a sense of heritage.

A third change centers in the shifting moral values of the society. Although America has always been a pluralistic society, the basic values were derived from the Judeo-Christian tradition. However, the society has become pluralistic not only in ethnic and religious background, but in value systems as well. Parents can no longer be assured that the teacher at school, the leader of the Scout troop, and the baseball coach live by Christian values or even acknowledge them at all. Consequently, the issues of homosexuality, abortion, drug usage, and premarital sex are offered to children and youth as alternatives. This presents a grave challenge to the family.

A fourth change is increasing technology. Almost every family owns an abundance of labor-saving devices: dishwashers, microwave ovens, trash compactors, automatic washers and dryers, vacuum cleaners, and power lawn mowers, to mention a few. What once was an all-day chore to cook and clean and keep a house now takes much less time. What once were chores for children are no longer practical demands for them. Changing technology permits more leisure time for parents and decreases the possibilities for teaching children about work and responsibility. In our consumer-oriented society, technology creates economic pressures as well. People are pressured to buy every new product or gadget advertised.

A final change is what some term an era of anti-childishness. In early American history, children were considered to be important primarily for their contribution to the family. At an early age, they were set to work to share in the family economy. Children were seen as miniature adults who existed to serve, not to be served. Yet they were not expected to be adult in every way: adults still made the decisions about values and religion and when the children could come and go.

Then parents became contributors to their children's livelihood, not just in childhood, but into adolescence and even young adulthood. Children existed to be given to, not so much to be received from. Parents were advised to protect a child's self-esteem and to beware of discipline that would damage the child's psyche. That condition still exists for many parents.

During the last few years, an added factor seems to have been added to the protection and giving cited above. Too many parents now see children as miniature adults once again, but this time as little adults who are capable of making their own decisions about use of leisure time, selection of values, and assimilation of sexual information. Children too often become confidants of the parents in matters too complex for children to decide. When parents abdicate responsibility in decision-making and discipline, a desperate threat to the family results.

All of these changes have brought about greater personal freedom, an advantage not enjoyed by previous generations. Yet in the pursuit of personal freedom, family solidarity suffers unless parents understand the pressures and deal with them.

Marriage was once an institution that survived for better or worse, because the institution superseded the individual identities of the two people in it. But marriage is now a companionship arrangement based upon internal cohesion more than on tradition. However, internal cohesion must be nurtured carefully—it is a quality not easily achieved in contemporary society. Some marriages—far too many of them—fail to survive.

The family is not doomed in contemporary society, but it is besieged. The family that succeeds will be the one in which the parents acknowledge the stresses, covenant together to meet and overcome the challenges, and observe biblical guidelines for communicating values to their children.

The Church and the Family

The church must help families realize their potential as "the church in miniature." With an effective teaching program, the church can provide strength and nurture for each member of the family. But by itself that is inadequate, for faith is transmitted more by the family than it is through formal instruction.

Larry Richards, writing in *Ventures in Family Living*, suggested three ways in which the church can help families in their task of teaching:

1. Train parents for their educative role.
2. Relate individual church ministries to the parental ministry.
3. Administer the church program to help rather than to hinder family life.[10]

Train Parents

Any congregation can train individuals for their role as parents. Such training begins in the youth department when teens explore the essentials of a Christian marriage, perhaps long before they seriously contemplate marriage for themselves. Training continues into the young adult and adult classes.

A minister who is concerned for the family can also help train parents for their teaching role. *Sermons* should reflect understanding of family life and application of biblical principles to family living. *Premarital counseling* can uncover areas of needed help before marriage takes place. Good *pastoral work* puts the minister in touch with the needs of families and provides opportunities for *marriage and family counseling*.

Teaching agencies such as Sunday school or evening discussion groups can feature periodic elective classes dealing with family topics. The possible topics are numerous: couple communication, conflict resolution, discipline, how to communicate faith, how to teach Scripture to children, understanding teenagers, how to be a single parent. Elective classes can provide an opportunity for exchange of ideas, and mutual support for those experiencing similar needs. One California church conducts a class for expectant parents in the church and community, then follows that up with contact at the time of the birth of the child and with quarterly contacts during the first two years of the child's life. Many churches conduct divorce recovery workshops for adults and children.

Many churches provide a wide variety of family resources in the *church library*. Books, tapes, and pamphlets should be made available for loan and/or purchase.

Some churches sponsor a *family month*, featuring the family and its needs and functions. Sermons, classes, films, and special family activities are often included. For example, one Illinois church observed family month with relevant sermons every Sunday for the month, two elective adult Sunday-school classes, more elective Sunday evening classes for adults, and a series of family fellowship activities.

Family camps and retreats are another way for families to be equipped for their teaching function. Materials and suggestions should be available not only for church-planned family camping activities, but also for families that go camping by themselves.

Resources for *family nights* and *family devotions* may also be suggested and made available by the church. A series of family night activities or devotions could be suggested for special occasions.

Relate Home to Church

Individual church programs should be tied together with the home. Too often the church teacher and the parent have no idea of what each other is doing.

Parent-teacher meetings help acquaint parents with what their children really do at church; they also serve to familiarize teachers with home situations. Such meetings may be regular and formal, or the same purpose may be accomplished with programs for parents in individual classes or programs. For example, one church planned at least one parent program per year at every age level of every program. These should be planned for different days, so that parents with more than one child can attend each.

Another helpful way of tying church and home together is for each teaching program to provide *quarterly curriculum previews* with suggestions of how parents can expand and reinforce curriculum concepts at home. At least one publisher provides such helps for Vacation Bible School through a family enrichment calendar.

Home visitation is another link between church and home. Teachers should be encouraged and equipped to do such pastoral work. The teacher who does his homework well will use curriculum far more effectively.

Careful Administration

The church intent on building families is a church that *evaluates existing programs* and plans for ways to improve. It is a church that administers carefully.

Careful administration calls for a *one-job-only policy.* Some churches fragment the family by overly involving parents in church activities, leaving little time for each other. A one-job-only policy recognizes the limitations of a volunteer's time and avoids using parents so much that their children are harmed.

A family-centered church will search for ways to combine meetings into fewer nights of the week. One or two nights per week can become focal points for committee meetings, board meetings, choirs, and other activities in the church calendar. This can be accomplished with careful scheduling.

Some church activities should be *activities for the whole family.* One Oklahoma church features three or four such programs per year. At Halloween, for example, each youth and adult class prepared and staffed a booth for a type of Halloween carnival that the children of the congregation and neighborhood attended. Creative planning will generate similar ideas.

Summary

The family was instituted by God. Its purpose was, and still is, to bring glory to God. But the modern family is besieged by many problems. The church must recognize its responsibility to help the family become the church in miniature, as God intended.

Projects

1. Analyze your home church to determine how well it helps prepare parents to teach. In what ways does it do so? In what areas can improvements be made?
2. Write a short paper outlining the biblical teaching about marriage and the family. How can the church help couples and parents to achieve this ideal?

Selected Bibliography

Getz, Gene. *The Measure of a Family.* Glendale, CA: Regal Books, 1976.

———. *The Measure of a Marriage.* Glendale, CA: Regal Books, 1980.

Guernsey, Dennis. *A New Design for Family Ministry.* Elgin, IL: David C. Cook Publishing Company, 1982.

Haystead, Wesley. *You Can't Begin Too Soon.* Glendale, CA: Gospel Light, 1974.

Howell, John. *Equality and Submission in Marriage.* Nashville, TN: Broadman Press, 1979.

Joy, Donald. *Bonding.* Waco, TX: Word, Inc. 1985.

———. *Rebonding.* Waco, TX: Word, Inc. 1986.

Lewis, Margie and Gregg. *The Hurting Parent.* Grand Rapids, MI: Zondervan Publishing House, 1980.

Nutting, R. Ted. *Family Cluster Programs.* Valley Forge, PA: Judson Press, 1977.

Sawin, Margaret. *Family Enrichment with Family Clusters.* Valley Forge, PA: Judson Press, 1979.

_______ . *Hope for Families.* New York: William H. Sadlier, Inc., 1982.

Schaeffer, Edith. *What Is A Family?* Old Tappan, NJ: Fleming H. Revell, 1975.

Sell, Charles. *Family Ministry.* Grand Rapids, MI: Zondervan, Publishing House, 1981.

Small, Dwight Hervey. *Christian: Celebrate Your Sexuality.* Old Tappan, NJ: Fleming H. Revell, 1974.

Ward, Ted. *Values Begin at Home.* Wheaton, IL: Scripture Press, 1979.

Wright, H. Norman. *The Pillars of Marriage.* Glendale, CA: Regal Books, 1979.

Zuck, Roy and Gene Getz. *Ventures in Family Living.* Chicago: Moody Press, 1971.

---

[1]Genesis 2:18, *NEB*

[2]Genesis 2:24

[3]Genesis 3:8

[4]Genesis 1:28

[5]Psalm 78:1-8

[6]Ephesians 6:4, *NEB*

[7]Proverbs 29:15; 13:24; 29:17; 22:6, *NEB*

[8]Ephesians 6:4, *NEB*

[9]Colossians 3:21, *NEB*

[10]From *Ventures in Family Living,* by Zuck/Getz. Copyright 1971. Moody Press, Moody Bible Institute of Chicago. p. 138. Used by permission.

CHAPTER 15

Building and Equipping for Christian Education

As you read, think about these questions:
—What are three trends for new church buildings?
—How should a congregation plan for adequate educational facilities?
—What space and equipment should be available for each age group?
—How can existing space be adapted to meet educational needs?

Good Christian education can occur in any kind of facility (or none at all), if teachers are committed models of faith who center their instruction in the Word of God. But to a great degree, the church building and facilities determine the kind of program that will take place within its walls. The congregation that is concerned with the teaching mission of the church will periodically analyze their use of space and equipment in an effort to enhance the efforts of faithful teachers. As Lois LeBar said, "Our building tells the community what we think of our God. It either aids or hinders the attainment of our goals."[1]

Current Trends in Buildings

Larger Classrooms

If a modern church building is to be planned for effective Christian education, it will feature larger classrooms than those traditionally available. Traditional teaching philosophy calls for learners to enter the classroom, find a chair, and sit for the remainder of the class session. The traditional method requires minimal space. Larger rooms become necessary, however, with a changing teaching philosophy. The use of an activity-oriented style of teaching requires more space than a traditional approach requires.

Multiple Use of Space

A second trend in modern church buildings is the multiple use of space. Church buildings are expensive structures that are often used only three to five hours a week. It is not economical, or even desirable, to provide separate space for every kind of church program. Therefore, gymnasiums become multipurpose rooms used for recreational, fellowship, and educational purposes. Fellowship areas double for fellowship and educational space, and several programs a week may meet in classroom facilities.

Some congregations plan new programs to make full use of facilities. For example, a congregation in Illinois uses preschool facilities not only for the usual Sunday school, graded worship, youth meetings, and Wednesday evening program, but also conducts two sessions of preschool each weekday. Other congregations conduct Christian schools during the week in facilities used by elementary children on Sunday. That kind of use calls for flexible room arrangements, but it makes efficient use of otherwise expensive space and equipment.

Effective multiple use of space rests upon four conditions:

1. Thorough analysis of the needs of all current programs and all anticipated needs.
2. Careful coordination of scheduling for the use of facilities.
3. Training of leadership for the coordination of use.
4. Provision for adequate custodial service.

Emphasis on Environment

Classroom environment is created primarily by a loving teacher who provides warmth and acceptance, but it is also affected by physical surroundings. Buildings today take into account the need for adequate lighting, cheerful colors, attractive floor covering, equipment appropriate to the age level, and picturesque landscaping. All of these environmental considerations affect attitudes toward learning. Older buildings can also be made to conform to this trend.

Planning for Building and Equipment

Develop a Statement of Teaching Philosophy

Harry Atkinson insisted on the necessity of a well-thought-out teaching philosophy: "The backbone of a good educational building is a clearly conceived program of procedures to be carried out within its walls."[2] A building should be planned according to the kinds of functions that will occur within it. Classroom requirements, for example, are directly related to teaching philosophy. The traditional style of teaching can be used well in small rooms, while an activity orientation to teaching demands more space per pupil and larger rooms that lend themselves to both large-group and small-group activities.

Teachers and educational leaders should formulate a workable teaching philosophy before facilities are planned and provided. Failure of a congregation to clarify its teaching philosophy leaves it vulnerable for an architect's philosophy to be imposed upon it. If the unstated philosophies of both congregation and architect are compatible, all is well. But should those philosophies turn out to be opposite, the congregation will experience undue disappointment and difficulty.

A Master Plan for Space and Equipment

The next step for effective space planning and utilization is to develop a master plan for space and equipment. A list should be made of the number of persons for which space is to be provided (both current and projected figures). This list will allow a projection to be made of needed rooms, required floor space, and essential equipment.

In *Building and Equipping for Christian Education*, Atkinson outlined probable needs for congregations of various sizes. Figure 15-1 adapts his suggestions to fit the organizational philosophy presented in earlier chapters of this book.

List Activities for Each Space

The next step toward efficient use of building and equipment is to list all activities, both Sunday and weekday, for each

	Sunday School Size				
	1-99	100-299	300-499	500-899	900+
Infants/ Toddlers	1	1	1 or 2	2	3
2's/3's	1	1	1 or 2	2 or 3	3
4's/5's	1	1	1 or 2	2 or 3	3
Grades 1-2	1	1 large	2 large	2 large	3 large
Grades 3-4	Same as Grades 1-2				
Grades 5-6	Same as Grades 1-2				
Grades 7-9	1	1	1 large	1 large	2 large
Grades 10-12	Same as Grades 7-9				
Adults	3	4 or 5	6 or 7	12	15

Figure 15-1. Classroom Requirements Based on Sunday School Size[3]

group. This list should include the times and frequency of use by community groups, like Scouts, that use facilities on a regular basis. This simple procedure allows for planned multiple use of facilities and omission of unnecessary space.

General Considerations for Usable Space

Every congregation should take the following considerations into account when planning for educational space. Observance of these guidelines will create comfortable, satisfying space.

1. *Circulation.* Access to the building should be easy. If possible, the entrance to a room should be from outside or from a hallway so that a working group need not be disturbed. Avoid winding hallways and limited foyer areas.

2. *Roomy classrooms.* A generally recommended room proportion is three feet of width to four of length. Window space is desirable.

3. *Floors.* Floor covering should be selected for durability, attractiveness, and ease of maintenance.

4. *Toilets.* Make separate provisions for young children so that facilities may be geared to their size. If such provision cannot be made, provide step stools to help the children.

5. *Heating and ventilation.* These should be provided for comfort.

6. *Lighting and electrical outlets.* Provide adequate lighting. Place light switches conveniently. Have at least one electrical outlet on each wall, more in large spaces such as fellowship areas.

7. *Coat hangers.* These should be convenient to classrooms and at an appropriate height for the age level using them.

8. *Storage.* Free-standing closets are recommended because of their flexibility. Open storage shelves are also valuable for children's areas.

9. *Drinking fountains.* These should be easily accessible and, if possible, at a height appropriate to the age level using them (a step stool could be provided for children).

10. *Acoustics.* Carpeting, draperies, and acoustical ceiling tile help to control sound.[4]

The Needs of Each Age Group

Preschool

The basic space requirement for preschoolers is 30 to 35 square feet of space per child, or rooms of 600-700 square feet for a class of twenty.

Babies and toddlers should be housed in bright, cheery rooms located on the ground floor near the worship center to provide easy access for parents. Cribs, play pens, and washable toys are essential; so are extra diapers, facial tissues, sheets, changing tables, shelves for diaper bags, and rocking chairs. A sink should be located in the room. A Bible, pictures, and mobiles create a warm environment. Rooms designed for toddlers only will add a few puzzles and books, cardboard blocks, trucks and cars, and a rocking horse or riding toy.

Rooms for children of ages two through five need the following items:

Art supplies
Autoharp
Bible
Blocks
Book rack
Books
Chairs (seats 10″-12″ from floor)
Child's rocker
Coatracks
Crayons
Doll bed
Dolls
Housekeeping equipment and furnishings
Nature materials
Pictures
Play dough
Puzzle rack
Puzzles
Record player
Records
Tables (20″-22″ high)
Tackboard (27″ from floor)
Trucks and cars
Wastebasket

Much preschool equipment can be built by individuals in the church.[5]

Elementary Children

Elementary children need 25 to 30 square feet of space per child if a church plans to follow the teaching philosophy suggested in this book. A room of 500-600 square feet is required for a class of twenty if all activity for a specific department occurs within a single room. These rooms should be on ground level or above, to provide adequate lighting and the most appealing environment.

A checklist of equipment and supplies provides guidance for planning:

Art supplies
Bibles
Book rack
Books
Cabinet
Chairs (seats 12″-16″ above floor)
Hymnals
Maps
Open shelves
Paper
Pencils
Piano or autoharp
Record player
Records
Scissors
Tables (22″-26″ high)
Tackboard
Wastebasket

Youth

Youth areas need to provide 20 to 25 square feet of space per pupil; that calls for classrooms of 400-500 square feet for a class of twenty. Although most teaching in youth departments is done in small permanent groups, a department assembly room would be helpful. A permanent group could meet in this room, too.

Use the following list as a guide for planning for equipment needs:

Art supplies
Bibles
Bible study aids
Cabinets
Chairs
Chalkboards
Hymnals
Pencils
Piano
Posters
Record players
Small tables
Tackboards

Adults

Adult learners require 15 to 20 square feet per pupil, or 300-400 square feet for a class of twenty. Rooms for young adults should be easily accessible to early childhood rooms. Older adult rooms must be accessible without the use of many stairs.

A checklist for equipment and supplies for adults is similar to that for youth:

Art supplies
Bibles
Bible study aids
Books
Cabinets
Chairs
Chalkboards
Hymnals
Maps
Pencils
Pictures
Tables
Tackboards

Administrative Space

Administrative space is essential for an education program. Offices should be provided for paid educational staff. A church library should be available (it may double as a classroom) as well as an audiovisual center. Central storage space is also essential. A small office is helpful for volunteer Sunday school administrators' use and for records and materials.

Adaptation of Existing Space

Not every congregation has ideal space and equipment. In addition, enrollment at various age levels fluctuates, requiring periodic analysis of space usage. How can less-than-ideal facilities be renovated?

Every congregation needs to analyze space requirements and assignments every year or two. With shifting enrollments, space can be reassigned to relieve crowded areas or for more efficient use by a different age group.

Be alert for ways to use adjoining rooms. Perhaps some walls could be removed to create larger areas. Separating a large class or department into adjoining rooms allows some large-group activity without excessive moving even if walls must remain in place.

Look for added space near the church building. Houses can be bought and converted into class and assembly rooms. Schools or club rooms can be rented. Small adult classes could meeting in nearby homes. Mobile homes can be placed on the parking lot and used for class areas. Where there is a need and a will to meet it, there is a way, however unorthodox it may be.

A good coat of paint will improve a room, even though it will not provide added space. A regular cleanup/paint-up day would be an asset for nearly every congregation. Removal of unused equipment and supplies can help use space to the fullest.

Most schools will be unable to acquire all needed equipment immediately. A priority checklist should be developed to guide future acquisitions.

Have some items built by individuals in the congregation. Cribs, home living equipment, chalkboards, bulletin boards, book racks, tables, shelves, and cabinets can be provided at great savings.

Appeals to the congregation will often provide donations of toys, homemaking equipment, books, and other items. Whatever is donated will have to be evaluated for usability. Usable items can be placed into service and unusable ones destroyed.

Summary

Adequate space and equipment contribute to effective teaching, but they seldom happen except by careful design. This chapter has presented a plan for determining what a congregation needs for each age level and suggestions for improving existing space. Do the best with what you have. Nothing substitutes for cleanliness, cheerfulness, and orderliness. Using the guidelines developed for space and equipment, make whatever changes are possible. Improvement will be evident before you know it!

Project

Take a tour of a church building and analyze the space and equipment you find in it. Determine the square footage in each classroom and how many pupils meet in each. Take along the checklist of suggested equipment and supplies to find out what is available for each age level. Comment on your general impressions of each room when you first saw it. From what you observed, how could the building and facilities be improved?

Selected Bibliography

Atkinson, C. Harry. *Building and Equipping for Christian Education.* rev. ed. New York: National Council of Churches of Christ in the U.S.A., 1963.

Boone, Eldon M., Jr. *Working with Preschoolers in Sunday School.* Nashville, TN: Convention Press, 1974.

Brown, Lowell. *Sunday School Standards.* Glendale, CA: Gospel Light, 1980.

Fulbright, Robert and Eugene Chamberlain. *Working With Children in Sunday School.* Nashville, TN: Convention Press, 1974.

---

[1]Lois LeBar, *Focus on People in Christian Education,* rev. ed. (Old Tappan, NJ: Fleming H. Revell, 1968), p. 91.

[2]Harry C. Atkinson, *Building and Equipping for Christian Education,* rev. ed., 1963. p. 12. Used by permission, Division of Education and Ministry, National Council of Churches of Christ in the U.S.A.

[3]Based on demographic proportions in the general population. The actual needs will vary according to the congregation's comparison with general population proportions.

[4]Atkinson, *op. cit.,* pp. 17-21.

[5]For suggested designs for children's equipment, see the books by Boone and by Fulbright and Chamberlain listed above.

Part Three

ADMINISTRATION OF CHRISTIAN EDUCATION

Section Outline

16. Christian Education in the Local Church
    A. Organizing the Local Church for Christian Education
    B. Educational Programs in the Local Church

17. Administering Christian Education
    A. The Nature of Administration
    B. The Purpose of Administration
    C. Planning in Administration
    D. Principles of Administration
    E. Organizing for Christian Education
    F. Personnel Recruitment and Development
    G. Leadership

18. Leadership for Christian Education
    A. Defining Leadership
    B. Kinds of Leaders Needed
    C. Developing Leaders

19. Evaluating Christian Education
    A. Why Evaluate?
    B. How to Evaluate
    C. What to Evaluate
    D. When to Evaluate
    E. Evaluation Questionnaire

20. The Minister and Christian Education
    A. The Minister as a Person
    B. The Minister as an Educator
    C. The Minister as an Administrator

21. The Minister of Christian Education
    A. Personal and Professional Preparation
    B. Responsibilities
    C. Interpersonal Relationships

The first section of this book dealt with the history and philosophy of Christian education and the social and demographic factors that affect it. The second section dealt with age level characteristics, special learners, teaching methods, curriculum, and facilities. These sections have laid valuable groundwork for the following chapters, which apply these theories and principles to the local church.

The testing point of any theory is in the local congregation, as it is put into practice in the lives of leaders and learners. Yet if one were to ask a typical congregation what its greatest weakness was, more likely than not its answer would be "lack of leadership." We can see the importance of good leadership, competent administration, and effective use of the educational agencies available to the local church.

If Christian education remains nothing more than an academic activity, a course to be taken to fulfill a requirement, then we have failed. Our times are too desperate to allow Christian education to be no more than scholarly inquiry. In the words of James DeForest Murch, we must "teach or perish!"

CHAPTER 16

Christian Education in the Local Church

As you read, think about these questions:
- —Why is a philosophy of education important for the church's educational program?
- —Why does a church's educational program need objectives?
- —What are some of the teaching programs a church may use?
- —How can various educational programs be correlated for a more effective educational program?

The educational mandate for the local church is a major element in the Great Commission.[1] Although the command to teach as a part of the church's mission is clear and precise, how the church is to carry out this mission is not made explicit in the Scriptures. This omission of specific instructions for carrying out the command to teach seems deliberate. Christ wanted His church to be able to adopt whatever methods were most appropriate to the cultural situation in which it found itself. We would hardly expect the church of the first three centuries, when it was an illegal religion and its meetings often had to be held in secret, to employ the same educational agencies that the medieval church used. In the Middle Ages, the church in western Europe enjoyed a place of prominence and privilege, but its educational efforts were hampered because most of the citizens could not read or write. And the educational programs the church finds most effective in our modern, thoroughly secularized society are quite different from those in either the third or thirteenth centuries.

Good stewardship requires that every congregation make the best possible use of the educational resources and opportunities at its disposal. The local congregation must be organized for its task. Various educational programs have developed over the years that are used in modified form by the modern church to carry out its educational responsibilities. Few congregations will conduct all of these programs, but an awareness of the most important of them is needed in order to understand how they can be used in the local church.

Organizing the Local Church for Christian Education

Philosophy and Objectives

Those who talk about a philosophy of education for the local church run the risk of being thought too scholarly and impractical. But preparing a philosophy is no more than an attempt to state in some orderly fashion what one believes about education in the local church: what authority determines its goals and methods, who is responsible for it, what is its content, and by what processes it is to be accomplished.

Once a congregation has settled these matters (the Scriptures provide the basic guidelines for the church's educational philosophy), then it is ready to turn its attention to its educational objectives. Objectives are statements of specific outcomes that a congregation intends to reach as a result of its philosophy. Programs are ways of implementing philosophy and achieving objectives. Every objective ought to be a positive element in the church's effort to fulfill its total mission.

The Sunday school, Vacation Bible School, youth meetings, and similar programs are not just separate organizations that happen to involve many of the same people and use the same facilities. Each of these programs has an important function to perform within the total framework of the church. These functions must be coordinated to avoid duplication and conflict.

Who's in Charge?

Ordinarily each congregation will be under the oversight of

some kind of a governing body. In some churches the governing body may be the board of elders or the board of trustees. In others, it may be called simply the church board. The educational activities of the church are one of the areas in which the governing board exercises its oversight. Often this responsibility is delegated to a board of Christian education or a Christian education committee. Under the direction of this Christian education board, the minister or the minister of Christian education (often called the director of Christian education), the youth minister, the minister of music, and the Sunday-school superintendent work to administer and help carry out the educational program of the church.

The board of Christian education should be responsible for coordinating all of the educational activities: scheduling (a master calendar of activities should be kept in the church office), recruiting and training leaders, selecting curriculum materials, purchasing supplies, and supervising facilities and equipment. Careful supervision of the program will eliminate unnecessary and wasteful duplication and insure that important areas of Christian education are not overlooked. The board of Christian education should also make sure that the doctrines proclaimed from the pulpit are not contradicted or obscured by the teaching done in the classrooms.

Educational Programs in the Local Church

In a typical congregation, a variety of programs will be used, each fitting into the church's total educational mission.

The Sunday School

When one thinks of the educational activities of the local church, one immediately thinks of the Sunday school (also called the Sabbath school, the church school, or the Bible school). The Sunday school dates back to 1780 when in Gloucester, England, Robert Raikes hired teachers to work with children on Sunday. The teachers imparted to them the rudiments of education along with some knowledge of the Bible. Raikes' efforts were soon copied by others. Before long the Sunday school began to receive wide acceptance, although not without considerable opposition from some quarters. The Sunday school made its appearance in the United States only a few years after Raikes' initial efforts and since then has become a firmly established program on the American scene.

At least three characteristics have marked the Sunday school during its 200-year history. Although clergymen have been involved in the movement during its whole history, the Sunday school has been largely a lay movement. Most of its leaders and teachers have not been professional religious leaders, but unpaid volunteers drawn from the membership of the church. The second characteristic of the Sunday school movement is that it has been ecumenical. Its organizations have reached across many denominations. The International Lesson Series outlines used in many Sunday schools have been and are still prepared by scholars from many denominations. The third characteristic of the Sunday school movement has been the strong emphasis it has put on Bible teaching. On this point, the Sunday school stands in contrast to other teaching agencies that have often stressed creeds, catechisms, or denominational doctrines.

In the typical church, the Sunday school meets during the hour before the Sunday morning worship, although some churches hold the worship service first with the Sunday school following. Rapidly growing churches holding multiple worship services may sandwich the Sunday school between the early and later worship services or hold it simultaneously with the worship service. In rare circumstances, Sunday school may be held Sunday afternoon or evening.

Even in the smallest Sunday schools some organization is required: a superintendent, a secretary (possibly doubling as treasurer if a separate Sunday school treasury is maintained), and a teacher for each class. Larger schools may have three departments—children, youth, and adult—each with its own departmental superintendent and other officers. Still larger schools may have even more departments—crib, toddler, nursery, beginner, primary, middler, junior, young teen, youth, young adult, middle adult, and older adult.

Schools are conducted in a variety of ways. Some begin with an opening assembly, which includes a brief devotional period of congregational singing, prayer, and Scripture reading, along with announcements and activities promoting the school. This is followed by a class period that runs from thirty to forty-five minutes. Some schools hold the assembly after class periods. In larger churches, each department might have its own assembly, preceded or followed by a class period.

For their printed curriculum materials a Sunday school may choose from a bewildering array of attractive quarterlies, leaflets, workbooks, and take-home papers. These are produced both by denominational publishing houses and independent religious publishers. Never has such a variety of materials been available to teachers. The biggest problem for a Sunday school is to select those materials that best support is educational philosophy and its theological stance.

Facilities for the Sunday school may vary from one open room that serves both for classes and a worship sanctuary to an elaborate and well-equipped educational plant that will accommodate hundreds of students. Teachers may vary from one person who is drafted on the spot though unprepared and reluctant, to teachers and helpers who are dedicated and often as skillful and highly trained as public school teachers. With such a range of facilities, curriculum materials, equipment, and teachers, there is little wonder that the results are spotty and often disappointing.

For this reason, the modern Sunday school is not without its critics. "The most wasted hour in the week!" charged one critic. "When is a school not a school?" another asked. "When it is a Sunday school!" But in spite of its weakness, which its critics point out and its friends lament, the Sunday school still has a lot going for it. How else can we explain its remarkable 200-year endurance?

Let us examine some of its strengths. First of all, the Sunday school has done more to teach the Bible and instill morals to more people than any other agency of the church during the past two centuries. A major thrust of the Sunday school is evangelism. Some estimates state that from eighty to ninety percent of the persons who are won to Christ are first reached through the Sunday school. Sunday schools are valuable because they afford an opportunity for fellowship. The relaxed and informal setting of the classroom, along with other class activities, allows for fellowship among members that cannot be enjoyed in the more formal atmosphere of a worship service. The Sunday school also provides excellent leadership training both through classroom learning and through in-service experience. In spite of its shortcomings, the Sunday school performs a function in the church's educational ministry that cannot be filled by any other agency. For this reason it is likely to be with us for many years to come.

Sunday Evening Programs

When we think of Sunday evening programs, we usually think of youth programs. Actually the educational opportunities on Sunday evening may include little children and adults as well as young people.

Today, Sunday evening youth programs have taken on a wide variety of forms and activities. Many denominations maintain their own youth organizations for which they provide printed curriculum materials. Independent publishing houses and youth organizations also have made available a wide selection of programs and materials. Programs are available for small children, teenagers, and adults. Next to the Sunday school, Sunday evening programs provide more Christian education opportunities than any other program.

Most Sunday evening programs are designed for children and youth. When there are enough persons involved to make this feasible, the Sunday evening program usually follows the same age divisions used in the Sunday school. A growing number of churches add a youth minister (who may serve on a full- or part-time basis) to their paid staff. Most of his effort is often spent on planning and supervising the Sunday evening program. Among his responsibilities are the recruiting and training of youth sponsors, the selection of curriculum materials, the planning of services and other programs including socials and recreation, the coordination of the youth program with other activities, the development of leaders among the youth, and the involvment of youth in the total church program.

Sunday evening youth programs are important for several reasons. They reinforce and supplement the learning gained in Sunday school. Since Sunday evening programs allow for more flexibility than the Sunday school does, it is possible to meet the needs of the students almost as soon as they become apparent. Sunday evening programs usually involve more student activity than the Sunday school does. Children and young people have more opportunities to develop leadership skills and other talents. The Sunday evening program also allows more opportunities for fellowship than the Sunday school.

The Sunday evening program is not without its problems. It is sometimes a struggle to recruit enough dedicated youth coaches. Printed materials, often lacking in real substance, must be carefully evaluated before they are used. Since the program attempts to meet a great variety of needs, probably no single set of curriculum materials can be used exclusively. Leaders and sponsors must maintain a high level of enthusiasm to hold the interest of young people. This makes severe physical and emotional demands on them, resulting in a rapid turnover in personnel. Young people often come under criticism for their dress and speech by adults. This leads to misunderstanding and tensions. Yet in spite of all of these problems, the Sunday evening program is well worth what it costs in time, effort, and money.

Vacation Bible School

The first Vacation Bible Schools were held in the 1890's. Since that time, the movement has grown to the point that thousands of schools involving millions of students are held every year. While the movement began among Protestant churches, today it also includes Roman Catholic and Orthodox churches, making it one of the most significant Christian education efforts of this century.

Vacation Bible School, as the name suggests, is ordinarily held during the summer vacation, although schools have been held during the Christmas and Easter vacations and on weekends. At one time schools sometimes ran for five or more weeks, but more recently this has been reduced to no more than two weeks, usually only one week. Schools have traditionally been held in the morning, but evening schools have gained great popularity during the last decade. Other time arrangements are sometimes made, such as holding the school one day a week for several weeks, holding two sessions during the day (one in the morning and one in the afternoon), holding it over a weekend, or splitting the school with sessions for small children in the morning and young people and adults in the evening.

Vacation Bible School offers several advantages:

1. It is a valuable supplement to the Sunday school, increas-

ing by up to fifty percent the amount of time available for teaching.

2. It affords an opportunity for concentrated learning where lessons may be reinforced daily rather than having a week lapse between lessons.

3. It offers a variety of learning, worship, and fellowship opportunities. Students learn through Bible storytelling, puppets, crafts, workbooks, and visuals.

4. It gives an opportunity to involve many church members who are not otherwise taking an active part in church activities.

5. It can be used to train new workers and teachers.

6. It offers many opportunities for evangelism and outreach for the local church. Many children will attend Vacation Bible School who do not attend the Sunday school, and as a result they can be reached for Sunday school and the church.

Vacation Bible School curriculum materials are produced by a number of denominational and independent publishers. These reflect a wide variety of theologies and educational philosophies. Many publishers have courses designed for either a five-day or a ten-day program. Along with the basic lesson materials, many courses offer visuals, worship program materials, prepared crafts, and promotional materials. These colorful and innovative materials make it possible for any church, regardless of size, to have an effective Vacation Bible School, even with inexperienced teachers.

Midweek Programs

Church members of earlier generations usually met on a weekday evening for prayer. The prayer meeting was usually followed by Bible study. This practice is still followed by some congregations, for it meets the needs of many for worship and fellowship. But increasingly in urban churches a different approach is being followed, if there is a midweek meeting at all. Opportunities for prayer and Bible study may still be featured, but often other church functions will also be carried on the same evening. There are likely to be graded classes for children and young people. The night may also be used for choir practice, teacher training programs, or teachers' meetings, officers' meetings, and other meetings. The practice of holding all meetings on one night solves some of the transportation problems that result from a multiplicity of meetings scattered through the week. It also allows the family to attend together, a significant consideration in view of the forces that seem intent upon shattering the family.

One of the chief weaknesses of the midweek program is that it is not well organized to meet specific needs in the church's total educational program. Since attendance is usually only a fraction of the attendance at Sunday school or church, it does not, in the thinking of many, warrant a great deal of time being spent on it. How unfortunate is this attitude! Properly planned and conducted, the midweek program can reinforce Bible learning gained through other agencies. It can supplement this learning by teaching in greater detail, or by exploring subjects that do not seem appropriate to the Sunday school. While few publishers have provided materials specifically designed for the midweek program, a great variety of elective courses are available.

Weekday Programs

Many churches are so located that they can reach many children through an after-school program, or in some communities where released time arrangements have been made, during school hours. These programs take several forms, but usually meet for about an hour and involve not only Bible study but also crafts and recreation. While some programs include students from elementary school through high school, most serve only elementary and junior high students. A variety of materials are used in these studies. Some churches prepare their own materials. Others use Vacation Bible School materials or Sunday school materials from a publisher other than those used in Sunday school. Some interdenominational organizations such as the Awana Youth Association, the Christian Service Brigade for boys, and Pioneer Girls for girls provide programs that are widely used. Some churches have been able to use other organizations such as the Boy Scouts, Girl Scouts, and Campfire Girls to reach young people for the church.

Weekday programs allow a church to supplement Bible learning gained through other programs. They also provide an avenue to help meet the legitimate social needs of children and young people. Since the learning situations are often less structured than those found in Sunday school, learning can be more spontaneous and enthusiastic. These programs also offer excellent opportunities for evangelism because they often attract many youngsters not reached by any other church program.

Children's Worship

Many churches provide separate worship services for children. These may be further divided into junior, primary, beginner, and nursery worship services. Although the main emphasis in these programs is on the worship experience, they still afford many excellent opportunities for Christian teaching.

Children's church has several distinct advantages:

1. It provides a worship service that is geared to the children's needs and to their level of understanding.
2. Children are sometimes a distractive influence in the adult worship. Since they are in their own service, this distraction is removed for adults.
3. Children's worship often relieves an overcrowded situation in the sanctuary. This allows better utilization of the facilities.
4. Adults working in the program develop their talents and are able to use them for the Lord.
5. Children, by participating in a service at their own level, are able to develop their talents.

It is difficult to hold a child's interest for an hour or longer in a worship service. Bible games, crafts, workbook activities, and other learning activities help to keep variety in the program. These may be interspersed with songs, Bible reading, prayers, storytelling, and object lessons. All of these helps and activities should be used in such a sequence that each child is led into an attitude of reverence toward God.

A variety of materials that will be helpful in children's worship programs is available from religious publishers. These include program books, Bible quiz and game books, children's songbooks, crafts, object lesson books, and both projected and nonprojected visuals.

Camping

While many phases of Christian camping take place outside the local church and beyond its immediate control, some types of camping can be conducted by the local congregation. In addition, the church's educational program is greatly enriched by those who are involved in camping activities outside the local church.

Camping offers some unique educational advantages (these are discussed in Chapter 23). Camping, perhaps more than any other educational agency of the church, involves a total person: spiritual, mental, social, and physical. It is a twenty-four-hour-a-day learning experience and its setting is more spontaneous and unstructured. In addition, camping can take advantage of an outdoor environment, a matter of growing importance as our population becomes increasingly urbanized.

Among the types of camping that may be effectively employed by the local church is day camping. In this type of camping, students spend all or part of a day in a camping situation, but are not at camp overnight. This type of camping may be carried on at a regular campground or in public parks or other such facilities. The local church provides the leadership and planned activities, often the transportation to and from the campsite, and sometimes a lunch if the program lasts all day. The program includes crafts, recreation, and Bible study. Since day camping does involve some expense, a small fee is often charged the students.

The local church may also employ other types of camping such as weekend trip camping such as backpacking and canoeing, and adventure camping such as whitewatering and rappelling. All of these can provide learning experiences for students and deserve a place in the church's educational program.

Summary

In this chapter we have discussed briefly some of the programs that the church may use in its total program of Christian education. Some of these are dealt with at greater length in other chapters. Others, such as the church kindergarten and the Christian school, have not been discussed because they require resources often beyond the reach of the local church. Other programs can and ought to be used by the church as the need and opportunity arises. The church is not limited to only a few traditional educational programs. Indeed, the church must not only modify traditional programs but seek new programs, if it is to meet future challenges.

Project

Interview the minister or other person responsible for the educational program of a local church. From this person learn what education programs are being used by the congregation and approximately how many students are involved in each. Indicate what programs the church might be able to use, but is not currently using in its programming.

Selected Bibliography

Bower, Robert E. *Administering Christian Education*. Grand Rapids, MI: Wm. B. Eerdmans Publishing Co., 1964.

Brown, Lowell. *Christian Educator's Manual*. Glendale, CA: Gospel Light, 1979.

________. *Sunday School Standards*. Glendale, CA: Gospel Light, 1980.

Daniel, Eleanor. *The ABC's of VBS*. Cincinnati, OH: Standard Publishing, 1983.

Evangelical Teacher Training Association. *Church Educational Agencies*. Wheaton, IL: Evangelical Teacher Training Association, 1968.

Lynn, Robert W., and Elliott Wright. *The Big Little School*. New York: Harper and Row, Publishers, 1971.

Murch, James DeForest. *Christian Education and the Local Church.*, rev. ed. Cincinnati, OH: Standard Publishing, 1958.

---

[1]Matthew 28:18-20

CHAPTER 17

Administering Christian Education

As you read, think about these questions:
—What is a definition for the phrase "administering Christian education?"
—What is the purpose of administration in Christian education?
—What style of leadership should characterize Christian education administration?
—What are the four major functions of administration in Christian education?
—What are the basic principles upon which Christian education administration is built?

Administering Christian education in a local church is a challenging, essential job. The variety, the involvement with people, and the interaction with the Word all combine to make administration an exciting and fulfilling type of work. Administration is an essential and holy responsibility. The goals of the church cannot be achieved without it.

The Nature of Administration

What is administration? Is it being the boss, as some think? Or is it simply keeping the machinery for Christian education greased and functioning? It is neither. Administration is mobilizing people and utilizing available resources in order to accomplish the stated biblical and congregational purposes for Christian education.

Administration includes four basic functions:

1. Managing resources—recruiting personnel, providing the necessary resource materials, and planning and supervising funds.

2. Educating—developing clearly stated objectives, communicating a biblical philosophy of education, modeling the philosophy of teaching in the training of leadership, and selecting and implementing curriculum.

3. Developing the educational program—planning and leading the expansion of the educational program, initiating and maintaining outreach efforts, assessing results, and planning long-range goals.

4. Ministering—caring for the needs of those serving in the educational program, planning ways to build a caring fellowship within the educational program, and guiding people to maximize their spiritual gifts in ministry.

This process should be biblical, systematic, and positive. Successful administration involves a thorough knowledge of human development: (1) how people learn, (2) what concepts can best be learned at each age level, (3) what atmosphere and methodology best fits the subject matter to be learned, and (4) how to coordinate and reinforce learning experiences so that maximum spiritual growth occurs.

Plans that are biblically-oriented, systematic, and positive result in programming. This programming also maximizes the effectiveness of Christian education.

The Purpose of Administration

The starting point for effective administration is a clear understanding of the purpose of the church. The purpose of the church is twofold: (1) to tell people the good news of Jesus Christ in order to bring them to faith and redemption and (2) to build up to maturity those who have become followers of Christ.

The process of administering Christian education (managing resources, educating, developing the educational program, and ministering) should always strive to disciple people for Christ. Each person touched by the Christian education program should be growing in likeness to Christ and in effective ministry for Christ's church. To be a disciple is a continual process of growth for every Christian until death ends the process and Christ grants perfection.

The Christian should grow as a disciple of Christ in four major areas: (1) love, (2) ministry, (3) purity, and (4) spiritual reproduction. The goal of administration is to achieve these goals in the Christian education program.

Planning in Administration

The administrator should devote plenty of time to thoughtful and prayerful planning. Good planning takes time, but it is essential if confusion and inefficiency is to be minimized. The curriculum planner, for example, should ask some key questions before attempting to develop a curriculum for his Sunday school or for a particular age group: What kind of learning experiences are needed? In what order should they occur? What resources are available to help achieve the specific objectives of these learning experiences? How can the teacher tell whether the desired learning has occurred? In order to relate these questions to the goal of achieving maturity Christian disciples, plans must be broken down into more specific categories.

As an example, one might take the category of love, particularly as it relates to increasing one's love for God. First, clearly specify the long-range goal (for example, to grow in love for God with all one's being—heart, soul, mind, and strength[1]). Second, set some short-range goals with dates attached to them. Third, determine to what extent the individuals have already achieved the short-term goals. (Written statements on "How I Feel About God" could help to assess the character and level of a person's love for God). Fourth, find prepared materials that will assist you in achieving the short-range objective. If you cannot locate adequate planned resources, adapt what you can from prepared resources and then prepare additional resources to fill in the gaps. Fifth, at specified times, evaluate what progress has occurred in reaching the goals. (For example, a second statement on "How I Feel About God" might be compared with the thoughts expressed in the first statement.)

Planning should be broken down into small manageable goals that can be achieved over specific time intervals. These goals should evidence faith, yet be tempered by realism. Discouragement comes quickly when one expects to accomplish too much in too short a time. But morale is heightened when realistic goals are achieved.

The planner should maintain proper balance between time given to planning and time spent in implementing the plan. There is truth in the statement, "If you are given three hours to chop down a tree, spend the first two sharpening the ax." Planning is the "ax sharpening." But one can plan too much and never get anything implemented.

Effective planning begins with prayer and is sustained by prayer. Trust God to help you through the process. If your plans are blocked by unforeseen obstacles, be flexible, but make your adaptations with your goals in mind.

Principles of Administration

Ten basic principles undergird the work of the administrator at whatever level he is working. The administrator should:

1. Regularly pray and study the Bible.
2. Build credibility, trust, and love with his co-workers.
3. Assess the needs of the people.
4. Make realistic, yet visionary plans based on biblical principles and the needs of the people.
5. Translate plans into clearly written statements of goals and time schedules.
6. Periodically evaluate the progress made toward achieving his goals and make any necessary adjustments.
7. Model the kind of person, procedures, and practices he wants the Christian education staff to exhibit.
8. Learn from other educational leaders.
9. Mobilize members for ministry.
10. Build a broad base of leadership.

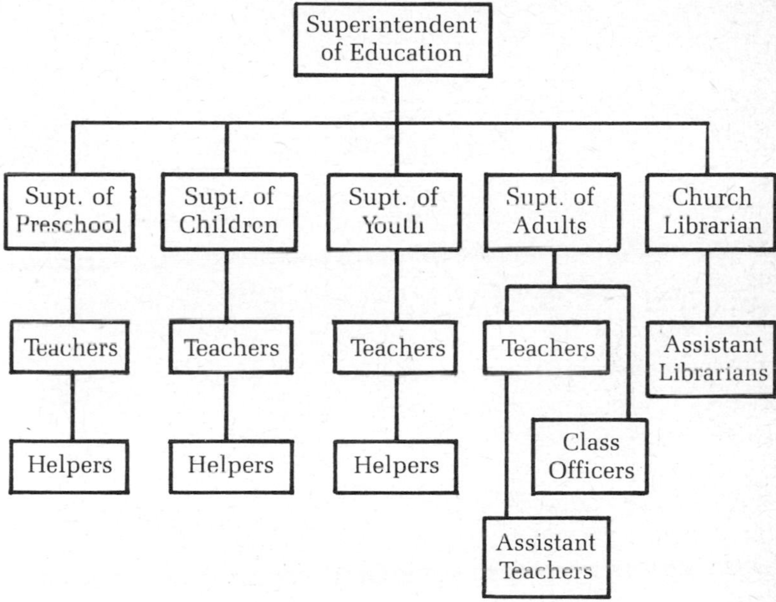

Figure 17-1. Organizational Chart for a Small Church (Under 200 in Average Attendance)

Organizing for Christian Education

Two organizational charts exist for every local congregation: (1) the way it is supposed to be, and (2) the way it really is. The effective administrator works to merge the two.

The larger the congregation, the more levels of organization are needed. Ideally, no supervisor should have more than six people directly responsible to him.

The *superintendent* in Figure 17-1 is a member of the local congregation and serves as a volunteer. The ministers mentioned in Figures 17-2 and 17-3 are paid staff members who have been trained for their particular responsibilities.

The *minister (or director) of education* in both figures serves as the supervisor for the six leaders directly responsible to him. The additional staff members in Figure 17-3 are responsible for the detailed planning and day-by-day operation in their areas. They meet together often to coordinate these individual minis-

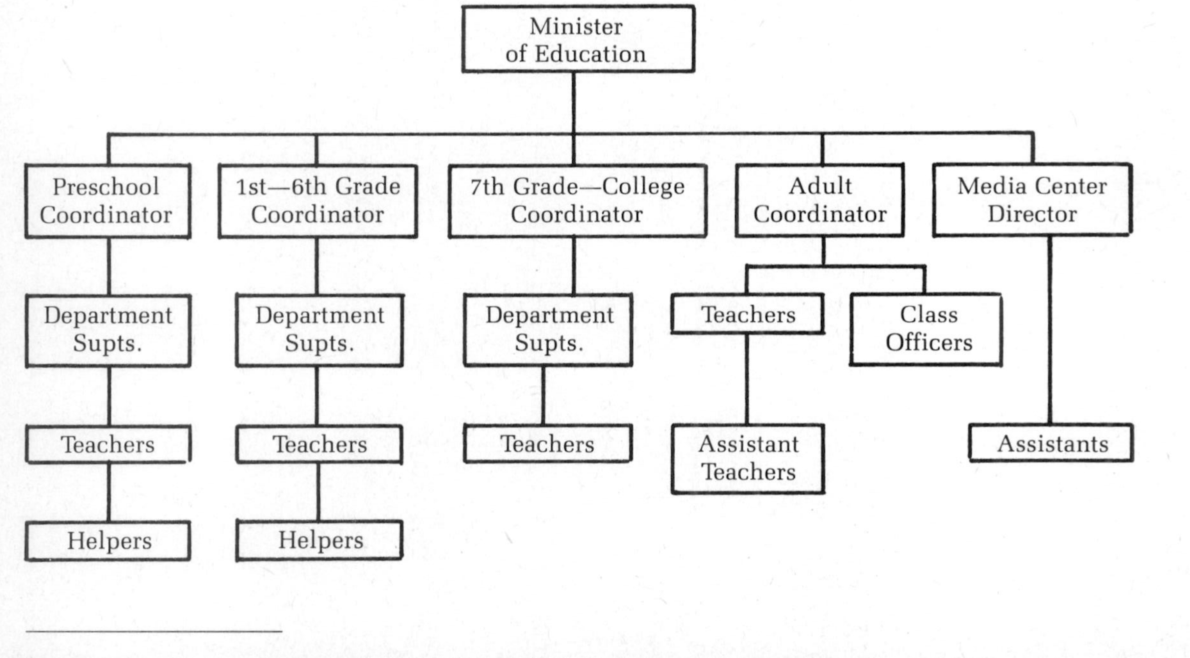

Figure 17-2. Organizational Chart for a Medium-Sized Church (Between 200 and 500 in Average Attendance)

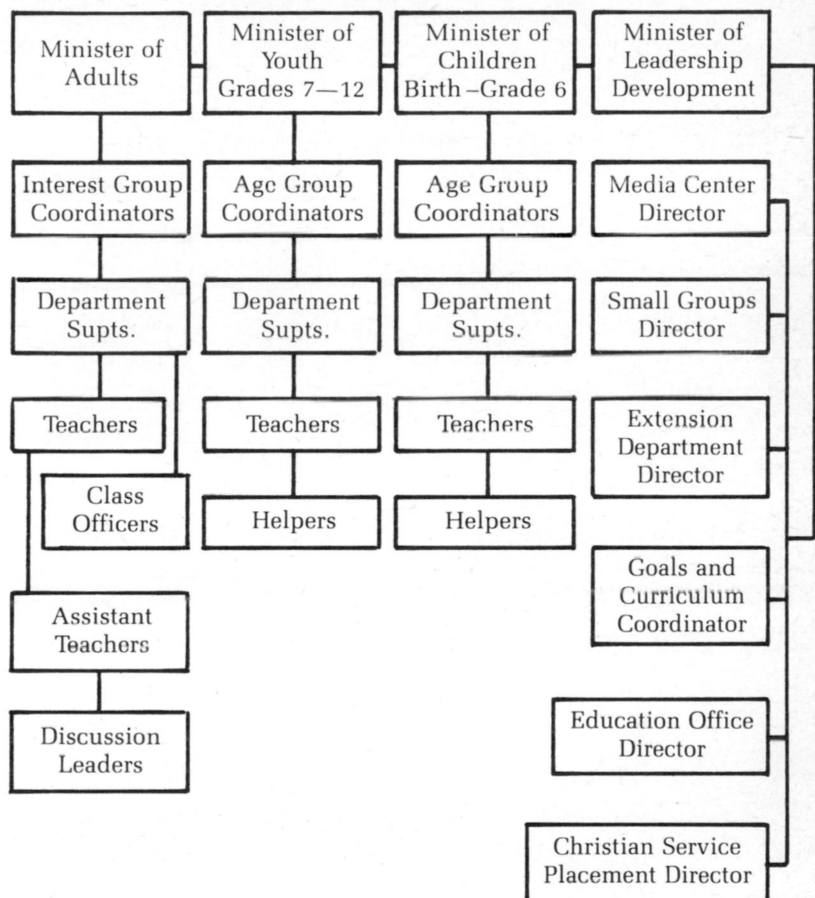

Figure 17-3. Organizational Chart for a Large Church (Over 500 Average Attendance)

tries into the church's total educational ministry. These staff members are responsible for supervising the Sunday morning, Sunday evening, Wednesday evening, and other special educational activities for that age group.

In Figure 17-2 the *coordinator* is responsible for administering the church's total educational ministry for a particular age group. This person is responsible for overseeing the Sunday morning, Sunday evening, Wednesday evening, and other special educational activities for that age group.

In Figure 17-2 the *department superintendent* is responsible for supervising the church educational ministry for a particular age group. In the preschool area, for example, there may be a department leader for crib babies, another for toddlers, still another for two- and three-year olds, and a fourth for four- and five-year-olds. This can be broken down even further as the church grows. Sometimes department leaders supervise all programs for their age level regardless of when these programs meet. At other times, department leaders are selected for each program.

The *teachers* may be structured in many different ways (lead teachers and assistant teachers, co-teachers, or team teachers). The structure of the teaching responsibilities should be determined by the number of class members and the abilities and temperaments of the teachers involved.

The *class officers* of each adult Sunday school class are responsible for overseeing, directing, coordinating, and contributing to the work of that class. In children's Sunday school classes, the teacher usually fulfills this essential role.

The *helpers* include such people as greeters, record keepers, class shepherds, classroom decorators, song leaders, interest center leaders, supply chairpersons, research assistants, and social directors. Helpers should be recruited and trained to fulfill every need of the class.

Personnel Recruitment and Development

Recruitment

Personnel recruitment is essential for a functioning, growing educational ministry. The following principles give direction to the administrator.

1. Recognize that all things are possible with God.[2] God can provide the leaders needed.

2. Pray for specific personnel needs to be met. Enlist other individuals to pray. Pray that God will bring to your mind the right person for each place of service and that He will prepare that person to respond positively when asked to serve.

3. Have one person coordinate recruit efforts. This person needs to keep accurate records of who is serving where. Competition between leaders for a particular worker can be elimi-

nated by clearing his name with the coordinator before asking him to serve. Discuss ahead of time the place where a particular person can best serve.

4. Be aware of personnel needs and the agreed-upon order of priority in which a person should be asked. If the person fails to accept the original ministry offered, the next possibility should be mentioned.

Normally, the one doing the recruiting should be the person with whom the one being recruited will work most closely. (For example, a teacher should be recruited by a department leader.)

5. Give a written job description to the person being recruited. Make it brief, yet have it cover the essential points. It is also helpful to have a printed organizational chart and a statement of educational goals so the person can visualize where he would fit into the total educational ministry of the congregation.

6. Find prospective workers by using a talent and interest survey, obtaining suggestions from those already serving, and checking through the church membership roll. One church follows the principle of asking *all* new members to serve a small but important ministry (such as the nursery or ushering). How they serve in those capacities will determine whether they will be asked to serve in more demanding areas of responsibility.

7. Visit in the home of the prospective worker when asking him to serve. This takes more effort than a phone call or a talk at the church building, but the dividends are worth the effort. You learn much about the person during a visit in his home and you deepen the ties that bind you together.

8. Place your appeal on a spiritual level. Talk about the task as a ministry for Christ.

9. Recruit for ministry for a specific period of time. Usually, this is for a year.

10. Provide training and shepherding for the workers.

11. Periodically recognize and honor those who serve in the educational ministry of the church. This can be done through installation services, services of commitment and recognition, articles in the church paper, special sermons and Sunday school lessons, personal notes of thanks, special seminars and retreats, and social gatherings.

12. Make worker recruitment a continuous endeavor. Keep this ideal before you: every member of the local "family of

God" should fulfill at least one specific Christian service responsibility for the growth and development of the "family."

Training

Both a pre-service and an in-service training program must be developed for the ongoing ministry of education in the local church. A good pre-service training program involves some or all of the following: observation of people doing their jobs, interviews with those experienced in the job (both in your congregation and other congregations), reading, listening to tapes, and viewing films and filmstrips about the job, taking a class relating to the job. These same items should also be included in an effective continuing education program.

A systematic plan for both pre-service and in-service training should be developed. This plan should be evaluated periodically and improvements made based upon past experience and the changing needs in your particular situation.

Delegating Responsibility

There is too much work in even the smallest congregation for one person to do all that needs to be done. When one person even attempts to do it all, he violates God's plan for the functioning of His church.[3]

Olan Hendricks accepts L. A. Allen's definition of delegation: "Delegation is entrusting responsibility and authority and establishing lines of accountability."[4] For the sake of the spiritual growth of both individual members and the church as a whole, members must be entrusted with responsibility. But responsibility cannot be given without also giving the authority needed to fulfill the responsibility.

The effectiveness of delegation can be increased by establishing clear lines of accountability and procedures to follow in certain situations. For example, a policy should be determined ahead of time that if poor teaching or any other unresolved problem arises in an adult class, the class president is responsible to inform the adult department leader. If the class president is negligent at this point, the problem should still be detected by the department leader when he periodically visits the class to observe how it is functioning. Then the department leader and the class president should confer and the results of their discussion should be reported to the person to whom the leader is responsible. Interaction should continue up and down this ladder of responsible authority until the problem is successfully resolved. Sometimes the problem is so difficult that the education committee or the elders must be consulted. Usually, however, a problem can be properly resolved at a level of authority near its source.

Leadership

Leadership Styles

Leadership style is frequently characterized as one of three kinds: authoritarian, laissez-faire, and democratic.

The authoritarian leader is a dictator. He may be a benevolent dictator who loves his people and works for their best interests. Nevertheless, he controls the decision-making process and the purse strings. He decides what is allowed and what is not allowed. The group is shaped and controlled by him.

The laissez-faire leader is really no leader at all. He is a leader in name only. People pretty much go their own way. Either inefficiency, confusion, and anarchy reign or some power "behind the throne" is actually functioning as the leader. Often the laissez-faire leader is the kind of leader people want—a "good old boy" who doesn't bother them, lets things take their course pretty much as they always have, and maintains the status quo (which, as one speaker put it, is a Latin phrase meaning "the mess we are in").

The democratic leader "does not necessarily differ from the authoritarian leader in amount of power, but he does differ in the way he exercises his power." As Krech, Crutchfield, and Ballachey further explain: "The democratic leader seeks to evoke maximum involvement and participation of every member in the group activities and in the determination of group objectives. He seeks to encourage and reinforce interpersonal relations throughout the group so as to strengthen it. He seeks to reduce intragroup tension and conflict. He seeks to prevent the development of a hierarchical group structure in which special privilege and status differentials predominate."[5]

The scriptural model of leadership in the church begins with Jesus Christ, the all-wise, loving, just, and perfect head of the church. He has imparted gifts of leadership to mankind.

The goal of the apostles' leadership along with the early evangelists, prophets, and pastor-teachers, was to equip Christians for the various ministries needed to upbuild and extend the church.[6] The example of Paul is instructive at this point. His goal was to work himself out of the central leadership position in a local church. He wanted elders to be appointed in every church he started as soon as men were qualified for that position. He wanted them to assume the leadership of that church so that he could leave and start another one.

Bible scholars do not agree as to how elders were selected in each congregation in the first century. But there can be little doubt in the first Christian congregation (Jerusalem), that deacons were selected by a process involving the members of the church.[7] It is plausible to assume that this same kind of process was used in selecting elders as well. When Paul instructed Titus to appoint elders in Crete,[8] perhaps he followed the Jerusalem church example in selecting deacons, and his "appointment" was merely a confirmation of the congregation's selections (similar to the setting-aside ceremony the apostles performed for the Jerusalem deacons in Acts 6:6).

From this brief scriptural overview, it appears that different leadership styles are appropriate at different phases in the life of the church. When a church was just starting, it needed some leader to function in a benevolent authoritarian style. When a church was established to the degree that men were qualified to become elders, the leadership style shifted to a more democratic style of leadership. That is, the elders attempted to carry out Paul's directive in Ephesians 4; as pastor-teachers, they equipped Christians to fulfill particular ministries in the congregation. By so doing, they encouraged a broadening of the leadership base and a sharing of the responsibility and authority. Authority still rested on the shoulders of the elders as the ones responsible before God for the spiritual welfare of the flock,[9] but the exercise of their authority was through their example, not their commands.

The Servant-Leader

When Jesus' disciples heard that the mother of James and John had asked Him to give her boys chief seats of authority in His coming kingdom, they were upset. Jesus called them together and told them about true leadership in God's kingdom here on earth: "You know that the rulers of the Gentiles lord it over them, and their high officials exercise authority over them. Not so with you. Instead, whoever wants to become great among you must be your servant, and whoever wants to be first must be your slave—just as the Son of Man did not come to be served, but to serve, and to give his life as a ransom for many."[10]

Leaders who "exercise authority over others" may have a place in society at large, but not in Christ's church. No matter what degree of rightful authority one has in the church (the total authority of Jesus or the delegated authority of the elders and deacons), the style of leadership is to be that of a servant. Even if authoritarian leadership is needed at some point, it should be carried out as a service to others. There is no place for self-seeking or personal advancement in any Christian leader.

Like Christ, leaders in the church are to view their roles as servants of others. They have not been placed in positions of leadership to be served by others. Their position of leadership provides opportunity to model the likeness of Christ for the sake of the church. They are to let Christ's ministering spirit pervade and transform the whole body of believers through them and through others whom they infect with the spirit of service. The church, when properly led, stands in bold and refreshing contrast to the world around it.

Lawrence O. Richards suggests three characteristics of the servant-leader:

1. "The servant is a person who is *among*, not over those whom he leads." As such, he is on the same level as the others; they perceive him as like them. Communication channels are open to two-way flow—either party can initiate communication, respond, or share. Within the church, either can minister and either respond.

2. The servant expends his life on behalf of others. "The servant task is to serve others in that which is important to God. . . . His primary concern and ministry is the building up of the body and its members."

3. The servant leads by example. He leads more by what he is and does than by what he says. Words are important only as they are undergirded by the servant's quality of life and spirit. The servant-leader is not a weak individual with little or no authority. He is an inwardly strong person who, by virtue of his Christlike example, bears a powerful authority.[11]

Summary

Administration in Christian education must be constantly growing. Administration takes all the wisdom, skill, and Christlikeness one can bring to the task. Because he is working with growing Christians, he must model a growing Christian. People will learn from him as they observe how he handles mistakes and failures, how he responds to obstacles, how he deals with changing situations, and how he solves personal and interpersonal problems.

The growing Christian education administrator is one who recognizes his weaknesses and takes specific steps to correct them. He chooses seminars to attend and keeps current on available resources (tapes, books) that will better equip him for service. He gets on the mailing list of churches that have a growing program of Christian education. He seeks out and interviews leaders in the field of Christian education. He gets to know fellow administrators and discusses their mutual ministry of Christian education. He continues learning, growing, and serving as long as the Lord gives him the opportunity to do so.

Project

Draw an organizational chart for the administration of Christian education in your local church. Be as complete as possible. How closely does your chart resemble the chart in this chapter that corresponds to your church's size. In what areas can administration function more efficiently?

Selected Bibliography

Brown, Lowell. *Christian Educators' Manual*. Glendale, CA: Gospel Light, 1979.

________. *Sunday School Standards*. Glendale, CA: Gospel Light, 1980.

Douglas, Stephen B. and Bruce E. Cook. *The Ministry of Management*. 2nd ed. Arrowhead Springs, CA: Campus Crusade for Christ, 1973.

Richards, Lawrence O. *A Theology of Christian Education*. Grand Rapids, MI: Zondervan Publishing House, 1975.

Schaller, Lyle. *The Decision Makers*. Nashville, TN: Abingdon Press, 1974.

---

[1]Mark 12:30

[2]Matthew 19:26

[3]see Acts 6:1-4, Ephesians 4:11-16, Romans 12:4-8

[4]Olan Hendricks, *Management for the Christian Worker* (Santa Barbara, CA: Quill Publications, 1976), p. 83.

[5]From *Individual in Society* by Krech, Crutchfield, and Ballachey. Copyright 1962, McGraw-Hill. Used with the permission of the McGraw-Hill Book Company.

[6]Ephesians 4:11-16

[7]Acts 6:1-6

[8]Titus 1:5

[9]1 Peter 5:1, 2

[10]Matthew 20:25-28

[11]A THEOLOGY OF CHRISTIAN EDUCATION by Lawrence O. Richards. Copyright © 1975 by the Zondervan Corporation. pp. 133, 134. Used by permission.

CHAPTER 18

Leadership for Christian Education

As you read, think about these questions:
—What is a definition for leadership?
—What kinds of leaders are needed in the church?
—How can the church develop leaders?
—What methods do churches use to train leaders? When can these methods best be used?
—How can the church maintain high standards for its leaders?

Ask almost any congregation about its greatest need. Almost invariably the reply will be, "Competent, dedicated leaders." The problem is universally recognized, but why has no one solved it?

Perhaps one reason is that *leadership* has not been clearly defined. Without a clear definition of leadership, we have not recruited or trained leaders, nor have we adequately identified those who are leaders even when they were available.

Defining Leadership

As God has dealt with His people through the centuries, He has chosen to do so through men and women, not through angels nor other celestial beings at His command. Those whom He selected were qualified to lead and were certified through training and commitment. We think immediately of people like Moses and David. Moses was schooled in all of the wisdom of ancient Egypt. Then God allowed him to mature for forty years in the wilderness of Midian. David learned to walk close to God as he kept his lonely vigil over his father's sheep. When God finally needed him to lead the nation of Israel, David was ready.

Problems in Defining Leadership

The meaning of leadership seems obvious. A leader is the person in charge, the dominant person, the man or woman standing up front. He is the one who wears the uniform or who possesses certain traits we have come to associate with leadership. But these traditional and widely accepted definitions or descriptions really explain little about leadership.

After only a few minutes of observing an elementary schoolroom, for example, it is often possible to discern the intellectual leaders within the group. They have not been appointed to any special position, nor do they wear a uniform to distinguish them as leaders. Yet other students and the teacher clearly recognize that they are leaders.

Then the same class goes out to the playground for recess and decides to play a game of baseball. Quickly the athletic leaders, who may or may not be the same as the intellectual leaders, become apparent. They, like the intellectual leaders, are not officially chosen, nor do they wear any special uniform. Yet everyone on the playground recognizes them as leaders.

One reason that we have difficulty in defining leadership is that we often confuse two aspects of leadership. On the one hand, we think of a leader as one who has been elected or appointed, formally or informally, to a certain role in a particular social setting. That setting can be a playground, a factory, an office, or a church board meeting. One the other hand, we sometimes define leadership in terms of his ability to function in a given role whether or not that role is an authoritative one. We further confuse the issue when we attempt to describe leadership in terms of certain innate qualities or attributes.

This leads us to another important questions: Are leaders born or made? We sometimes comment that a person is a "born leader;" at first glance we may decide that leaders are born. Heredity (nature) is decisive in some leadership situations. One is not likely to become a leader on the football field unless nature has endowed him with a large, sturdy body, quick reflexes, and a strong heart. Nor is one likely to become a nuclear physicist unless he has an I.Q. considerably above average.

Yet nurture (training) is also important in developing leaders. Not every three-hundred-pounder becomes a football star, nor does everyone with an I.Q. of 140 succeed as a nuclear physicist. Nature may limit the areas in which one may exercise leadership, but nurture determines whether or not one becomes a leader in those areas (or what kind of leader he becomes).

Some Contemporary Concepts of Leadership

In recent years a great deal of research has been done in the area of leadership. Because of the highly competitive nature of our secular society, business, industry, government, and education must have capable leadership if they are to survive and grow. This research can also help Christians develop insights into the recruiting and training of leaders for the Lord's work.

Much of this research centers on group behavior or group dynamics. Persons behave differently when they are involved in different groups situations. A calm, sedate member of a Sunday school class may have been a screaming, arm-waving fanatic at a football game the day before. Leadership grows out of a group situation. The person who best meets the needs of the group in that situation is likely to emerge as the leader.

Modern concepts of leadership put great emphasis upon creativity. In a more stable, tradition-bound society, leadership could spend its energies defending and maintaining the status quo. But in our modern, rapidly changing world, such a stance is difficult to maintain and, if maintained for very long, can be disastrous both to the organization and to the leader himself. Most of us are familiar with dying churches whose motto is "We've always done it this way" or "We've never done that before."

Another important aspect of leadership is communication. Rare indeed is the leader today who can isolate himself from his fellow workers, appearing only occasionally to dictate orders. Research clearly indicates that a group performs better when it is knowledgeable about the organization and is involved in setting goals and making decisions. Christian leaders should apply this insight to the work of the church.

Numerous studies have also been made of the personality traits displayed by leaders. These intangible qualities are often difficult to identify and evaluate. How can one person be a dynamic leader while another, just as talented, intelligent, and well-educated, lacks this personal dynamism? We have come to call these intangible qualities "charisma." Perhaps in this area we are getting close to the "gifts" Paul spoke about in 1 Corinthians 12.

Biblical Concepts of Leadership

Since God chose to carry out His mission to the world through human beings, the Scriptures have a great deal to say about leadership. What God reveals to us about leadership comes both from positive teaching and from many examples of God-led men.

God's leaders were people who had been cleansed and transformed. We immediately think of Isaiah and his confrontation with God, or Saul of Tarsus on the road to Damascus.[1]

God's leaders were dedicated persons, not willing to allow inconvenience or suffering to turn them aside from their calling. Jeremiah could endure all kinds of ridicule and mistreatment because he had a fire that burned in his bones.[2] The apostles could face the threats of religious officials, counting it joy to suffer for their Lord.

God called men who were prepared to carry out the tasks He assigned them. Moses had an excellent education when God called him; Paul was an outstanding scholar. Some dismissed the apostles as poor, unlearned peasants, even though they had spent three years at the feet of the greatest teacher who ever lived. God may be able to use a person who has little education or preparation for leadership, but God can make greater use of people who are prepared.

The Scriptures suggest several other qualities that God looks for when He chooses leaders. Among these are humility, enthusiasm, perseverance, compassion, creativity, vision, and the ability to work with others. God also seeks persons whose lives are open to the leading of the Holy Spirit.

A Working Definition of Leadership

How can we define leadership? From a Christian perspective, a leader is one who possesses the biblical characteristics defined in the preceding section, and who can mobilize people and use available resources to accomplish the stated biblical and congregational purposes of the church. This person may be appointed or selected for the task, although some leaders function in that capacity without official appointment.

The function of leadership is far more important than the titles designating leadership, although it is a fortunate congregation that has leaders who are both appointed and function as leaders. Even then, others may well function as leaders in the biblical sense of the word without holding any official position of leadership. Every person ought to be encouraged to exercise his gifts to accomplish the purposes of the church.

Kinds of Leaders Needed

Paul appropriately compared the church to the human body, in which each member fills an important role that cannot be filled by any other member. Eyes can see but they cannot hear; feet can walk but they cannot talk. If this was true of the first century church, it is even more true of the church today. Advanced technology has forced us to become specialists, and even the church in its educational work cannot escape those pressures for greater specialization. As a result, persons involved in the educational program of the local church must give increased attention to preparing persons to meet these needs, some of which we will discuss in greater detail.

Church Officers

There may have been a time when a church, especially a small congregation, could have gotten along with a hit-or-miss approach to carrying out its mission, using whatever volunteers might have been available. But that day is past. Even a small congregation needs officers who understand their tasks and have some preparation for fulfilling them. Every congregation should develop elders, deacons, financial officers, and persons serving in the areas of evangelism, missions, fellowship, education, and benevolence. Sometimes this preparation will involve classes for these areas. In other cases it will require directed reading and personal study or internships and on-the-job training.

Workers in the Church's Educational Programs

The education programs of the typical church will involve more people in more different activities than any other church program. For this reason, those who lead in this area need special preparation. Since the Sunday school is the largest and most visible educational activity of the church, capable leadership in all of its activities is important. A Sunday school ordinarily will have a superintendent, assistant superintendent, secretary, and sometimes a treasurer if a separate treasury is kept for the Sunday school. Most adult classes within the school will have their own officers as well.

As important as these officers are, the teachers are even more important. The effectiveness of the teachers in communicating God's Word to their students will largely determine the effectiveness of the church's educational program. Yet teachers are often selected in a haphazard fashion, thrust into the classroom with little or no training, and left largely to their own initiative and resources. Is it any wonder that so little learning takes place in some Sunday schools? (Yet, amazingly, much learning occurs in many circumstances.) Persons who would serve as teachers need instruction in Bible content, teaching methods, and educational psychology. While teachers can, and often do, acquire this information on their own, it can be more readily and quickly acquired in regular classes or directed studies.

Youth Workers

A church that neglects its youth is a church that is failing an important part of its mission. Trained leaders are vital if a youth program is to succeed. Even with a youth minister on the staff, the typical church needs volunteers to work in various youth programs. Youth coaches or sponsors will need special training to prepare them for their work. They will also need on-the-job training to learn how to help meet the needs of young people.

Worship Leaders

The public worship services of the church afford many people meaningful religious experiences. Yet if these services are disorganized or clumsily carried out, they have other, less desirable results. For this reason, we need to be concerned about those who lead or participate in public worship. The educational program of every church should provide training in such areas as music, song leading, public prayer, ushering, taking the offering, and serving the Lord's Supper.

Miscellaneous Activities

Numerous other activities of the church require trained leaders. A congregation should feel responsible for developing these leaders and requiring that trained leaders fill these positions. Among these are activities such as children's worship services, Vacation Bible School, nurseries, recreation programs, retreats, camps, calling, and women's programs.

Developing Leaders

While certain skills or abilities that the church needs (organists or pianists, for example) can be gained from outside the church, most of a church's skilled leadership must be trained by the church. Several steps are necessary to build an effective leadership training program within a local church.

Discovering Potential Leaders

The first step in any program is to find those who have skills or who have the potential to gain these skills needed by the church. The minister, church officers, and especially Sunday-school teachers should be alert to those who have such potential. The Sunday-school teacher is usually the key person in recruiting leaders. Because the class is usually a small group and because class meetings and socials often provide opportunities for informal discussions, the teacher can come to know his students better. This gives him a chance to evaluate a student's talents or sometimes to discover hidden talent.

Many congregations use a talent survey questionnaire to discover potential leaders. Such a survey should be taken at least once a year; people sometimes acquire new skills or develop new interests that can be used by the Lord. New members can be encouraged to fill out the questionnaire at the time they join the congregation.

A church must not overlook children and young people in its search for capable volunteers. Every congregation should try to involve as many of them as possible both in service activities and in various training programs. These experiences prepare them for the day when they can accept larger responsibilities.

Leadership Training Programs

Leadership programs should be of two types: pre-service, that is, training to motivate and prepare individuals to assume specific ministries; and in-service, training to encourage, support, and develop added skills in the one who is already involved in a specific ministry.

Pre-service training programs should include opportunities for individuals to assess their talents and capabilities for service. It should also include systematic Bible survey courses to give the participants an overview of the Scriptures. It must also include an introduction to age characteristics, basic lesson development, classroom management, and curriculum use. These topics need not be offered in one comprehensive class, but in several short segments to allow people to fit in at the place of their needs.

In-service training programs will often be accomplished in the educational program through the monthly teachers' meetings. These meetings should include introduction to new teaching skills, times of encouragement, Bible studies of value to the teachers involved, observations, field trips, and practice sessions.

Four principles must be observed in planning for leadership training programs. To ignore even one is to weaken the training program substantially.

1. *Effective training is age- or program-related.* Preschool teachers learn principles, techniques, and skills that are useful for work with preschoolers; teachers of adults learn about adults. Likewise, training for ushers need not explore the same materials as training for missions leaders.

2. *Effective training is curriculum-related.* Curriculum materials used by the teachers should conform to the subject matter being taught. If the person is being trained in storytelling, the teacher should use a story in his curriculum. This principle is perhaps less applicable to training areas other than teachers, youth coaches, and worship leaders, but it should be heeded when it is appropriate.

3. *Effective training is experiential.* The person being trained should have opportunity for experience doing the tech-

nique being explored. The trainee should actually prepare and tell a story if that is the topic. The person learning to call should go calling with an experienced caller before his training is complete.

4. *Effective training is regular and systematic.* Training is never a one-time class or event. It must be done regularly, a little at a time, adding skills and motivation for ministry.

Below are some suggested times and methods for training along with their advantages and disadvantages.

1. During the regular Sunday-school hour. More students are likely to be available at this time than at any other time during the week. Training conducted at this time would need to be pre-service experiences.

2. Sunday evening. Sunday evening training sessions have become popular in many churches. These may be held at the same time as the youth meetings. This time period would be good for either pre-or in-service training.

3. Midweek evening. Some churches have found this to be a good time for training sessions. Probably the most serious drawback to the midweek evening session is that it usually has fewer participants than sessions conducted at other times.

4. Weekday sessions. This has worked successfully in some churches. These have the same disadvantage as sessions conducted on a midweek evening.

5. Vacation Bible School. Many churches now hold Vacation Bible School at night. It is often possible to have classes for youth and adults at a night VBS. This affords an excellent opportunity for training sessions.

6. Weekend leadership training seminars. One or two sessions can be held on Friday night, Saturday morning, and occasionally Sunday afternoon. Thus on a weekend it is possible to attend several training sessions. Often two or more churches hold the seminar cooperatively. These sessions can be led by Christian college personnel and other experts.

7. Cooperative training programs. In some areas several churches pool their resources and training sessions that may meet one night a week for six or eight weeks. Outside experts may be used as teachers or resource persons.

8. Christian college sponsored programs. Many Christian colleges offer classes designed to train leaders for the local

church. These may be available on the college campus or through extension programs.

9. Camp leadership training programs. Many Christian camps offer these in their summer camping schedule. These may be for a week or perhaps for a weekend.

10. Religious publishers. Some publishers offer a variety of programs and published materials designed to strengthen leadership in the local church.

11. Conventions. Denominational conventions and conventions sponsored by Sunday-school associations often provide clinics for leaders and teachers.

12. Correspondence courses. Some publishers and Christian colleges offer correspondence courses for teachers and leaders. Even if one is not able to participate in any of the other training programs, he can (in his own home for a nominal expense) prepare himself for more effective Christian service.

13. Church library. The church can provide materials in the church library to help teachers in their ministries. This allows a person to study on his own to develop needed skills.

Maintaining Leadership Standards

One of the most dangerous pitfalls of leadership in any organization is that is often becomes complacent. It is normal for a leader to attempt to reduce his repeated activities to routines. This allows one to go through his normal activities without spending a great deal of time and energy thinking about them. But routines often become ruts, and, as someone has observed, a grave is nothing but a rut with both ends filled in. To avoid getting into ruts, we need to make ample provisions for regular training programs.

Maintaining Spiritual Standards of Leaders

One might suppose that once a leader reached a high level of spiritual maturity he could rest secure in the knowledge that further spiritual struggle was unnecessary. But such is not the case. God requires absolute moral perfection of us. Since we don't even begin to come close to perfection in this life, we must constantly struggle to keep reaching higher. Our surroundings do not help us to do this. When one is content to stand still spiritually, he is actually losing ground.

Teachers and leaders must be encouraged and helped to look

to their own devotional lives. Various helps (such as devotional guides or systematic Bible reading schedules) can be made available to help them in their Bible study and prayer.

While one's private spiritual growth is essential, there is also a place for sharing together in achieving spiritual growth. Many churches provide regular opportunities for spiritual growth through prayer and Bible study sessions. Teachers' meetings afford opportunities for inspiration and spiritual guidance. Some churches plan retreats for their teachers and leaders. These are most effective when conducted away from the busy routines of life. Such retreats can be used for instruction, for planning, and for spiritual renewal. Leaders return to their tasks for new enthusiasm and resources for the challenges before them.

Evaluating Leaders

Still another aspect of preparing and maintaining good leadership is evaluation. Unfortunately, evaluation has negative overtones for many people. It sounds like testing or inspecting. As a result, many seek to avoid evaluation. But the members of a congregation are continually evaluating their leaders, though not in a formal way. When attendance in the Sunday school class declines, the students may be indicating by their actions that the teacher is not meeting their needs. Or when the members of the congregation fail to meet the budget, they may be telling the leaders that they are not satisfied with their leadership. Though some may seek to do so, leaders cannot avoid being evaluated.

While informal evaluation goes on all of the time, there is also a place for regular formal evaluation of teachers and leaders. Leaders can be evaluated by others, but self-evaluation is also helpful. Many persons, especially those who feel insecure in their positions, fear evaluations as some kind of an inquisition. But a positive emphasis can help them to look upon evaluations as opportunities to improve their skills for the Lord.

Summary

The need for competent leaders in the local church has never been greater. Church leaders today must function in a variety of roles: organizer, planner, decision maker, promoter, inspirer, counselor, model. Christian stewardship demands that we give our best to the Lord—and then do better. For this reason, then, the Christian education program of every church must include a comprehensive plan for recruiting and training leaders. To do less is to invite disaster.

Projects

1. Determine the leadership needs of a local congregation.
2. Design a leadership program that would meet the needs of the congregation you analyzed, including the types of leadership needed, the number of potential trainees, instructors, curriculum materials, and time of meeting for training classes.

Selected Bibliography

Books

Brown, Lowell. *Sunday School Standards*. Glendale, CA: Gospel Light, 1980.

Ellis, Joe S. *The Church On Purpose*. Cincinnati, OH: Standard Publishing, 1982.

_______. *The Church On Target*. Cincinnati, OH: Standard Publishing, 1986.

Leavitt, Guy P., rev. by Eleanor Daniel. *Teach with Success*. Cincinnati, OH: Standard Publishing, 1978.

_______., rev. by Leon Langston. *Superintend with Success*. Cincinnati, OH: Standard Publishing, 1980.

Sources for Training Materials

David C. Cook Publishing Company, 850 N. Grove, Elgin, IL 60120.

Evangelical Teacher Training Association, P.O. Box 327, Wheaton, IL 60187.

International Center for Learning, 2300 Knoll Dr., Ventura, CA 93003.

Scripture Press, 1825 College Ave., Wheaton, IL 60187.

Standard Publishing Company, 8121 Hamilton Avenue, Cincinnati, OH 45231.

---

[1]Isaiah 6:1-10; Acts 9

[2]Jeremiah 20:9

CHAPTER 19

Evaluating Christian Education

As you read, think about these questions:
—Why is evaluation of the church's education program important?
—What are some ways to evaluate?
—What should be evaluated?
—When should evaluation be carried out?

A person carefully studies his cancelled checks and compares them with his check stubs. He is evaluating. A business firm closes down for two days to take inventory. It is evaluating. A teacher averages scores in her gradebook and finally puts down a grade. She is evaluating. A coach watches players practice as he makes out his starting lineup. He is evaluating. The process of evaluation goes on almost constantly and takes numerous forms.

We not only evaluate physical things that can be counted, weighed, or measured, but we often evaluate mental activities as well. Every pop quiz or final examination is a form of evaluation for the student—and the teacher. As Christians we must also be involved in various types of spiritual evaluations. Paul wrote, "A man ought to examine himself before he eats of the bread and drinks of the cup."[1] John had in mind another kind of evaluation when he wrote, "Dear friends, do not believe every spirit, but test the spirits to see whether they are from God, because many false prophets have gone out into the world."[2]

Why Evaluate?

To Determine Whether Goals Have Been Reached

An effective Christian education program must have goals or objectives. These goals may be very general or quite detailed. They may be short-term or long-term. They may deal with such readily measurable items as attendance or offerings, or with the spiritual growth of students, something much more difficult to measure. But goals serve little real purpose if no provisions are made to see whether they are being met.

Unless definite goals have been established, we have no basis for evaluating whether progress has been made. For this reason, goals ought to be as specific as possible and in terms that can be readily measured wherever possible.

To Help Establish New Goals

Goals are like mileposts along a road. They are to be reached and then left behind as new goals are met. Suppose an attendance goal is set for the Sunday school. When that goal is met, a new goal must be set. But suppose the goal is not reached, and attendance falls substantially below the goal. This may indicate that the goal was unrealistically high and should be revised downward. Whether the new goal is higher or lower, it has been changed because of a process of evaluation.

To Help Determine Personnel Efficiency

Neither the Sunday school nor any other education program of the church is stronger than its leaders. The best leaders available should be involved in every program. To make sure that the best leaders are involved, we must evaluate them and the alternative leaders at hand.

The most capable people we have need to be busy and working in the Christian education program. Therefore, we evaluate a person's capabilities before we assign him a job. But the evaluation process continues as he continues in that job.

To Discover Weaknesses

The most obvious use of evaluation is to determine weaknesses. A failure to reach a goal is apparent to everyone, but it is important also to know why the failures occurred. Suppose that we had set an attendance goal for a certain Sunday, but fell short of reaching the goal. If there had been a ten-inch snowfall on the previous night, we could readily understand the poor attendance. But suppose the weather was excellent and there were no other conflicts that might interfere with attendance. Then we would need to probe deeper to find the reason for the failure to reach the goal. Once we were able to isolate the reason for the failure, we could take appropriate action to avoid similar failures in the future.

To Discover Strengths

Although we are inclined to think mainly of the negative aspects of evaluation, the positive aspects are just as important. When a program is successful, we need to be made aware of that fact. We need to know why the program succeeded so that we can use the ideas to help make future programs successful. The reasons why a program succeeded may not always be obvious, so we may have to spend some effort finding them.

To Stimulate Growth and Learning

Most of us work better when we know what we are working for. We also work better when we know how well we are doing in reaching our objectives. A lagging student, for instance, might be motivated to work harder by a failing grade on a test. The evaluation gave him a basis for understanding what the teacher expected of him and how well he measured up to those expectations. But in the same way a high grade can lead a student to work harder to maintain the high average. Similarly, when one evaluates his prayer life or his stewardship, he might be stimulated to work to improve them.

How to Evaluate

Once we have established reasons for evaluating our Christian education programs, we need to establish definite methods of carrying out the process. We must have definite methods of gaining the facts we need, and we must have ways of determining what these facts mean.

Two Kinds of Evaluation

Our approach can be confined to two different kinds of evaluation: process and results. In the first of these, we are concerned about how the established goal is reached. For example, we may observe how a teacher teaches his lesson. How does he introduce the lesson? How does he get his students into the Scripture? How does he lead the students to apply the Scripture to their lives? How does he get student involvement in the teaching-learning process? How does he close the lesson?

All of these questions deal with process. We are concerned about the process or method in order to find ways of doing the job better. If the job is being done well, we want to be able to share good ideas with others.

We are interested in the process, but we are also interested in the end results of that process. No matter how effective a song leader seems to be, if he does not lead people into worshipful praise of God through his song leading, then his efforts leave something to be desired. A teacher may be an exciting storyteller or be adept at using audiovisuals, but if the lives of his students are not changed, then something is wrong.

We must also, then, measure for results in the lives of those we serve. Is attendance and participation in various church programs increasing? If so, this usually tells us that the people's interest and commitment is growing. Is there greater concern about the missions and benevolent activities of the church? If so, this may indicate that our teaching is taking root in the lives of the members. In this kind of evaluation, we are measuring results.

Use Measurable Goals

If evaluation is to be meaningful, we must begin with goals that establish a basis for comparison. Statistical goals (attendance figures, offerings, number of baptisms) can be easily measured as long as accurate records are kept. Each organization within the church should have someone designated to keep records. Records should be checked regularly for accuracy. Standard forms are helpful for maintaining these records in the same form from year to year even though different persons keep them. Copies of these records should be kept on file in the office of the director of Christian education or the person who is responsible for the church's educational program.

Not all of the important goals in Christian education can be reduced to statistics. Cognitive learning, that is, learning that deals with the acquisition of factual information, can be measured by tests. But affective learning, the kind of learning that deals with the change of attitudes and emotions, cannot be as easily measured. About the best we can do is to measure the change in people's outward behavior or changes in the pupil's report of his attitudes. We can set up goals that will measure this change in behavior. Such goals will then let us evaluate certain phases of our education program.

Personnel Feedback

One helpful way of evaluating a Christian education program is to determine how the teachers and leaders involved in it feel about it. Can they cite specific evidence that students are involved and learning? Are they satisfied with their own efforts? Can they find ways to improve their teaching? Are there adequate supplies and equipment to do the job?

The answers to such questions as these can be helpful, not only to the teachers or leaders involved, but also to those who plan and administer the programs. These evaluations, which ought to be conducted regularly, can be used in many ways to improve the total work of the church. (The evaluation questionnaire included at the end of this chapter will assist in these evaluations.)

Student Feedback

The students themselves are in a better position than anyone to know whether their spiritual and educational needs are being met. Student feedback can be observed in several different ways. Attendance and attitudes in class are means commonly used. Interviews or questionnaires can also provide helpful information.

Suppose that the attendance in the junior girls' class has suffered a steady decline during the past several months. The matter is discussed with the teacher, who began teaching the class a year ago. She indicates that there seems to be a lack of interest on the part of the students and an increase in discipline problems (these two trends usually go together, by the way). Then we interview some of the students. They indicate a lack of interest in the lessons, confirming the teacher's report on the situation. Then one of the students indicates that the teacher always reads the lesson, there is little discussion, and little application of the lesson to life.

This kind of evaluation helps us to pinpoint the source of the problem. Once we know that the problem lies in the lesson presentation, we may now suggest tactfully some ways in which the teacher can make her lessons more interesting.

What to Evaluate

Since the purpose of evaluation is to find ways to improve the total education program of the church, we need to evaluate the entire program. But this is often an overwhelming undertaking if we try to do it all at once. The various aspects of the program should be evaluated one by one over a period of time. Below are listed some of the areas that may be profitably evaluated. Since some of these areas are discussed in other chapters or covered by the survey form at the close of this chapter, this listing does not go into great detail.

Goals

An effective program for Christian education within the local church will have both general, overall goals and specific goals for each area. These goals ought to be reexamined at least once a year (more often in many situations). In almost every congregation, some changing or restatement of objectives will be necessary. Regular evaluation of goals will prevent their becoming out-of-date or impractical.

Programs

Separate programs within the total program need to be evaluated frequently. For example, Vacation Bible School should be evaluated as soon as it has been concluded while information and attitudes are still fresh in the minds of the participants. A teacher training class should be evaluated not only when it is concluded, but also several weeks or months later to determine its long-range effectiveness.

Organizations

Organizations within the church should be subject to regular evaluation. Are they performing a useful function? Can they be made more effective? Are they duplicating activities that can be more efficiently carried out by other organizations? Even the most elaborate organizational charts and detailed job descriptions for all positions within the educational program can soon become useless without frequent evaluation and updating.

Personnel

Persons serving within the various programs are always being evaluated, at least informally, by their peers and their students. Because so much of this evaluation is informal, it is not useful. But formal evaluation of teachers and leaders is often feared and resented, and so it must be done tactfully.

Facilities

Since the available physical facilities play a great part in shaping and limiting the church's educational program, facilities and equipment should be evaluated at regular intervals. Equipment can be updated or kept in good repair and facilities can be remodeled and used more efficiently.

Records

All church records, especially those dealing with educational work, should be checked frequently to keep them up to date and accurate. It is helpful to keep them available in one central location and on standard forms.

Curriculum

In its broadest sense, curriculum concerns all the activities within the church that help the church reach its educational objectives. Certainly this is a subject for constant evaluation. Sometimes people restrict the use of curriculum to printed lesson material. Such materials should be kept under close scrutiny to ensure their doctrinal fidelity, their educational soundness, their usefulness to the teachers working with them, their attractiveness to the students, and their appropriateness to the church's educational objectives.

Students

In the final analysis, nothing is more important than what happens to the student in the educational program. Unless there is clear evidence of Christian growth, with each person becoming more Christlike in his attitudes and behavior, then the program has fallen short of its primary objective.

Testing for cognitive learning is relatively simple and should be done more frequently than it is. Admittedly, tests have a negative connotation for many people, but with the proper approach testing can be done regularly in the Sunday school and similar formal learning situations. Testing for spiritual growth is far more difficult, but it should be done if we are to help people meet their needs.

When to Evaluate

Many churches do not take evaluation seriously until they are faced with a serious problem. Then hastily and often with less than happy results, leaders try to find out what went wrong. Assuredly, evaluation is necessary in a crisis situation, but frequent and regular evaluations can often head off problems before they become real crises.

Methods of systematic evaluation should be set up within the congregation. Carried out in this way, evaluations do not seem nearly so threatening to the persons involved. In many aspects of the program, annual evaluations are adequate. Others may require quarterly or monthly attention. Teachers should be encouraged to evaluate their lessons each week, at least for their own benefit.

Summary

When we talk about evaluation, it may seem idealistic, impractical, or unimportant in the typical congregation. But nothing could be further from the truth. As we have already noted, some types of evaluation—at least informally—are always taking place. Our main concern, then, becomes one of going about the process in a more systematic and efficient manner. The form that has been included with this chapter may help teachers and leaders do that.

Project

Evaluate the Christian education program of a local congregation, using the evaluation form beginning on the next page (or any appropriate parts of it).

Evaluation Questionnaire

A. *Objectives*

1. Does the church have objectives for its total program?
   _____ Yes _____ No
2. Are the objectives written and readily available?
   _____ Yes _____ No
3. By whom were the objectives designed? (Check all that apply.)
   _____ Minister
   _____ Committee chairperson
   _____ Church board or other governing body
   _____ Members of the congregation
4. Does the church have objectives for its educational program? _____ Yes _____ No
5. Are these written and readily available? _____ Yes _____ No
6. By whom were these objectives designed? (Check all that apply.)
   _____ Minister _____ Committee chairperson
   _____ Church board or other governing body _____ Sunday school superintendent
   _____ Teachers _____ Students
7. Have objectives been established for each department?
   _____ Yes _____ No
   For each class? _____ Yes _____ No
8. When were these objectives last evaluated and revised?
   _____ Within the last year
   _____ The last five years
   _____ Never

B. *Teaching Philosophy and Plan*

1. Do teachers involve learners in the learning process?
   _____ Yes _____ No
2. Does every department/class use total session teaching?
   _____ Yes _____ No
3. Does every department/class use Bible learning activities to involve learners in purposeful Bible study? _____ Yes _____ No
4. Does the curriculum used support the church's philosophy and plan for teaching? _____ Yes _____ No

C. *Organization and Administration*

1. Does the Sunday school have a superintendent?
   _____ Yes _____ No
2. Does each department have a superintendent?
   _____ Yes _____ No

3. Fill in the following chart.

Class

No. of Teachers

No. of Learners

Adult Caring Units

4. List the leaders who are directly responsible for more than five workers.

5. Is there a written job description for each position? _____ Yes _____ No
   List those who do not have a job description.

6. Is there an administrative group to carry out the functions of Christian education? _____ Yes _____ No
   It fulfills these tasks (check all that apply):
   _____ a. determining goals
   _____ b. developing plans to carry out goals
   _____ c. communicating with the staff
   _____ d. implementing decisions
   _____ e. evaluating implementation and programs
7. Do the teachers meet together regularly? _____ Yes _____ No
8. Does the church have a regular pre-service leadership training program? _____ Yes _____ No
   An in-service program? _____ Yes _____ No
9. In addition to the Sunday school, what other regular programs does the church use in its educational ministry?
   (Check all that apply.)
   _____ Sunday evening classes
   _____ Youth meetings
   _____ Children's church or extended Sunday school sessions
   _____ Midweek classes
   _____ Camp
   _____ Retreats
   _____ Kindergarten
   _____ Weekday classes
   _____ Vacation Bible School
   _____ Other
10. Are attendance records kept for various church activities?
   _____ Worship
   _____ Sunday school
   _____ Sunday evening service
   _____ Midweek service
   _____ Youth meetings
   _____ Other

11. Are records kept in such a way that comparisons can easily be made with last year's figures? _____ Yes _____ No
    Figures from five years ago? _____ Yes _____ No
12. Are records kept in a convenient location? _____ Yes _____ No
13. Are records regularly used to evaluate the progress of the church's educational program? _____ Yes _____ No
14. Are detailed records kept on individual students? _____ Yes _____ No

D. *Facilities and Equipment*

1. Do the educational facilities allow for easy departmentalization of the Sunday school? _____ Yes _____ No
2. Fill in the following chart.

Classroom

No. of Square Feet

Permanent Equipment

3. Indicate which of the following are available to teachers.
   _____ Flannelboards
   _____ Flannelboard materials
   _____ Pictures
   _____ Slide projectors
   _____ Filmstrip projectors
   _____ Overhead projectors
   _____ Overhead transparencies
4. Is there an established procedure for regular, systematic maintenance of facilities? _____ Yes _____ No
5. During the past year, has each teacher evaluated his rooms and disposed of materials not currently used? _____ Yes _____ No

E. *Growth*

1. Fill in the following chart for the past ten years.

Year

Baptisms

Transfers

Average Sunday
School Attendance

2. Does the church have an outreach director to implement outreach in the educational programs? _____ Yes _____ No
3. What classes have shown enrollment decreases in the past ten years?

Check the factors contributing to those losses.

_____ lack of purpose	_____ poor organization
_____ weak Bible study plan	_____ inner frictions
_____ poor teaching	_____ lack of staff commitment to growth
_____ inadequate teacher training	_____ personal needs not met
_____ lack of adequate staff	_____ lack of commitment to Sunday school by elders/minister
_____ lack of prospect enlistment	_____ sporadic outreach efforts
_____ lack of visitor follow-up	_____ others:_____

4. Have new classes been created when it is advisable? _____ Yes _____ No
5. Is there an up-to-date list of prospects? _____ Yes _____ No
6. Does each class follow up on prospects and absentees? _____ Yes _____ No

Selected Bibliography

Brown, Lowell. *Sunday School Standards*. Glendale, CA: Gospel Light, 1981.

Bower, Robert K. *Administering Christian Education*. Grand Rapids, MI: Wm. B. Eerdmans Publishing Co., 1964.

Leavitt, Guy P., rev. by Eleanor Daniel. *Teach With Success*. Cincinnati, OH: Standard Publishing, 1978.

[1] 1 Corinthians 11:28
[2] 1 John 4:1

CHAPTER 20

The Minister and Christian Education

As you read, think about these questions:
—What qualities and commitments should the minister have?
—What qualities should the minister have as an educator?
—What qualities should the minister have as an administrator?

The modern minister must be many things. He is expected to be a preacher, pastor, evangelist, counselor, administrator, teacher, and family man. The minister is also expected to have time to work at, if not excel in, all these pursuits.

Faced with impossible demands on his time and talents, the wise minister seeks to assign priorities to the tasks he is expected to do. This gives him a logical basis for allotting differing amounts of time for his duties. When he establishes job priorities, a minister must look to the needs of the situation rather than his own preferences. He must resist the temptation to allot a disproportionate amount of time to the activities that he enjoys the most, or at which he is most skilled.

The minister's academic preparations for his job rightfully emphasizes exegetical and language preparation. But practical skills—especially administrative and teaching skills—are not always developed, even though he will be expected to provide significant leadership in both areas.

A study conducted by the Accrediting Association of Bible Colleges indicated that ninety-six percent of the ministers responding would include more Christian education courses in their academic programs if they were preparing for the ministry again.

In most congregations the minister is the key to the educational program. Persons preparing for the ministry will have many opportunities in the area of Christian education. As part of their preparation for the preaching ministry, they should consider taking other courses in Christian education or doing further study on their own.

The Minister as a Person

Usually a person can separate his personal life from his professional life, but the minister cannot. Every aspect of his work is influenced by the kind of person he is.

He must be a committed Christian. Because the temptations to pride and to routine professionalism are constant, every person preparing himself for the ministry needs to be reminded that his every activity stems from this commitment. He will encounter subtle pressures to sacrifice integrity to expediency, to compromise convictions, to settle for the good rather than insisting upon the best. The best antidote for these temptations is a frequent reminder of whose we are and whom we serve.

He must be a student of the Bible. Church members expect their minister to be an expert in the Scriptures. A Bible college or even a graduate seminary education can do little more than introduce a person to the Scriptures and give him a few tools that will help him do independent study. The holy Word will yield its sweetest fruit only to those who engage in regular study over many years. If a primary task of the minister is to share these sweets with his people, he must be prepared to study diligently.

Early in his ministry, a wise minister will establish study routines that bring him into an in-depth relationship with God's Word. He will set aside a special time each day or each week for Bible study according to some systematic plan. One will want to occasionally follow a book-by-book study plan. At other times, topical studies may prove helpful. But almost any planned study is better than a hit-or-miss approach.

A minister will study the Scriptures for the purpose of sermon preparation. He will also study the Word to prepare to teach classes to the Sunday school, Sunday evening or mid-week studies, or various special classes. But while the minister must study the Word in order to share it with others, he must also allow it to speak to him and to his personal needs. To neglect this devotional study of Scripture is to come to look upon it as little more than a professional tool.

He should be committed to sound doctrine. One who is a student of God's Word will be concerned about sound doctrine, because in our day so many forces are at work to erode our doctrinal foundation. Basic Christian doctrines are under attack both from inside and outside the church. An even more serious danger may be posed by the subtle forces that would have us not repudiate, but compromise these crucial doctrines. The minister must resist the temptation to allow his feelings, rather than the Scriptures, to become the final authority in matters of doctrine. If the minister is to play his proper role in the educational program of the church, he must be a guardian and teacher of sound doctrine.

He should be a man of prayer. Like the apostle Paul, he must learn to "pray without ceasing." And learn he must, for one does not build an effective prayer life just by wishing for it or talking about it. He must pray about his own personal needs, the needs of the congregation, and the needs of the community and the world.

Every program of the church ought to be planned in prayer, developed in prayer, and consummated in prayer. There is no way to measure the power that prayer can impart to a church program. Yet as important as prayer is, it must not become a convenient way to avoid the careful planning and hard work that successful church programming requires.

He should be a growing learner. The minister must be a student of the Scriptures, but he must also be a student of history, literature, sociology, psychology, science, politics, and current events. Guided by the Scriptures, he must build a Christian philosophy of life that allows him to give proper evaluation to all these areas of knowledge and to use them in his ministry to his people. Although his own interests and aptitudes will lead him to emphasize some areas more than others, yet no area of knowledge is beyond his proper concern. Since all truth is God's truth, every particle of truth in the universe is important to him and may be useful as he attempts to meet the needs of his people. In no profession is a well-rounded education more important than in the ministry. It is a part of becoming "all things to all men." And to achieve this well-rounded education, a minister must be a lifelong student, not only of books, but of life.

He must love people. No man can effectively serve his people if he does not love them. He may perform many of the duties associated with his office, yet this service alone will never exude the warmth and enthusiasm that comes from a service of love. Such an attitude of love is nowhere more necessary than in the minister's relationship to his educational program and the people involved in it. It takes patience and understanding for one to lead others to grow in faith and knowledge. Love allows one to develop this patience and understanding.

He must understand and appreciate his role in Christian education. The minister must understand that he is the key to the success of the congregation's educational program. His attitude toward that program will go a long way toward determining whether it will fail or succeed. He needs to realize that his enthusiastic support for Christian education can become contagious, infecting the whole congregation.

The minister also needs to understand that a great deal of the support for his ministry will be generated by the educational program. A congregation that has been nurtured on God's Word will respond favorably when the Word is proclaimed from the pulpit. It will rise to meet the challenge of evangelism, stewardship, and service.

The Minister as an Educator

In many congregations the minister will be more knowledgeable about Christian education than any other member. In such situations, he must exercise considerable leadership in Christian education. In other congregations, many competent educational leaders are available. In these congregations, the minister's leadership need not be so prominent. But regardless of the specific role he is required to fulfill, in every congregation the minister needs to be an educator.

He must have a sound philosophy of Christian education. To be effective, a Christian education program must be built upon a sound philosophy of education. Every person involved in Christian education has a philosophy of education that provides the basis for the decisions that he makes. Such a philosophy may be sophisticated and detailed or it may be simplistic and disorganized, perhaps not even articulate.

The minister should take the lead in establishing a philosophy of Christian education that is grounded in Scripture and meets the needs of the congregation. He would be wise to organize and write out his philosophy of education. In this way he can more readily share it with others, refine it, or improve it.

He should understand the importance of educational objectives. The minister needs to be involved with the leaders of the congregation as they develop the overall objectives for the congregation. Specific educational objectives should also be established by every agency, department, and Sunday school class in the church.

He should have some understanding of educational psychology. It is hardly fair to expect the minister to be an expert, but he must understand some of the basic elements of psychology if he is to provide leadership for his congregation. He should know something about age level characteristics. He should understand how learners are motivated and the processes by which they learn.

An alert minister will soon find that the knowledge of educational psychology needed for the church's educational program will also be useful in other phases of his ministry. Many of these principles are applicable to preaching as well as teaching, for example.

He should have some understanding of teaching methods. Probably more Christian education programs fail in local churches because of poor and monotonous teaching methods than for any other reason. One reason teachers fail to use better teaching methods is the age-old problem of lethargy. Teachers have fallen into the habit of teaching in a certain manner and they stubbornly resist all suggestions for change. Most teachers tend to teach the way that they were taught, thus perpetuating poor teaching methods. Further, teachers often feel a sense of security in using certain teaching methods. The lecture method often provides such a feeling of security. The teacher can present his position without being challenged by class members as he might be were he to use a discussion method that encourages feedback from students.

The minister may be qualified to conduct training courses for his teachers. If not, he should be concerned enough to see that teacher training courses are provided for them. But more important than teacher training classes is the example the minister sets. Some ministers prefer not to be tied down to teaching a Sunday school class regularly. Others may consider this a very important way to become close to some of their members. This is a matter for each minister to decide on the basis of his own interests and the needs of the congregation. He will, however, almost certainly teach some classes, such as a class for new members or one for church officers. If he knows and uses a variety of good teaching methods, he can create a persuasive model for others to follow. In the long run, a good model is likely to be a far more effective method in improving teaching than is any number of training classes.

He must be a counselor. Teachers and leaders in the church's educational program are certain to have problems even under the best of circumstances. They need someone to whom they can go for help and encouragement. If a minister is knowledgeable about Christian education, he is the logical person to provide such counseling.

The minister is often in a position to serve as a resource person for teachers. Most members of a church will look to the minister as the best Bible student and theologian in the congregation. But they will also turn to him for information about curriculum materials, supplies, equipment, and the newest trends in Christian education.

The Minister as an Administrator

In a congregation that has a minister of education, the minister may not be involved directly in the administration of the education program. But most congregations do not have a minister of education, and the minister must carry out many of the administrative duties that would ordinarily fall to the minister of education.

He must be an organizer and planner. Even the smallest congregation must be organized if its educational program is to be effective. The minister is usually best qualified to provide the leadership necessary for good organization. He is also in the best position to see the church program as a whole and to understand how education fits into it.

A good organizer first evaluates the resources of the congregation in terms of its objectives. He evaluates the persons available to work, and employs the agencies best suited to help the church achieve its objectives.

The minister also needs to be a good planner. He must work with the congregation to formulate long-range plans for achieving the church's educational objectives. He must also develop short-term plans to meet needs that arise each week and each month. Plans and coming events should be recorded on a master calendar. The church office is usually the best place to maintain a master calendar for all church activities.

He must work with others. One mistake that many ministers make is to take too many responsibilities upon themselves. They feel that because they are better qualified than most of the members, they must do the work. But the whole membership needs to be involved, not just to relieve the minister of many jobs, but that they too may learn and grow through experience.

An important task of the minister is to recruit and train leaders. Once leaders have been trained, the minister must be willing to delegate responsibilities to them.

The minister must learn to work effectively with others in the church. He must not see himself as a boss whose chief job is to give orders. The leaders with whom he works are volunteers; coercion is ineffective with them. The minister should consider himself a member of a team on which each member has different, yet significant, responsibilities. He will frequently have to work with or through a board or committee of Christian education. While ordinarily he should not serve as chairman of this committee, he should be an *ex-officio* member of it and all other committees involved in education. If the minister does not learn to work harmoniously with others in the church's educational program, then other phases of his work will be hampered.

He must coordinate the educational program. Unless all educational agencies within the church are coordinated, serious overlapping or omissions may result. Since the minister is in the best position to see the church's total program, he is the best qualified member of the congregation to coordinate all aspects of it.

Some coordination is done in the organizing and planning activities previously mentioned. The choice of curriculum materials is another way that the program may be coordinated. Unfortunately, in some churches each teacher is free to select his own materials. Since different publishers may have different philosophies of education and different theological stances, such a cafeteria approach to the selection of curriculum materials can lead to confusion and even disaster. The minister should provide wise leadership in helping select and use curriculum materials.

Coordination is also important in the use of facilities. By careful planning a church can learn to make the best possible use of the facilities it has. Occasionally a church may have to alter its programs to fit its facilities. When new facilities are planned or older facilities remodeled, the minister should be involved in developing and coordinating the plans and carrying them out.

He must promote the educational program. A minister who understands the importance of Christian education to his ministry will be an enthusiastic promoter of all the church's educational activities. He must regularly explain these activities to the congregation, since many members will not understand them nor appreciate their value.

This support for education must be made from the pulpit, in the church bulletin and church paper, in committee meetings, and in private conversations. The minister should use every opportunity to praise those who work in educational programs. He should also seek for ways to show how Christian education has influenced the lives of the church members.

Summary

The specific ways that a minister is involved in the educational work of his church will vary depending upon his own talents and the needs of the congregation. But he must be involved, for every phase of his ministry will be vitally affected by what happens in the educational program. Evangelism, stewardship, pulpit work, counseling, and pastoral work are all influenced by how effectively the Word is learned by the members of the congregation.

Project

Interview a minister and find out how he is involved in Christian education in the congregation where he ministers.

Selected Bibliography

Bower, Robert K. *Administering Christian Education*. Grand Rapids, MI: Wm. B. Eerdmans Publishing Co., 1964.

Gangel, Kenneth O. *Leadership for Church Education*. Chicago: Moody Press, 1970.

LeBar, Lois E. *Focus on People in Church Education*. Old Tappan, NJ: Fleming H. Revell, 1968.

Lentz, Richard, Paul H. Vieth, and Ray L. Henthorne. *Our Teaching Ministry*. St Louis, MO: Christian Board of Publication, 1967.

Miller, Randolph Crump. *Christian Nurture and the Church*. New York: Charles Scribner's Sons, 1961.

Person, Peter P. *The Minister in Christian Education*. Grand Rapids, MI: Baker Book House, 1960.

Towns, Elmer. *The Successful Sunday School and Teachers Guidebook*. Carol Stream, IL: Creation House, 1976.

CHAPTER 21

The Minister of Christian Education

As you read, think about these questions:
—What qualifications should the minister of Christian education have?
—What are the different responsibilities of the minister of Christian education?
—What are the relationships of the minister of Christian education with paid staff, church officers, and volunteer workers?
—What are some of the possible sources of stress in the life of the minister of Christian education?

"What is a dearie?" asks a member of a congregation.

"A dearie?"

"Yes, you know, the new D.R.E."

So begins one chapter in Rolf Aaseng's clever little book *Anyone Can Teach (They Said)*. And so one congregation was introduced to a new paid staff person—the professional Christian education minister/director, in this case called a Director of Religious Education.

Realizing the importance of Christian education, churches in increasing numbers are calling persons especially trained to provide leadership for the educational program of the local church. And though the person is more often called a minister or director of education rather than a D.R.E., the question still remains: who is this person and what does he do?

Personal and Professional Preparation

Commitment

The primary qualification of a minister of Christian education must be a mature and growing commitment to God and Jesus Christ. God calls a minister of education, like any other minister, to know God, so that he "may be filled to the measure of all the fullness of God,"[1] to become "mature, attaining to the whole measure of the fullness of Christ."[2] The minister of education must grow more like Christ and help others to do so by his example.

Age and Experience

Age	Males	Females	Total	Cumulative %
21-25	2	0	2	3.2
26-35	24	7	31	52.4
36-45	17	2	19	82.1
46-55	6	4	10	98.4
56-65	1	0	1	100.0
Total	50	13	63	

Average Age = 36.5   Median[3] Age = 35

Table 21-1. Age of Professional Educators

Years	Males	Females	Total	Cumulative %
1-5	17	3	20	32.7
6-10	12	5	17	60.6
11-15	10	3	13	81.9
16-20	6	0	6	91.8
21+	3	2	5	100.0
Total	48	13	61	

Average Years = 9.2[4]   Median = 7.5

Table 21-2. Years in Educational Ministry

Years	Males	Females	Total	Cumulative %
1-5	25	7	32	50.0
6-10	17	4	21	82.8
11-15	6	2	8	95.3
16-20	2	0	2	98.4
20+	1	0	1	100.0
Total	51	13	64	

Average Years = 6.2[5] Median = 5.0

Table 21-3. Years in Present Educational Ministry

A survey was done among professional Christian educators in Christian Churches/Churches of Christ in early 1986. It assessed the professional characteristics of 64 people who were randomly sampled from throughout the United States. (A total of 75 questionnaires were sent; 13 females and 51 males responded.)

Christian education professionals tend to be young in age and experience, as Tables 1—3 reveal.

Job Titles

The titles by which these professional educators are designated vary widely. Some are generalists with a broad range of

Title	Number	Cumulative%
Associate Minister	21	32.8
Minister/Director of Education	14	54.7
Minister/Director of Adult Education	4	60.9
Minister/Director of Youth	5	68.8
Minister/Director of Children	12	87.5
Minister of Discipleship	0	87.5
Other Titles (usually combinations of those above)	8	100.0

Table 21-4. Job Titles

responsibilities in Christian education, while others are specialists with responsibility for specific age ranges. The designations for the sample are indicated in Table 4.

The 1986 study also revealed that forty-nine of those responding were ordained. Not all were male, though most were. Table 5 summarizes the findings.

Sex	Ordained	Not Ordained	Total
Males	46	4	50
Females	3	10	13
Total	49	14	63

Table 21-5. Ordination[6]

Professional Training

The professional training of the minister of education should include work in education and administration. A good background in Bible and theology is basic, since this is what he will teach others. A thorough knowledge of educational philosophy, psychology, and principles of teaching is also essential.

The 1986 survey reveals the level of professional preparation for educational ministry. The results are reported in Table 6.

The minister of education must continue to grow and develop through refresher courses, seminars, conferences, reading, observation, and other similar experiences. The educa-

Educational Level	Males	Females	Total	Cumulative %
Bachelor's degree in Christian education or youth	7	5	12	18.7
Some seminary work	17	2	19	48.4
Seminary degree	19	1	20	79.7
Other	8	5	13	100.0

Table 21-6. Educational Preparation[7]

tional leader who continues to grow professionally not only equips himself for more effective service, but also sets an example for those who work with him.

Personal Qualifications

A college degree does not mean that a minister of education is automatically capable of leading a local church. Evaluation of his qualifications should also be made on the basis of his Christian education, professional training and experience, personal qualities, and past performance as a leader. Desirable qualities (not necessarily in order of importance) include:

Spirituality	Humility	Love for people
Neat and clean appearance	Studiousness	Unselfishness
Emotional maturity	Self-control	Foresight
Leadership ability	Patience	Obedience
Good health	Cooperativeness	Growth in grace
Attractive personality	Special talents	Sincerity
	Sense of honor	Diligence
	Common sense	

The minister of education should be able to lead others. He should not only know where he is going and how to get there, but he must also be able to influence others to cooperate with him. Flexibility on the part of a leader is absolutely essential in meeting the changing demands of a congregation. A leader who can adjust his leadership approach when the situation changes is more effective than one who functions in the same way in every situation.

Financial Considerations

The Christian education professional can realistically expect to receive a living wage, though females may be compensated somewhat less attractively than males. The same is true when benefits are considered. Tables 7 and 8 summarize the findings of the 1986 survey.

Adding in the approximate value of benefits, the average salary reaches approximately $23,074 annually. This is considerably lower than the figures revealed in a 1985 survey in Indiana in which the average total compensation was $29,328 for an education minister and $23,460 for a youth minister.

Salary Range	Males	Females	Total	Cumulative %
$12,000-$14,500	12	7	19	29.6
$14,500-$17,000	7	2	9	43.7
$17,000-$19,500	7	2	9	57.8
$19,500-$22,000	6	0	6	67.1
$22,000-$24,500	7	2	9	81.2
$24,500-$27,000	2	0	2	84.3
$27,000-$29,500	5	0	5	92.1
$29,500-$32,000	2	0	2	95.3
$32,000+	3	0	3	100.0
Average	20,409	19,150	20,156	
Median	18,250	14,500	18,250	

Table 21-7. Salaries

Benefit	Males	Females	Total	Percentage
Housing Allowance[8]	35	3	38	59.4
Life Insurance	19	5	24	37.5
Health Insurance[9]	39	8	47	73.4
Retirement	20	3	23	35.9
Car Allowance	31	5	36	56.3
Convention Expenses	40	7	47	73.4
Secretary	36	6	42	65.6
Other Compensation	13	2	15	23.4

Table 21-8. Benefits

Responsibilities

Developing an Educational Program

The minister of education is primarily responsible for the development and success of the church's educational program, which is primarily concerned with developing people. The minister of education is expected to lead the church to:

1. Develop a philosophy of Christian education.

2. Build and implement a curriculum to meet the needs of the church.
3. Evaluate the educational program.
4. Recruit and train leaders.

An effective professional in Christian education will lead the church to determine appropriate educational objectives and then plan to meet them. Two types of planning are necessary. The first is short-term planning, which takes place on a week-to-week basis. Second is long-term planning, which may cover a period from one to five years. The long-range plans provide the framework for short-term planning.

Once the church has determined its educational objectives, the minister of education will lead church members to develop abilities that will assure the achievement of these objectives. Ordinarily he should not teach a Sunday-school class or direct a youth group himself. His primary responsibility is to be a teacher of teachers and a leader of leaders. If the entire church program is to profit, he must be free to observe and evaluate the program in action in order to correct weaknesses.

His success at achieving the church's educational objectives depends largely on his ability to build a cohesive team of workers. He must recognize that he is not primarily attempting to motivate individuals, but to build work teams that are committed to the attainment of the church's objectives. He must involve people in problem solving and decision making.

Rather than attacking the apparent weaknesses of the church program, the minister of education should build on the already existing strengths of the church. People will change, but slowly. It is best not to rush people into accepting a new concept unless the change is an emergency measure. Under these circumstances, he should get as much support as possible for his proposed change and monitor the change closely to be sure of its effectiveness.

The minister of education serves as an education resource expert and as advisor for the entire church program. Part of his duties involve not only the workers in the program, but all the other resources available to the church. He will also help lead the church to become closer in fellowship with one another. In addition, he will help the church determine what ministries can be developed to meet the unique needs of the community served by the church.

The minister of education needs to be cautious in his allocation of time and duties. Because of his background, experience, and abilities, he might most enjoy the part of his ministry that is related to administration. Some ministers of education spend so much time in administration that they neglect those areas of ministry concerned with outreach, teaching, and counseling. It is easy to become sheltered behind a desk.

Evaluating Education Programs

The minister of Christian education must be constantly alert to changing trends in his field. New forms of Christian education continue to emerge. For example, there is an increasing focus upon relationships. In a society that has become more and more impersonal, people have a desperate hunger to relate to one another. The purpose of relational Bible study is to deal with the Scriptures on a highly personal level rather than on an abstract verbal level. Another trend stresses educating the affective domain (attitudes and emotions). A third new emphasis in education is active pupil involvement in learning. Christian educators view involvement learning as preparation for daily engagement with the traumas, struggles, and sufferings experienced in this world. This is accomplished through discovering how the Bible can be applied to the learner's lifestyle. Yet another trend is the growing use of modern technology to develop various types of teaching situations.

As they become available, the minister of Christian education must study and evaluate new techniques and materials in light of the Scripture. He must be able to distinguish fads from effective new concepts, adapt these new ideas to his own programs, and persuade and train workers to use these new ideas and equipment.

Knowing About Available Materials

The professional in Christian education must lead the church in an awareness of available educational and curriculum materials. He needs to be able to lead church program leaders in evaluating, selecting, adapting, and producing curriculum materials appropriate for use in all aspects of the church's total educational program.

The minister of education should constantly be aware of the needs of his teachers and learners. The behavior of an individual at any particular moment is usually determined by his own needs.

Selecting, Enlisting, and Training Workers

The church's educational program will succeed only to the extent that it has dedicated, trained workers led by a dedicated, trained leader.

One of the greatest challenges to the minister of education is the selection, enlistment, and training of workers. He should keep a list of potential leaders and teachers who could, if trained and/or challenged, fill vacancies. With the help and direction of God, all such positions can be filled. The minister of education must also provide pre-service and in-service education for his volunteer teachers and workers. Likewise he must promote and direct regular teachers' planning sessions.

Encouraging Use of Facilities and Equipment

The environment in which teachers instruct can be either an asset or a liability. The minister of education is responsible to see that teachers use the facilities and equipment most advantageously. He will seek ways to improve the educational facilities while making the best use of those he has.

Keeping Records

The Sunday school that knows its past has a future. Trends in attendance reveal a great deal about the educational program of a church, but such evaluations can be made only when accurate records are kept. The minister of education should regularly study and interpret records.

Planning for Visitation

Records must be reinforced with a good visitation program of personal visits, phone calls, and post cards. People come when callers go. The minister of education plans and develops a strong visitation program.

Summary

Table 9 summarizes the reported responsibilities of the Christian education professionals who returned questionnaires in the 1986 survey. Interestingly enough, only about three-fourths (47 out of 64) of the sample group had their responsibilities clearly outlined in a written job description.

Task	Yes	No	Percentage
Recruitment	63	1	98.4
Training	62	2	96.9
Organization	64	0	100.0
Planning	63	1	98.4
Planning for Growth	64	0	100.0
Coordination	63	1	98.4
Promotion	63	1	98.4
Supervision	61	3	95.3
Budgeting	58	6	90.6
Teaching	62	2	96.9
Hospital Calling	55	9	85.9[10]
Pastoral Work	54	10	84.4[11]
Other	32	32	50.0

Table 21-9. Job Responsibilities

Interpersonal Relationships

With the Paid Staff

Much of the minister of education's work will be done behind the scenes; few will notice or give credit for what he does. He must be able to remain the background while others enjoy the limelight, and so he must be constantly alert to the temptation of jealousy. He will respect the authority of his superiors, but at the same time he will not compromise his convictions just to maintain the appearance of harmony that does not really exist. In an aggressive program, disagreements among staff members may develop, yet even these tensions that occur can become creative opportunities for Christian growth.

The 1986 survey revealed that the majority of Christian education professional were in positive, harmonious staff settings. Table 10 summarizes the findings.

With Church Officers

The minister of education must maintain open and effective lines of communication with the elected representatives of the congregation: the church board, the board of Christian educa

Quality of Relationship	Males	Females	Total	Cumulative %
Excellent	28	8	36	56.3
Good	15	4	19	85.9
Fair	7	0	7	96.9
Poor	1	1	2	100.0

Table 21-10. Staff Relationships

tion, and the Sunday school council. He must work with the finance committee of the church to provide adequate resources for curriculum materials, equipment, supplies, and leadership development.

The minister of education should also involve department leaders and appropriate staff members in the resolution of philosophical, procedural, and scheduling problems. It is his task to see that there is coordination and balance among the various educational programs of the church.

With the Volunteer Staff

Working with the volunteer staff from the congregation is a *must* if the minister of education is to be successful. The average volunteer has a greater desire to be put to use than church leaders often realize. These volunteers require a greater amount of help and training than most church leaders believe. It is in the role of equipping others for service that many ministers of education find their greatest satisfaction. Continuing emphasis must be given to this training process.

Summary

The "Minister of Education" or "Director of Christian Education" is a man or woman called by a local congregation to lead and supervise its educational program. He is an individual called to a specific form of ministry, requiring adequate preparation to do the job. His responsibilities are to plan programs, recruit and equip workers, and coordinate the work of teaching in the local church. He is a key figure in his congregation.

Project

Interview a director of Christian education. How does his work compare to what is described in this chapter?

Selected Bibliography

Brown, Lowell. *Christian Educators' Journal.* Glendale, CA: Gospel Light, 1979.

_______ . *Sunday School Standards.* Glendale, CA: Gospel Light, 1980.

Getz, Gene A. *Sharpening the Focus of the Church.* Chicago: Victor Books, 1984.

Harrington, Arthur. *What the Bible Says About Leadership.* Joplin, MO: College Press Publishing Company, 1986.

Leavitt, Guy P., rev. by Leon Langston. *Superintend with Success.* Cincinnati, OH: Standard Publishing, 1980.

Richards, Lawrence O. *A Theology of Christian Education.* Grand Rapids, MI: Zondervan Publishing House, 1975.

---

[1]1 Ephesians 3:19

[2]Ephesians 4:13

[3]The median is the midpoint in the age range from oldest to youngest. Half of the sample lies below the median, half above.

[4]This is somewhat lower than a 1985 survey done among Christian Churches/ Churches of Christ in Indiana in which the average was 11.2. However, when youth ministers are included in that survey, as the present one, the average would be approximately the same in both samples.

[5]*Ibid.*

[6]The differences between ordination of men and women is significant, with women far less likely to be ordained for the same position as a man. This reflects the general position of the church group represented about ordination of women. It is not an impossibility, but it is not a likelihood either.

[7]Significant differences exist between males and females, with males more likely to pursue additional education.

[8]Significant differences exist between males and females, with females less likely to have this benefit. This is directly linked to lack of ordination and tax rulings relating to ministerial housing.

[9]Significant differences exist between males and females with females less likely to receive this as a part of their compensation. This is due, in part, to the fact that several of the women are married and have health insurance coverage through their husbands' jobs.

[10]Significant differences exist between males and females, with females less likely to be involved in this facet of ministry.

[11]*Ibid.*

Part Four

BEYOND THE LOCAL CHURCH

Section Outline

22. The Christian School
    A. History of the Christian School Movement
    B. Has the Christian School a Right to Exist?
    C. Philosophy of the Christian School
    D. Organizational Structure
    E. The Christian School Teacher
    F. The Future of the Christian School
    G. Sources of Additional Information

23. Christian Camping
    A. Definition and Purpose
    B. Objectives of Christian Camping
    C. A Brief History of Christian Camping
    D. Forms and Varieties of Camping
    E. Administering Camp
    F. The Camp Program

24. The Campus Ministry
    A. History of Campus Ministry
    B. Philosophy of Campus Ministry
    C. Types and Programs of Campus Ministry
    D. The Campus Minister

25. Christian Higher Education
    A. The Beginning of Colleges in America
    B. The Teaching of Religion in American Colleges
    C. Professional Training in Christian Education
    D. The Rise of Bible Colleges and Institutes

The local church is the focus of Christ's mission to the world. We stress that mission in terms of evangelism and education, the two basic thrusts according to the Great Commission. This volume has been concerned mainly with the program of Christian education that local churches need to develop to accomplish Christ's will for His people.

Some areas of Christian education lie beyond the local church. They may be cooperative ventures of several churches or groups of churches, such as Christian camping, campus ministries, colleges, and seminaries.

Many have doubts about the continuing value of the public school. Christian schools are involved with the education of children and youth, and should be understood and evaluated in terms of the mandate of Christ to teach. The chapter on the Christian school presents this option.

Christian education begins in the local church, but it need not end there. In this section, attention is given to those agencies and activities that are beyond the local congregation. They contribute to the local church's program of nurture, and in some cases, the local church can develop cooperative programs. As such, these programs must be considered and evaluated.

CHAPTER 22

The Christian School

As you read, think about these questions:

—Who were the significant people in the development of the Christian school movement?

—What are the arguments for and against a Christian school?

—How is the philosophy of integration applied within the Christian school?

—Identify the significant roles that the teacher must play in the Christian school.

History of the Christian School Movement

Religion in the schools is not new in America. In fact, its roots are to be found in early American history. The first American schools, at St. Augustine (1606), Boston (1635), and New Amsterdam (1638), educated individuals in Christian truths. This practice remained the norm even after the emergence of public education and the establishment of independence in the American republic. However, with the increasing secularization of society and education along with the waves of immigrants from all kinds of ethnic backgrounds, Christian education was gradually replaced in the public schools.

Until recently, the development of the independent Christian school has been primarily influenced by the leadership and support of the National Union of Christian Schools located in

Grand Rapids, Michigan, and the National Association of Christian Schools in Wheaton, Illinois.

The National Union of Christian Schools grew out of the Christian school background in the Netherlands. Christian schools were developed in reaction to a ruling by King William II of the Netherlands, which decreed that public schools were to have a social and educational task only. Prior to this time, schools had been under the direction of the church. The first Christian school was established in Nijmegen in 1840, followed by one in Greda in 1842. Several leaders in Christian school education, including Henry Beets, H. P. Scholte, and A. C. Van Raalten, later emigrated to America, taking with them their tradition of Christian schools.

The earliest Christian day school professional organization was founded in 1892 and was known as the *Vereenigin Voor Christelik Onderwijs Op Gereformerden Grandslage* (Society for Christian Board on the Reformed Faith). Ten or twelve schools were charter members of this organization, which later developed into the Chicago Alliance. This alliance appointed a committee consisting of Mark Fakkema, the first principal of Chicago Christian High School; Andrew Blystra, and Henry Kuiper to assess the standards of education in their schools. The committee reported that the need to standardize the curriculum, train better teachers, and issue textbooks were universal problems in the Christian schools, and it recommended that a national union be formed.

On September 1, 1920, representatives of 37 school associations met in Chicago and formed the National Union of Christian Schools. The task of the National Union was clearly defined in articles Three and Four of the constitution of the Union. Article Three read: "The purpose of the Union is to further the interests of Christian Education which our schools have in common." Article Four read:

> This purpose of the Union shall be achieved by:
> (a) Aiding the cause of Christian Normal Training
> (b) Encouraging the publication of literature of a pedagogic nature
> (c) Raising the standard of education
> (d) Improving the economic position of the teacher
> (e) Aiding one another as schools when necessary
> (f) Supervision of the individual schools.[1]

From its inception, the National Union was to be a service organization. In no way would it seek to dictate to individual schools.

Most of the independent non-parochial schools were within the Reformed tradition until 1940 (an exception was the Portland School in Louisville, Kentucky). But by the early 1940's, the influence of the Christian school movement had extended well beyond the Reformed churches. In 1945, groups from non-Reformed church backgrounds bought a majority of the promotional literature sold by the National Union. Warren Benson describes this situation:

> It became clear that with so many denominations seeking to develop Christian schools that a new type of organization was needed. The organization envisioned was to embrace all Christian schools which were parent-controlled or private, rather than parochial in polity. Membership in such an organization was to be based on a general doctrinal statement such as we identified with the National Association of Evangelicals.[2]

At the National Association of Evangelicals convention in Omaha, Nebraska in 1947, Frank Gaebelein of the Stony Brook School was appointed chairman of a committee that dealt with elementary and secondary education. This committee recommended the formation of the National Association of Christian Schools. This association was founded in 1947 with Mark Fakkema as its chief official. It became the guiding influence in the development of Christian day schools over the next 25 years.

At the height of its expansion in 1971, the National Association of Christian Schools had a membership of 364 schools, a growth of 120 schools in four years. In July, 1978, four months after its formation into a new organization, the Association of Christian Schools International had a membership of approximately 1,200 schools representing more than 150,000 students.

In 1950, the Christian school system was rare. Now city-wide systems, such as those found in Memphis, San Diego, and Los Angeles, are increasing. Briarcrest Baptist School System in Memphis, Tennessee, is an example of this trend. Established in 1973, the schools now meet in a dozen locations and have a total enrollment of about 4,000. The system has been described as "having just about everything: a lavish $6.5 million building and a well-educated corps of teachers (40 percent have masters degrees)."[3] Concerning this school, the *Wall Street Journal* commented:

> Briarcrest's concern for quality education is another difference. It offers all the standard academic subjects in addition to religious training, but above all, Briarcrest is financially sound.[4]

This development of the Christian school movement has been described as "an explosion" of unprecented size. Two decades ago, Henry Buchanan and Bob Brown made the following observation about the growth of Christian schools:

> The most exciting development in education today is the rise of the Protestant church school. A rarity three decades ago, Protestant church schools are now being organized at the rate of 225 per year. If the enthusiasm does not wane, they will soon take a place of equal importance alongside the public and parochial schools.[5]

During the past decade or so, enrollment in Christian day schools affiliated with the national professional association has soared. Christian day schools are now coming into existence at an estimated rate of two to three new schools a day.

Has the Christian School a Right to Exist?

While Christian schools have existed in America throughout her history, their right to exist has been constantly challenged. Some of the arguments raised on both sides of the debate are listed here.

Arguments for the Christian School

1. God's revelation is the basis for all truth.[6]
2. God gave parents the responsibility to control the education of their children.[7]
3. God gave religious leaders a responsibility for teaching children.[8]
4. Christian education must be education for the whole person.[9]

5. God's education is always in contrast to man's education.[10]

6. Biblical education requires a submission of the intellect and will to the lordship of Christ.[11]

7. Every part of the educational process is related to God, and, therefore, education cannot be divided into "secular" and "religious." It can take place only in an atmosphere where this relationship can be implemented.

8. The person to be educated is a unified personality. He is one as God is one. Therefore, his education cannot be compartmentalized into "secular" and "religious."

9. The goal of all education, in church or school, is to help man more fully achieve the purpose of his life, that is, to know and serve God. Only the Christian school can eradicate the false dualism of "sacred" and "secular" and bring the two together, thus presenting a unified Christian world view.

10. Higher academic standards are possible because of devoted teachers, limited enrollment, and increased efficiency due to the wise stewardship of limited resources.

11. The small percentage of time children spend at home and church reinforces the needs for the Christian school.

12. For the Christian, the highest incentive in learning and conduct is to glorify God. This incentive can be stressed in Christian schools in a way that is not possible for a Christian teacher in a public school. Thus the standards of the Christian home are reinforced and emphasized.

Arguments for the Public School

1. The public school is the only way the Christian voice may be heard in a tangible way in education. The Christian has a great responsibility toward his town's public schools. Withdrawal from them will abandon them to secular humanism.

2. Christian children should attend public schools in order to present a witness and to avoid being overly sheltered from the world. This promotes evangelism and a realistic point of view.

3. Public schools have better physical, financial, and transportation facilities and therefore provide better education.

4. A strong parent-child relationship and a virile Christian home life coupled with public school offers the best educational combination.

5. Public school offers the traditional American way of education.

6. The public school offers full academic and athletic programs. In all, a much broader form of education is available in the public school.

7. Parents are already paying for public education with their tax dollars. Rather than use its money to establish schools, the church should devote this money to the cause of world missions and encourage parents to use the educational facilities that are already available to them.

Philosophy of the Christian School

What, then, are the specific features of Christian schools? W. J. Lanouette described them this way:

> These Christian schools aren't the familiar parochial schools of the main line religions: Roman Catholic, Episcopalian, Presbyterian, Lutheran, and the like. And, with few exceptions, they're not the all-white private academies begun to avoid public school desegration. Rather, those in the movement apply the term "Christian Schools" to new and independent entities, most founded since World War II. All are evangelical, and most are conservative in outlook.[12]

Much criticism in the past has centered around the idea that parents who send their children to Christian schools shelter them from the real world. Both Paul Kienel, executive director of the Association of Christian Schools International, and Roy Lowrie, president of the Association of Christian Schools International, have vigorously protested against such criticism. An education that leaves out teachings about God, they say, gives the student an incomplete and erroneous picture of reality: it does not depict the "real world" at all. Especially teachings about man himself must be considered in the full light of Scripture. Further, any educational system that leaves God out of its teachings is itself making certain presuppositions that it takes on faith, and in this sense is also giving children a "religious" education, only this religion is one of secular humanism.[13]

The National Association of Christian Schools, under Mark Fakkema's leadership, developed an overall philosophy of education that is widely accepted among Christian schools today. This philosophy can be summarized as follows:

> The non-Christian philosophy has an integrating center in man, but the center of the Christian philosophy is God. . . . It is understood that the two resultant programs which are so separated in the beginning will never reach agreement, but rather, in the main, will stand in antithesis. It is because of this philosophic divergence that many Christian educators have concluded that the Christian day school is the only answer to the problem of providing a theocentric and thus Christocentric educational program for children.[14]

Certain examples substantiate this contention. Mathematics reveals a God who is unchangeable. Grammar speaks to us of God's law and order of plan. The child also recognizes something of God as He reveals himself through nature. History is man in the laboratory of life demonstrating to himself and to his fellow man that he is a sinner in need of God's plan of redemption.

A true philosophy of education integrates all truth in God, and demonstrates the relationship of all subject matter to Him in a manner that honors God. Since all truth is God's truth, all curriculum material must be thought through from a Christian frame of reference.

Organizational Structure

Four types of organizational structures can be distinguished within the Christian school movement.

1. The *private school* is owned by an individual or family. Usually it is operated either by that individual or by a self-perpetuating group of trustees. The role of the board, if one exists, is advisory. Many of these schools are at the secondary level, and some evangelical boarding schools also fit into this category.

2. The *church-organized school* is organized by a church or denomination. A majority of the schools founded in the last decade are owned or operated either by one or a group of churches. This type of school is often run by a school board that is itself responsible to and appointed by the church board.

It often uses the church's educational property. Church members frequently play an active role in various areas of the school's life and regard the enterprise as a part of their educational mission outreach.

3. The *parent society school* is an independent Christian school started by a group of parents who form a legal corporation that owns the school property and appoints a board to manage the school. This corporation is often called a school society. An individual may have a child in the school and not be a member of the corporation, and some corporation members may not have immediate family members in the school.

4. The *multigrade individualized education school* is a recent development. Companies have prepared materials that allow for the development of a school that has very few pupils. Generally these companies train church leaders and administrators and sell them a complete curriculum package. These curriculum materials frequently use programmed textbooks through which the student moves at his own pace with needed help given by a supervisor. It is possible for several grades to meet in one room and for one supervisor to help all of them. This type of structure has made possible a Christian school with only a few pupils. In most cases churches sign a three-year contract with the production company that provides all that is needed to establish and operate the school.

The Christian School Teacher

The key person in the training of a child is the teacher. The teacher must reflect God's glory as he teaches Scripture. Mark Fakkema ascribed roles of privilege and responsibility to the teacher; the teacher must take seriously James' statement: "Not many of you should presume to be teachers . . . because you know that we who teach will be judged more strictly."[15]

The concept of the Christian school makes special demands on the teacher. Not only must he be living the life a growing, maturing Christian, but he must also be academically competent. Only the very best in all areas of the school life can truly bring glory to God.

When Paul talked about his role as a teacher to the church in Thessalonica, he said: "You know how we lived among you for your sake. You became imitators of us and of the Lord. . . . and so you became a model to all the believers in Macedonia and Achaia."[16] In Paul's life there was harmony among what he taught, how he taught it, and the life he lived. The same harmony is demanded of each Christian day school teacher. A truly Christian school is one staffed by Christian teachers where Christian values and a Christian world view permeate every part of its life.

Curriculum

The only satisfactory curriculum to the Christian teacher is one that has two components: a horizontal one (a relationship among facts) and a vertical one (a relationship with God). Scripture relates all things vertically to God in a threefold way. "All things" are said to be of God, through God, and for God. Every system of instruction that ignores or bypasses this vertical relationship (as secular instruction does) is inadequate, for not to know things in their vertical relationship is not to know their true origin and real purpose.

The importance of curriculum development and the role of curriculum in the Christian school were discussed in the 1920's by the National Union. At that time, a need was expressed for the development of curriculum guides for teachers in order to help them to perform the necessary integration of the Bible and biblical material with other subjects.

Current writers continue to emphasize the need for an integrated curriculum. John Burgess, chairman of the Division of Education at Gordon College, has sought to identify two types of integration—isolated and structured. Isolated integration is that which occurs when no comprehensive objectives guide the selection of biblical elements to be introduced into the learning activity. This results in a curriculum containing a series of unrelated biblical concepts. There is no conscious planning for one element to support another.

Burgess says that the structured integration approach involves long-range planning:

> This approach is characterized by the careful planning of Biblical integration over a significantly large portion of the curriculum. Objectives are identified and the Biblical elements are structured so as to support each other and to contribute to the

> accomplishment of common Biblical goals. . . . Structured integration should be accomplished at two major levels. It should take place as a corporate effort by the entire faculty of a school in the organization of the total curriculum and by an individual teacher over that portion of the curriculum which is his responsibility.[17]

Robert Miller, superintendent of a Christian school, presents the following scenario to illustrate what is implied by structured integration:

> A school is concerned with the subject of government. In the Christian school, we cannot delete the normal material included in a government course but must first consider what Biblical principles apply to this area. As a result of a student's research and discussion with his peers, he will discover such truths as the following:
>
> 1. God is the supreme ruler, controlling nations and rulers.
> 2. When men refuse God's rule, He lets them rule themselves.
> 3. The powers that be are ordained of God. Since God has a hand in the placing of leaders, they should be respected and obeyed.
> 4. Believers must pray for their leaders.
> 5. Believers must support the government in taxes.
> 6. Civil authorities are a deterrent to evil, not to good.
> 7. When civil authorities conflict with God's Word, we are to obey God.
> 8. God holds nations accountable for their actions.
> 9. God expects kings and government leaders to keep the promises they have made.
> 10. When a godly nation turns from God, its sins are often worse than those of the heathen, and its judgment is greater.
> 11. The Bible encourages patriotism and love of country.
> 12. The Bible discourages rebellion and rioting.
>
> For the Christian teacher these Biblical principles do not become an interesting supplement to the course but rather the basic propositions which will shape his planning and instruction. To be worthy of the name "Christian education" the course must not only analyze the inter-working of our governmental structure but see it as it fits into God's plan and purpose. Only as these Biblical principles become an integrated part of the government course can it be said that the subject begins to reflect

> the unique philosophy of the Christian school. The heart of integration in Christian education is no less than "the living union of its subject matter, administration, and even its personnel, with the eternal and infinite pattern of God's truth."[18]

This underlying fact of God's authorship and purpose of government must be clearly presented to the student as a part of each subject he is taught. The student should see each subject from a God-centered instead of a man-centered perspective. This integration must be communicated to the student in such a manner that it becomes his frame of reference. He must be exposed not only to the results of the teacher's study, but to the whole process of integration. He himself must learn to put together the pieces of the puzzle. In this way he will develop his own Christian world view.

A factor that must be considered in any discussion of Christian school curriculum concerns regulations imposed by various states. At present this is a sensitive issue. Some states apply only regulations concerning health and safety to the private schools within their area, while others require the use of approved textbooks and curricular materials. This issue is currently before the courts in several states. Many Christian schools regard these regulations as a contravention of the principle of the separation of church and state. They suggest that the philosophy of integration demands the freedom to use Christian textbooks in all subject areas.

Until recently this ideal has been hard to achieve. Few quality textbooks have been written from a Christian perspective for elementary and secondary education. With the growth of the Christian school movement the demand for this type of text has grown. Some Christian textbook publishers are beginning to offer fairly complete sets of materials, at least at the elementary level. The rate of production of quality secondary texts is also accelerating. A partial list of Christian school textbook publishers is included at the end of the chapter.

The Future of the Christian School

Diversity is a feature of Christian schools, so it is impossible to generalize about them. Schools founded for inadequate reasons or on an unsound financial, biblical, or administrative basis will experience problems and tend to bring criticism to the movement as a whole. On the positive side, there are signs that the movement is developing maturity. At the present time questions concerning the tax exempt status of these schools, racial integration, and curricula are among the issues being tested in lawsuits. The decisions that are finally reached in some of these areas will affect the future of the Christian school, but will not cause the end of the movement.

In the next decade, there will be more teachers and administrators trained for ministry in the area of Christian schools. Better specialized curriculum materials will continue to be made available. More professional help will be offered to the schools through organizations such as the Association of Christian Schools International. The school has the potential of being a meaningful agent, together with the home and the church, in providing for the total education of the child. Ministry within the Christian school, whether as a teacher, administrator, counselor, or one of the many auxiliary helpers, will provide an increasing opportunity for meaningful Christian service.

Summary

The development of Christian schools in the last decade has been just short of phenomenal. The Christian school movement has roots back to the early settlement of this nation, even as far back as Europe for some religious groups. Public education nearly supplanted the evangelical Christian school movement for a hundred years, but the past decade has been the era of a return to private education. Even so, the quality of these schools depends upon a sound philosophy of education, effective teachers, and appropriate materials.

Project

Visit a Christian school in your community. Find out its origins and goals as well as teacher qualifications and textbooks. Observe a class in action. How does this class differ from one in a public school?

Sources of Additional Information

Professional Organizations

American Association of Christian Schools
6601 N. W. 167th Avenue
Miami, FL 33193

Association of Christian Schools International
P. O. Box 4097
Whittier, CA 90607

Christian Schools International
865 28th Street, S. E.
Grand Rapids, MI 49508

Southern Baptist Christian School Association
Nashville, TN 37201

Curriculum Publishers

A Beka Book Publications
Pensacola Christian College
125 St. John Street
Pensacola, FL 32503

Accelerated Christian Education
P. O. Box 2205
Garland, TX 75041

Alpha Omega
P. O. Box 3153
Tempe, AZ 85281

Association for Bible Curriculum Development
1515 N. Los Robles Avenue
Pasadena, CA 91104

Association for Christian Schools International
P. O. Box 4097
Whittier, CA 90607

Beacon Enterprises
P.O. Box 1296
Santa Cruz, CA 95061

Bob Jones University Press
Greenville, SC 29614

Christian Education Music Publishers
2285 W. 185th Place
Lansing, IL 60538

Christian Light Publications
P. O. Box 1126
Harrisonburg, VA 22801

Christian Schools International
865 28th Street, S. E.
Grand Rapids, MI 49508

Creation-Life Publishers
P. O. Box 15666
San Diego, CA 92115

Rod and Staff Publishers
Crockett, KY 41413

Selected Bibliography

Blanchard, John F., Jr. *Education That Is Christian*. Wheaton, IL: National Association of Christian Schools.

Clark, Gordon H. *A Christian Philosophy of Education*. Grand Rapids, MI: WM. B. Eerdmans Publishing Co., 1947.

Gaebelein, Frank. *The Pattern of God's Truth*. New York: Oxford University Press, 1954.

Haycock, Ruth. *Bible Truths for School Subjects*. Whittier, CA: Association of Christian Schools International, 1979.

Kienel, Paul A. *The Christian School: Why It Is Right For Your Child*. Wheaton, IL: Victor Books, 1974.

________ . *The Philosophy of Christian School Education*. Whittier, CA: Association of Christian Schools International, 1977.

Van Dusen, Henry P. *God in Education*. New York: Charles Scribner's Sons, 1951.

---

[1]Henry Kuiper, "The National Union Begins to Function," *Christian Home and School,* XXXII (June, 1954), p. 16.

[2]Warren S. Benson, "A History of the National Association of Christian Schools During the Period of 1947-1972," unpublished Ph.D dissertation (Loyola University, 1975), p. 25.

[3]Wayne Allen, "How We Began Our Christian Day School Ministry." From *Church Administration,* June, 1978. © Copyright 1978 The Sunday School Board of the Southern Baptist Convention. All rights reserved. Used by permission.

[4]*Ibid.*

[5]Henry A. Buchanan and Bob W. Brown, "Will Protestant Church Schools Become a Third Force?", *Christianity Today,* XL (May 12, 1967), p. 3.

[6]Luke 11:52; Proverbs 1:7

[7]Deuteronomy 6:7; Ephesians 6:4; Genesis 18:17-19

[8]Deuteronomy 31:9-13

[9]Proverbs 22:6

[10]Colossians 2:8

[11]1 Corinthians 1:18-31; 2 Corinthians 10:5

[12]William J. Lanouette, "Christian Schools Boom by Stressing That the Fourth R Is Religion," *The National Observer,* January 15, 1977, p. 1.

[13]Paul Kienel, "Should Parents Shelter Their Children From the Real World?", *Christian School Comment,* VIII (September, 1977), p. 1.

[14]Benson, pp. 83-84.

[15]James 3:1

[16]1 Thessalonians 1:5-7

[17]John Burgess, "Considering the Individual in Structuring Biblical Integration," *Christian Teacher,* 12 (March-April, 1975), p. 17. Official publication of the National Association of Christian Schools, P.O. Box 550, Wheaton, IL 60187.

[18]Robert M. Miller, "Implementing the Christian Philosophy in Textbook Selection and General Curriculum Development," *The Philosophy of Christian School Education,* ed. Paul A. Kienel (Whittier, California: Association of Christian Schools International, 1977), pp. 132-33.

CHAPTER 23

Christian Camping

As you read, think about these questions:
—What are meant by the terms, *camping, conference, centralized*, and *decentralized*?
—What are the objectives of Christian camping?
—How are objectives and program related?
—What are the elements of an effective camp program?
—What is the value of camper-counselor relationships?

Camping in twentieth-century America is big business. Mitchell and Crawford estimate that five to six million young people are involved in camping each summer. As many as 190,000 persons find vocational opportunities in camping. When various other kinds of camping (such as retreats and family camps) are added to this figure, it is conceivable that some ten to fifteen million people are involved in some form of camping.[1]

Of these millions involved in camping, most are involved in camp programs sponsored by religious groups. These groups have found that camping is an exciting experience through which the goals of the church can be accomplished. As a result, camping has become a vital thrust of the Christian educational program.

Definition and Purpose

Robert Rubin has defined *camping* as "communal living close to nature with a set purpose."[2] The American Camping Association's definition expands on Rubin's:

> Organized (Resident, Day) Camping is an experience in group living in a natural environment. It is a sustained experience under the supervision of trained leadership. Camping provides a creative, educational experience in cooperative group living in the outdoors. It utilizes the resources of the natural surroundings to contribute significantly to mental, physical, social, and spiritual growth of campers.[3]

Christian camping is a specific type of camping with definite biblically-oriented goals. It is "a Christ-centered program of small-group living in a simple, controlled out-of-door environment where the camper is enabled to develop recreational, educational, and social skills and to know Christ as Savior and Friend."[4]

Christian camping is an activity the church uses to help fulfill the Great Commission Jesus gave it. In Bible-oriented churches, the camping experience stresses both initial Christian commitment and Christian growth. Its uniqueness is in the setting and the varied programming that can reach and motivate persons who otherwise would remain uninterested or uninvolved.

Objectives of Christian Camping

The objectives of Christ-centered camping grow out of this basic purpose. Four major objectives should be common to all Christ-centered camps. These objectives correspond to that statement of Jesus' balanced growth recorded in Luke's Gospel: "Jesus grew in wisdom and stature, and in favor with God and men."[5] Each camp program must have clear objectives for the *physical well-being and growth* of its campers, the *social relationships* it attempts to cultivate, the *educational growth* its Bible study programs are intended to foster, and the *spiritual commitments and qualities of life* that the total camp environment is designed to produce.

A Brief History of Christian Camping

Abraham and the other patriarchs pitched their tents and sojourned in a land into which their God had guided them.[6] Here was living out-of-doors under the guidance of the Creator-Lord of self-disclosing love. Moses directed what must have been the greatest family camp that ever existed.[7] The law that Jehovah gave His people provided for an annual time of short-term camping when all Israel was to come to Jerusalem and dwell in tents. During this time, they would remember how God had led and provided for them after they had departed from Egypt.[8]

Although camping may have a long past, it has a relatively short history. Christian camping has its immediate background in the camp meetings of the nineteenth century. These meetings developed out of the revivalism associated with the Second Evangelical Awakening, particularly the phase that took place on the American frontier. Even after the initial wave of revivalism had passed, the camp meeting survived as a popular religious institution, especially in the South and West. Camp meetings served both religious and social purposes. As Hall notes in *Texas Disciples*, "Scattered settlers with little preaching available found it advantageous to gather at some camping spot, camp out for a week or two, and hear preaching day and night. Travel was slow and tedious and camping was congenial to the pioneers."[9]

These camp meetings, particularly among Methodists and Baptists, became annual affairs and were held at centrally located campsites. Evangelism was emphasized. Preaching, Bible study, and prayer were included in the religious activities of the campers. In a natural setting, religious nurture was provided for persons of all ages.

The first camping experience specifically for youth occurred in 1861. Frederick Gunn, headmaster of the Gunnery School for Boys in Washington, Connecticut, led his young cadets to nearby Milford-on-the-Sound, where they camped. For two weeks, he led them in a series of activities including military training, hiking, boating, and fishing. This proved so successful that he continued this each summer until 1879. Gunn has been dubbed the father of the American camping movement.

The first church-sponsored camp was an informal program

conducted in 1880 by George Hinkley. He took seven boys camping on Gardiner Island, Rhode island. He believed that the informal living outdoors would break down barriers between these young men and himself, and enable him to win them to the Lord. The informal program he conducted included Bible teaching, sports and recreation, and an evening worship hour.

In 1885, the Young Men's Christian Association began its first summer camp. Sumner F. Dudley organized this camp on the banks of New York's Lake Champlain. This camp, now known as Camp Dudley, is the oldest boys' camp still in operation. Other parachurch and character-building agencies followed the YMCA example. After the turn of the century, the YWCA, Boy Scouts, Girl Scouts, Campfire Girls, Salvation Army, the 4-H, and other agencies began organized camping programs.

Sometime in the 1880's, Dwight L. Moody began summer conferences at his home in Northfield, Massachusetts. The Mountain Retreat Association, later known as Montreat, near Asheville, North Carolina, began a similar program in the 1890's. Other conference centers, such as the one at Winona Lake in Indiana, were also begun. These were not strictly camping, but were leisurely paced programs of Bible study set in a natural atmosphere. The founders of these programs felt that such Bible teaching was not being carried out as it should be within the local churches, so vacation time and in-depth Bible study were combined at these centers. Later, several of these conferences began to sponsor boys' and girls' camps on the outskirts of their properties.

Similar in nature was the Chautauqua Conference for Sunday school teachers established in 1874 at Lake Chautauqua, New York, by Methodist bishop John Vincent and Lewis Miller school enthusiasts. This original summer program of Bible study and teacher training was expanded to include many other religious and cultural elements. It became the springboard of the Chautauqua lecture program that helped to provide adult education for many communities for several decades.

In 1912, the International Sunday School Association under the leadership of John Alexander began a leadership training conference at Lake Geneva, Wisconsin. After this, various denominations began their own camping and conference programs. Cynthia Pearl Maus inaugurated the Disciples of Christ's first conference in 1919. Other denominations began programs in the 1920's and 1930's. By the mid-thirties, many independent and evangelical groups were developing camping-conference programs. Camping is now as universal among religious groups as the Sunday school.

Forms and Varieties of Camping

Much that is done in the name of camping is not really camping, but an adaptation of the older conference idea. The Todds outline those elements that are characteristic of camps and conferences:[10]

A Church Camp	*A Conference*
Leisurely pace	Fast-moving
Simple, relaxed life	Designed for inspiration
Controlled environment	Less controlled environment
Small-group activity	Mass activity
Counselor centered	Platform centered
No "prima donna" speaker	Expert speakers
Better-trained counselors	Counselors mainly disciplinarians
Simple outdoor setting	Often elaborate facilities
Nature emphasis	Nature only incidental
Emphasis on personal evangelism	Mass evangelism
Informal worship	Formal worship
Personal counseling	Group instruction
Individual worship stresses private devotions	Mass approach to worship
Development of the individual	Leadership training
Informal program	Formal program
Participation by all	Spectator status for most

Kenneth Gangel notes that a conference is meeting-centered: "The entire program—recreational, instructional, and spiritual—is superimposed upon the site so that the resulting activities are structured very carefully and centered in the meetings of the day."[11]

Most church camps are largely conference-type experiences that include some camping for variety, interest, and individual emphasis. This has come about because many evangelical churches and parachurch organizations that sponsor camping "consider the indoctrination and evangelization of their youth more important than teaching how to char a potato in coals or to sleep in a bumpy bough bed."[12]

There is probably more variation in church camping than in any other agency designed to achieve Christian educational goals. Types of camping programs range all the way from strict Bible conferences to outdoor adventure or wilderness camping; from trip camping (backpack, bicycle, horseback, canoeing) to resident camping; from camps run by an individual to extensive camp programs under strict denominational control.

Types of camping can be classified as to their sponsorship, the various age groups and other interests that they serve, and the duration and location of the camp program.

Sponsorship

Camping programs have a variety of sponsorship. Some successful Christian camps and conferences are operated by individuals who own the campground, control the program and personnel, and offer their services to churches and individuals.

Several parachurch organizations sponsor camping programs. Young Life camps and Fellowship of Christian Athlete camps are conducted with evangelistic and nurturing goals in mind, along with the specific aims of the organization (Fellowship of Christian Athlete camps are sports-oriented, yet aim for evangelism and nurture).

Probably the largest number of camping programs are church sponsored. The local camp is sponsored and controlled by a large local church, a group of cooperating churches, or a denomination.

Age Groups and Special Interests

When camp programs first began, they were mainly for adults and college youth. In more recent years camping has been expanded to serve other age levels. Day camping, which is becoming popular, has been offered for six- to eight-year-old youngsters. Family camping, encouraged by secular as well as religious interests, involves all ages in family units. The emphasis is upon helping families to grow spiritually and become a stronger Christian witness.

Research conducted jointly by Christian Camping, International and Scripture Press noted that 26.3 percent of all camps researched were for junior age children (ten and eleven). High school camps made up 21.5 percent of all camps, and junior high 17.1 percent. Family camping logged in at 8.1 percent, followed by college-age at 6.7 percent. Leadership training groups at 6.2 percent, and married couples at 4.5 percent.

Special interest camps range from sports activities camps to camps for the handicapped and retarded. Other special interest camps include camps and retreats for the underprivileged or the delinquent, music and/or drama camps, work camps (painting, repairing), college-credit camps, retreats for the elderly, and various kinds of youth and adult retreats (for example, engaged couples' retreats and church leadership retreats).

Duration and Location

Camping programs can also be classified as to their duration. In the research conducted by Christian Camping, International and Scripture Press, it was found that almost half (47.5 percent) of all camping programs were one week in duration. Another two out of five were weekend camps and retreats. The week-long camp seems to be more popular among juniors and young teens, while the weekend camp or retreat was more popular with the high school and college ages.

More and more camp programs are conducted year-round as facilities are winterized for more extensive use. Whereas only about 15 percent of the programs had year-round camping in 1964, in 1969 almost 40 percent did, and camp directors were projecting year-round camping in 70 percent of all camps surveyed by 1974.

In times past, camping was often limited to a resident campsite. This is still the most popular. However, in recent years trip camping has grown rapidly. Campers, whether hiking, in canoes, on horseback, or in camper-trailers, do not settle in one location but keep on the move, pitching camp in different spots. Day camping and overnight camping do not need a resident camp location either, but can use a farm, a city or state park, or a friendly wooded area.

There are more church camps in the Midwest (31.6 percent) and West (29.8 percent) than in the South (18.7 percent) or East (13.5 percent). Only 6.4 percent of camps are in Canada. Almost 80 percent of all camps surveyed owned their own campsite, and 70 percent of these camps had been in existence for more than eleven years.

A wide range of camps exists, from platform to wilderness, from centralized to decentralized. Some camps are like plush country clubs with excellent modern facilities. Others are rugged, back-to-nature, rustic, and primitive. But when it comes to lasting results, what matters most is people, not facilities. When God works, He works through people sharing their commitment to God with others in the camp experience.

Administering Camp

The administration of a camp program is usually accomplished by a camp board or committee. A camp director and/or deans implement the plans made by the committee. Planning should be done in an orderly, businesslike manner, for much of the administration of the camp relates to budgets, food service and purchasing, maintenance, and securing a competent staff. The camp committee could be divided into subcommittees that would plan and carry out certain phases of camp work. Committee workbooks with guide sheets could be developed to aid in the planning process.

The camp director or manager is responsible for putting basic decisions into action and generally overseeing the camp itself. In some situations the director is the overall administrator, but each week's individual program is planned by a dean who selects his teachers and counselors and directs the actual camp program.

Better planning for camping will result when a definite planning schedule is developed. This calendar will schedule specific items that need to be done by a certain time. As the summer program is finished, for example, evaluation should be made at various levels. Reports and follow-up ideas should be forwarded to the participating churches. All bills should be paid and the books audited. As the fall months come, next year's program should be planned. The planning calendar should give direction to the camp board and director and provide continuity and guidance for any new director or board member.

Other essential items must be administered effectively. Publicity and promotion is one of those areas. Various media must be used to share information, motivate potential campers, and secure good will and financial support among the camp's constituency. An effective public relations program will help create a favorable public image. This, in turn, helps to recruit campers and staff and to undergird a program with prayer and financial support.

The camp administrator must be aware of governmental and legal regulations that affect camping. The camp must meet government health and safety standards. The administrator must provide Social Security and unemployment compensation for salaried employees and collect sales tax on canteen items sold to campers. Membership in such organizations as American Camping Association[13] and Christian Camping, International[14] can provide beneficial information on many of these items. By meeting the standards set out by these organizations, member camps will generally also meet all government regulations, with the exception of local laws and codes.

Other items must also be given careful attention. They include insurance (for campers, staff, buildings, grounds, and vehicles), food services, and bookkeeping. These items must be carefully planned for and the plans must be effectively executed.

Since there are many different phases of organizing and administering a camp program, the camp committee and director should outline those tasks that should be done before, during, and after each camp session. This outline could be coordinated with a planning calendar. Regular meetings of the camp committee should be held to assess the progress of planning and performance. Such administrative tools and tasks are designed to develop a better program and accomplish the spiritual objectives for which Christ-centered camping exists.

The Camp Program

Success is measured in the program of each camp week. The program includes everything that happens at camp, planned or unplanned, so planning can help ensure a program's success. The following are some essential guidelines for program planning:[15]

1. Provide opportunities for adventure, achievement, and social adjustment.
2. Encourage the participation of all campers, not just those who are highly skilled or athletic.
3. Allow for individual needs and unscheduled situations—be simple, balanced, and flexible.
4. Take full advantage of both the campsite and staff resources.
5. Grade activities and subject matter to the ages, interests, and abilities of the campers.
6. Provide opportunity for individual creativity, so that each camper may develop his own special interests and abilities.
7. Stay within the expectations of those churches supporting the camp, so that the camp produces compatible and contributing members for the churches.
8. Expand the program for young adults to include a wide variety of interests. Such features as music, fine arts, and exploring social problems should be provided as well as all types of outdoor activities.
9. Create and maintain favorable camp traditions.
10. Safeguard the health and well-being of the entire camp community.

Since programming is variable, an ideal program cannot be defined. What would be ideal for a more activity-centered program might not be ideal for a small-group, counselor-centered camp week or for a week whose program centers in some theme. Camping that is conference-oriented would demand a different program than a camp that is decentralized.

However, certain general features of programming for Christ-centered camping should be included whatever the camping pattern.

The Bible should be central. Bible classes, discussion groups centering on biblical themes, and applications of Bible truth to young people's problems are essential to Christian camping.

Evangelism must also be stressed. Whether on a one-to-one basis or a more traditional, platform-centered approach, every young person of accountable years needs to be led to a relationship with Jesus Christ as his Lord and Savior.

Music is important. A singing camp is a happy camp. All kinds of music have their place in the camp program—camp songs, silly fun songs, folk songs, choruses, gospel songs, and hymns. Camp can also be a time for training older young people in music leadership.

Camps should provide opportunities for *worship*. Individual, small group, and total camp worship experiences should be planned carefully.

Campfires are traditional at camp. In fact, they are so commonplace and often poorly done that their value has been eroded. It is better to plan only one or two campfires, and make them highlights of the camp week, than to have a campfire each night with little or no planning.

Recreation of various kinds is a universal feature of camping. Often it is organized around team sports and carried out in organized, competitive recreation. Other informal kinds of recreation are provided that cater to individual interests. In addition, more Christian camps include general recreational activities as swimming, crafts, and various well-planned nature programs that combine recreation with learning. A special emphasis upon *world missions, development of Christian service,* or *leadership training* should be programmed into every camp week, particularly those serving older youth.

The planners of a camp program must be aware of the camp objectives and the nature of the campers. Johnson and Kingsley stress that those formulating the program should be sensitive to overlapping, overlooking, and overloading.[16] A camp program should not *overlap* on what the Sunday school or regular youth program in the local church is doing. Neither should planners *overlook* any possible program feature that could be developed for their campsite by the wise use of resources, both personal and financial. *Overloading* can apply to the program and staff as well as the campers. A program should stress variety and balance, wise use of staff time and energy, and the eliminiation of program pressures from campers.

The key to the program is the camp staff. They are program leaders who make the program effective. They help the camper to grow spiritually. The staff includes deans, who usually are the overall leaders of a week of camping, Bible instructors, worship and activity leaders, and cabin counselors.

Camp counselors are key personnel, especially in decentralized camps. Counselors are not professionals. They are mature, spiritually committed people (at least nineteen years old, say most standards). Counselors may assist with program activities, teach assigned classes, and share in other program areas. Their main function, however, is to live with their assigned campers. As they share living quarters, they become proxy parents to them. In these informal times, campers will have opportunity to share problems, insights, and feelings. In cabin devotions, rap sessions, and informal living, counselors can guide campers to develop better attitudes and grow spiritually.

How can such counselors be developed? Camp personnel can be led to see that they all should be counselors. They can show their concern, share with the campers in the week's experiences, and be available whenever needed.

A counselor training program can be developed by each camp organization. Joy MacKay's excellent volume, *Creative Counseling for Christian Camp* (Scripture Press, 1966), sets forth a program that any camp could inaugurate. It features training by correspondence, with special weekend sessions and pre-camp sessions. Through these means, counselors are led to explore camp objectives, take part in specific camp programs, learn more about campers as persons, and discuss ways of handling specific problems. As the counselors actually work with campers, counselor meetings could be held each day for further instruction, discussion, and evaluation. Whatever training plan is followed, a rule of thumb is—a job description *before*, supervision *during*, evaluation *after*.

A camp that is conference-oriented could modify its program to allow opportunity for more small-group and one-to-one experiences. Camps that are already locked into traditional facilities can assign counselors to a certain group, housing them together in a certain area of the dormitory. The program can allow time for the counselor and his group to be together.

Every camp should have training sessions for teachers and counselors. They should be made aware of the importance of interpersonal relationships, and instructed in the principles of counseling and working with small groups.

Summary

Christian camping is growing and making a spiritual impact. Thousands of decisions leading to spiritual conversion are made each year. Through the camping experience, many young adults are led to decide that their lives should be devoted to specialized, church-related vocational service. Hence, Christian camping is a recruiter for the Christian college and for the formal ministry of the churches. Indeed, the church camp is not just a place, but an experience with God. This experience may have lifelong consequences, issuing into eternity. Christian principles, creative freedom, and sound administrative practice must be joined together to make this experience with God even more significant in the future.

Project

Read at least three periodicals pertaining to Christian camping. Write a brief report.

Selected Bibliography

Ensign, John and Ruth. *Camping Together as Christians*. Richmond, VA: John Knox Press, 1958.

Graendorf, Werner and Lloyd Mattson (ed.). *An Introduction to Christian Camping*. Chicago: Moody Press, 1979.

Johnson, Ted and Lee M. Kingsley. *Blueprint for Quality: Administrative Guidelines for Camping*. Chicago: Harvest Publications, 1969.

Peters, Raymond. *Let's Go Camping*. Elgin, IL: Brethren Press, 1945.

Todd, Floyd and Pauline. *Camping for Christian Youth*. rev. ed. Grand Rapids, MI: Baker Book House, 1968.

---

[1]Viola Mitchell and Ida B. Crawford, *Camp Counseling* (Philadelphia: W. B. Sanders, 1961), p. 8.

[2] Robert Rubin, *The Book of Camping* (New York: Association Press, 1949), p. 1.

[3]*Camping is Education* (Martinsville, IN: American Camping Association, 1960), p. 8.

[4]From CAMPING FOR CHRISTIAN YOUTH by Floyd and Pauline Todd. Copyright 1963 by Floyd and Pauline Todd. p. 34. Used by permission of Baker Book House.

[5]Luke 2:52

[6]Genesis 12ff

[7]Numbers 9:17ff

[8]Deuteronomy 16:13-15

[9]Colby Hall, *Texas Disciples* (Ft. Worth, TX: Texas Christian University Press, 1953), p. 202.

[10]Todd and Todd, p. 30.

[11]Kenneth Gangel, "Christian Camping," *Voice,* 42:21 (June, 1969).

[12]Todd and Todd, p. 31.

[13]The American Camping Association is the professional association for organized camping in America. It grew out of a coalescence in 1935 of the Camp Directors' Association (1910), the National Association of Directors of Girls' Camps (1916), and the Midwest Camp Directors Association (1921). It serves camps by providing information, instilling professional attitudes, setting up standards and accrediting camps that meet these standards.

[14]Christian Camping, International is a similar organization growing out of previous evangelical camping groups. It functions for Christian camping as the American Camping Association does for general camping. It also sponsors national and regional workshops so that help can be given at the grass roots level.

[15]Ted Johnson and Lee M. Kingsley, *Blueprint for Quality: Administrative Guidelines for Camping.* (Chicago: Harvest Publications, 1969), pp. 83, 84.

[16]*Ibid.,* pp. 76, 77.

CHAPTER 24

The Campus Ministry

As you read, think about these questions:
—Why are campus ministries significant in our country?
—How did campus ministries develop?
—What are the objectives and programs for campus ministries?
—What qualifications are necessary for the campus minister?

Higher education is no longer Christian higher education. The church gave birth to higher education in medieval times and continued to nurture it for several centuries, but now most higher educational institutions are secular.

More than 70 percent of all college students are enrolled in state or public institutions. Churches can no longer depend solely upon their own higher educational institutions to educate students about Jesus Christ. It became apparent that churches would have to follow students to the secular campus, to help preserve their faith in an alien surrounding and to help them witness to others in that surrounding. For this purpose, campus ministries developed.

History of Campus Ministry

At the time of the Civil War, only 19 of America's 182 colleges were public institutions. The remaining colleges had been brought into existence by the churches and religiously-oriented private groups. They invested heavily in these private, denominational, and church-related colleges. Most young people entering college were enrolled in these institutions, and the religious flavor that dominated their atmosphere was seen as sufficient to keep these young people committed to the church.

But the Morrill Act of 1862, which granted land for the establishment of state colleges, was destined to change this picture. By the beginning of the twentieth century, the state colleges established through the impetus of the Morrill Act were taking the lead in higher education. In 1910, only two of the largest dozen schools were not state-supported, and the rate of student enrollment gain in state colleges and universities was three times the rate of gain in private and church-related institutions. This flood of students into secular institutions, including more and more church youth, alerted church leaders to a new need—to follow the students to the state campus and minister to them there.

Some student work (as campus ministry was called in those years) was being done, however. The Student Volunteer Movement, grew out of the Haystack Prayer Meeting of Williams College students in 1806. By the close of the nineteenth century, it had permeated many colleges with its religious fervor, particularly its concern for foreign missions. In a quarter of a century, 4,500 missionaries sailed from the North American continent, given impetus by the Student Volunteer Movement. The Northfield, Massachusetts Conference, called by Dwight L. Moody in 1880, gave permanent form to this movement. Under the leadership of John R. Mott, a young Cornell graduate, it became the parent body to the World Student Christian Movement with twenty-two national Student Christian Movements formed throughout the world.

The bulk of religious work, even at the many private and church-related colleges, was done by the Young Men's and Young Women's Christian Associations. The first student YMCA began at the University of Virginia in 1857. Twenty years later, delegates from forty colleges gathered in Louisville, Kentucky, to form the national student YMCA. A similar organization was formed by the YWCA in 1886. By 1900, these two organizations had 1,300 associations with a total membership of 100,000—nearly one-half of all American college students. At this time the Y's still saw themselves as "arms of the church" that served the general interests of Protestant churches. Denominations were willing to let the Y's care for their students enrolled in state institutions.

The denominational churches themselves attempted various forms of campus ministry with volunteer leadership. Most programs centered in local churches and not on the college campus itself.

Another denominational approach was to organize student guilds or societies upon the college campus. In 1887, the Tappan Association for Presbyterians and the Hobart Guild (Episcopal) were formed at the University of Michigan. This plan was quickly adopted by the major Protestant denominations and by the Roman Catholics (Newman Clubs) at state universities in Illinois, Texas, Pennsylvania, Wisconsin, and elsewhere. These campus guilds or clubs became the basis for current patterns of campus ministries.

Another approach was the development of a Bible chair or professorship at the university. This plan was pioneered by the Disciples of Christ at the University of Michigan in 1893. Other Bible chairs were begun at the University of Kansas. These were sponsored by the Christian Women's Board of Missions. Soon this plan became generally accepted and the Bible chairs grew prevalent. College credit offered through the chair was accepted by the university, but the chair itself was supported by an organization outside the university. The Churches of Christ throughout the south began to establish Bible chairs at every major college and university.

The most significant effect of Bible chairs was not that accredited instruction was given, but that men with ecclesiastical standing and academic preparation were sent to work full-time on major campuses. This paved the way from the student associations and denominational guilds, with their nonprofessional, voluntary leadership, to the professional leadership of university pastors and campus ministers.

The Bible chairs came at a propitious time. They began when religious education was seen largely in terms of Bible study, and were located in the geographical and cultural area known as the "Bible belt." The Bible chair was regarded as an acceptable device for teaching religion at a state institution without violating the principle of separation of church and state. Bible chairs or their equivalent arose among many of the major denominations, with Disciples, Churches of Christ, and the Mormons leading the field. At various places in the 1920's and 1930's, some of these Bible chairs banded together to form a school of religion. In a few instances these schools of religion offered accredited work through the university toward majors at baccalaureate and master levels. In one institution, the University of Iowa, a doctorate in religion is available.

However, the Bible chair thrust has lost much of its impetus, because many state institutions have developed departments of religion. Academic study, in those areas provided earlier by the Bible chairs, is done through the university with no qualms about church-state problems.

By the close of World War II, various kinds of campus ministries existed. Most denominations had established departments of campus ministry and had begun campus clubs or foundations at most major university centers. Bible chairs were present in certain institutions, frequently joined to a denominational club or foundation. Local churches also ministered to the college campus, either through their own college departments or cooperatively with other local churches. In some instances, places for religious instruction, Christian fellowship, and other programs and activities were built adjacent to the campus.

On June 22, 1944, the Rankin-Barden bill became law. This bill produced what is generally called the "GI Bill of Rights." By 1957, 2,350,000 World War II veterans had received college training, and almost 6,000,000 had taken advantage of some other kind of schooling (vocational, skill-oriented, or apprentice). This impetus was to have lasting effects upon the college population.

By the end of the 1960's, 55 percent of all high school graduates enrolled in colleges, and most of these (70 to 80 percent) were in public institutions. Though other forms of higher education have become increasingly popular in the 1970's and the college population has leveled off, it continues at a high level. This continuing college population has challenged the churches and concerned Christians. Church youth need help in developing Christian maturity while they attend college, and the state campus is itself a mission field.

Certain evangelical organizations such as Inter-Varsity Christian Fellowship began their ministries on American campuses in the late 1930's. Bill Bright, a product of the college department of First Presbyterian Church in Hollywood, California, formed Campus Crusade for Christ in 1951. Young Life, the Fellowship of Christian Athletes, Navigators, and others soon entered campus work. Almost all of these operate on a club basis and are oriented toward evangelism.

American denominations have continued to promote campus ministries. Some, like the Southern Baptists in their Baptist Student Union, have done so independently with great success. Others have joined together in ecumenical partnership. In 1960, the student ministries of the Disciples of Christ, the Evangelical United Brethren Church, the United Church of Christ, and the United Presbyterian Church brought into being the United Campus Christian Fellowship. This organization and the National Student Christian Fellowship (an umbrella agency related to the National Council of Churches) began sponsoring united ministries on campuses. They tend to emphasize an ecumenical program, not in the sense of denominational cooperation, but the loss of denominational identity in a united ministry.

Because of the need for professional workers in campus ministries, Christian colleges and seminaries have developed courses and programs to prepare individuals for such ministry. Internships, workshops, and other kinds of learning experiences have also been developed to aid in this preparation.

Philosophy of Campus Ministry

The church's concern with higher education is based upon the conviction that God is the author of all truth and that He is concerned with every level of life. In the past, campus concerns of the churches were directed toward conserving the faith of church youth and providing an evangelistic witness on campus. Such concerns must be stressed continuously, but in a sense the church must also attempt to *reclaim* the colleges and universities for God. The church must present to the university a visible and influential example of the Christian community on campus.

In this ideal sense, a campus ministry is involved in the total academic community, not just with students. As a result, the church's ministry on campus is the same as its ministry in the local church or in the Christian college: to promote Christian education. "In the special context of higher education, a Christian is helped to see all truth and values in relationship to the Biblical truth of Jesus Christ, and is thereby freed to live as a whole person and to participate responsibly in the world of *academia*." [1]

Any underlying philosophy and practice of campus ministry must be concerned with people. On any secular campus, the persons uncommitted to Jesus Christ must be evangelized. The Christians who teach or administer must be challenged by an effective campus ministry to take seriously their Christian responsibility. People who are hurting, confused, and caught up in problems unique to the college context must be led to see that in the Christian community on campus there is genuine love, care, and concern that can provide help for their problems. By the very nature of the current secular campus, there will be students and faculty members who operate on a faith level borrowed from family or community. An effective campus ministry will provide a robust and open exploration of biblical and theological themes and implications.

With these basic principles in mind, the campus minister must set out specific objectives for his particular campus ministry. He must consider the type of institution (multiversity, regional college or university, community college, commuter or resident college) at which the ministry operates and the specific needs of area churches. The following is a list of guidelines for developing a specific statement of objectives.[2] An effective campus ministry:

1. Recognizes the validity of every sincere effort to reach the academic community with the gospel and welcomes every opportunity for cooperative effort.
2. Recognizes that the college campus must be dealt with not as a homogeneous unit but as a highly stratified, fragmented, diverse community.
3. Avoids a sectarian posture.
4. Understands the sociological aspects of the student's background, the community environment, and the climate of the individual campus.

5. Establishes a cordial working relationship with administrative officials, faculty members, and student body officers and attempts to enlist their active support for its program.
6. Strives to make its program an integral part of campus life. Consequently, the program is tailored for high and low points in campus activity.
7. Recognizes the unsophisticated religious background of the average student and adjusts its doctrinal arguments to an appropriate level.
8. Identifies itself with the highest ideals of the university.
9. Is positive in approach and attitude.
10. Presents a life-affirming and culture-affirming faith.
11. Identifies itself primarily with the students.
12. Experiments, innovates, and adapts its methods.
13. Establishes itself as a ministry within the campus rather than beside the campus.
14. Rallies the effort and energy of the existing community of faith within the academic community.
15. Exercises great discretion in identifying itself with any campus issue.

Types and Programs of Campus Ministry

Each campus minister must make a thorough study of its situation and develop programming and activities accordingly. He must consider place of residence, academic relationships, extracurricular activities, and the academic environment. Although different campus ministries use different methods and activities, some areas of program should be universal.

Evangelism is a primary objective of the campus ministry. Evangelistic activities on the campus may range from those traditionally used in local churches to a one-to-one style in which a student or faculty member shares his faith with another. Whatever methods are used, the heart of the evangelistic task is the same—the presentation of the good news of God in Jesus Christ so that all people may accept Him as Savior and obey Him as Lord. This is the central task of the church and the campus ministry. Christian students, faculty, and university staff members must actively present Christ to other persons on campus.

Most campus ministries have developed a core group concept. Any active campus Christian group has a center or core group who are genuinely committed to Christ. These people can become the radiating influence on campus for that ministry. The campus minister himself should disciple these young people and send them forth, as Jesus did with His disciples, to minister and serve on the campus.

Much of the work of an effective campus minister will be *counseling*. In spite of the presence of professional counseling services in the university complex, many young people never consult professional counselors. Here is the campus ministry's unique opportunity. Sensitive Christian students may themselves function as counselors or refer needy students to a campus minister who is more skilled at counseling than they are. Group discussion of common academic and moral problems may well become group therapy. Students who are helped with their problems will share with other students facing similar situations. The counseling service can become an informal, yet vital public relations tool.

Every campus ministry must stress *biblical and theological study*. Such study can be done in programs accredited by the university or an accredited Christian college. Other ministries prefer non-credit, short-term religious study. Inter-Varsity Fellowship has done much to provide non-credit Bible and theological study, and their publishing arm, Inter-Varsity Press, provides excellent resources for study. Evangelical campus ministries can cooperate in this area by bringing in special lecturers on relevant themes or sponsoring debates on crucial religious or scientific issues. Frequently the campus ministry may share sponsorship of a special lecturer with one of the university departments.

On some campuses, a campus house where Christian students live has also become a study center. The house not only provides the place for special formal programs, but it involves residents in a deepening of their convictions through discussion and small group worship.

If a campus ministry is to be concerned with the total academic community, it must not ignore the *university faculty*. Many of these people are nominally Christian, and need a renewed and revitalized faith. Under the aegis of the National Council of Churches, the Faculty Christian Fellowship has provided an ecumenical effort toward reaching the university campus. Such publications as the *FCF Bulletin, The Christian Scholars* (a journal of the Commission on Higher Education of the National Council), and *Faculty Forum* (published by the Methodist Church to serve the whole faculty movement), are auxiliaries to this program. The Inter-Varsity Christian Fellowship, through its Faculty Fellowship, provides an ecumenical platform for those whose convictions are more biblically conservative. Both of these groups stress the importance of vocation, the need to be Christian in all of one's relationships, and the problems and opportunities of Christian witness as a faculty member.

American college and university campuses have become the training ground for many *foreign students* in recent years. The Smith-Mundt Act, passed in 1948, providing for a cooperative higher educational exchange program, and the Fulbright Act of 1946 resulted in an increase in the number of foreign students. In 1946, 15,000 foreign students were studying in United States higher educational institutions. By 1964, this number had risen to 75,000. The number continues to increase. These students have come from more than 152 countries and are enrolled in almost two thousand different colleges.

Here is a golden opportunity for the church through its campus ministries. Many of these foreign students are lonely and in need of friendship. A campus ministry could provide opportunity for acquaintance and friendship, sponsor a "host family" program, and help foreign students adjust to the American culture. But here is also a tremendous evangelistic opportunity with world mission implications. These foreign young people are the higher-class, more intelligent youth of their countries. If they are led to Christ, they may have greater influence in their home countries than dozens of American missionaries. In some instances in which a nation is closed to traditional missionary work, this may be the only way to send a Christian witness to that country.

In the past it has been assumed that a ministry to college students would necessarily be carried out by a ministry on campus or by a church located in the university town. The development of regional universities and community colleges has made it possible for almost every church to minister to the college student. It is estimated that some kind of college exists within twenty miles of every citizen. In such urban areas as Los Angeles, churches have college people in their membership even though these college people do not know one another as a part of the academic community. This has led to area-wide campus ministries, even though no attempt has been made to form structured ministries on the university campuses in the area.

These developments mean that "every church is going to be faced with the problem of ministering to the academic community."[3] Churches must recognize that they minister to people whatever their context or subculture. Campus ministry, then, is a ministry to persons who are involved in the academic life of the country. To be true to its Lord, the church must devise ways of reaching the people within that special context.

The Campus Minister

In most instances the key to success in a campus ministry is the campus minister. He is the motivator, the discipler, and the teacher who provides the driving force for those involved in the ministry. Because of the environment of the secular campus, the Christian commitment and leadership ability of the campus minister may need to be greater than that of other kinds of ministers.

The campus minister should be young enough to understand the students. At the same time, he needs to be emotionally and spiritually mature. He should be well-educated, with both undergraduate and graduate degrees. Work at the graduate level in counseling, apologetics, history, and theology is extremely helpful. As he ministers, he may wish to take graduate classes at the university. This gives him a feel for the academic atmosphere at the university and provides opportunities for interaction with students and faculty. He should seek other opportunities in continuing education—workshops, reading, and a perusal of the various higher education journals to keep abreast of the trends.

Above all, the campus minister must be motivated by the love of Jesus Christ. He must have a deep abiding faith and carefully-thought-through convictions. He must also be intellectually honest and sympathetic toward students.

Activity	Frequently	Occasionally	Rarely
1. Engaged in informal theological discussions with students	71%	26%	1%
2. Gave personal counseling to students or faculty	68%	29%	1%
3. Helped students to organize religious programs	60%	32%	6%
4. Led study groups on religious topics	48%	40%	10%
5. Entertained students in your home	47%	45%	6%
6. Conducted worship services for the campus	32%	24%	42%
7. Was active in your denomination's regional or national meetings on matters other than the campus ministry	20%	45%	33%
8. Had sessions for students becoming baptized, confirmed, church members, and so forth	16%	23%	59%
9. Was liaison for local church to get faculty or other adults into the life of the church	15%	37%	46%
10. Engaged in theological discussions with the faculty	14%	60%	24%
11. Helped students organize social events	13%	43%	42%
12. Helped students organize some sort of social action effort	10%	50%	38%
13. Took stands you knew your denomination would disapprove of	6%	44%	48%
14. Took stands you knew the college administration would disapprove of	5%	50%	43%
15. Guest-lectured for faculty member	1%	23%	74%
16. Had meetings for college alumni to discuss religious and social issues	1%	9%	89%

Figure 24-1. Activities of Campus Ministers

Each campus minister should be given a job description that will help define his role, his responsibilities, and his relationships to various groups. This job description must be developed in relation to the needs of the individual campus and the abilities of the campus minister. Figure 24-1 indicates the tasks in which Hammond found campus ministers involved.[4] It suggests some elements for the development of a job description:

Summary

Campus ministries are a vital part of the church's thrust in evangelism and education. If the church is to affect the future, it must influence those centers of influence in American higher education. American churches must invest in a ministry to college and university people. We must accept and implement the challenge of reaching the university with the gospel.

Project

Write to or interview a campus minister. What does he do in his work?

Selected Bibliography

Ambrose, W. Hayden. *The Church in the University.* Valley Forge, PA: Judson Press, 1968.

Beach, Waldo. *Conscience on Campus.* New York: Association Press, 1958.

Bolin, Gene. *Christian Witness on Campus.* Nashville, TN: Broadman Press, 1968.

Cantelon, John. *A Protestant Approach to the Campus Ministry.* Philadelphia: Westminster Press, 1964.

Chamberlin, J. Gordon. *Churches and the Campus.* Philadelphia: Westminster Press, 1963.

Earnshaw, George W. (ed). *Campus Ministry.* Valley Forge, PA: Judson Press, 1964.

Garrison, Charles. *Forgotten Christians.* Joplin, MO: College Press Publishing Company, Inc., 1967.

Guidelines for the Development of United Campus Ministries. Department of Higher Education, NCCCA, 1965.

Hammond, Phillip E. *The Campus Clergyman.* New York: Basic Books, 1968.

Hummel, Charles E. *Campus Christian Witness*. Chicago: Inter-Varsity Press, 1958.
Miller, Alexander. *Faith and Learning*. New York: Association Press, 1960.
The Study of Religion in College and University and Its Implications for Church and Seminary. New York: Department of Higher Education, National Council of Churches, 1967.

[1]George W. Earnshaw (ed.), *Campus Ministry* (Valley Forge, PA: Judson Press, 1964), p. 20. Used by permission of Judson Press.

[2]Adapted from a paper presented by K. Don Clark for a class in Campus Ministry, Emmanuel School of Religion, 1967.

[3]Earnshaw, p. 63.

[4]Phillip E. Hammond, *The Campus Clergyman* (New York: Basic Books, 1968), pp. 65, 66.

CHAPTER 25

Christian Higher Education

As you read, think about these questions:
—What role has religion played in higher education in America?
—What has been done to prepare professional workers in Christian education?
—Define a *Bible college*. Why did these institutions come into existence?
—What is the Evangelical Teacher Training Association?

Higher education was born in the church and nurtured at her bosom for centuries. It has its roots deep in medieval European society. Ancient universities developed out of medieval scholasticism and the cathedral schools of the church; these have set the pattern for modern higher education. Degrees, faculties, and courses of study still reflect the ancient pattern. In Europe, universities are still religiously oriented and often church-related. Their departments of theology are integral and vital parts of the general faculty.

The Beginning of Colleges in America

Religious Motivation

The first colleges established in America were established by the church. Harvard College was established in 1636 to train a literate ministry. Harvard's mottoes, program of studies, and religious fervor in its early years bears witness to the religious motivation for its establishment and continuation.

Yale University, William and Mary College, Dartmouth, and many other early higher educational institutions came into being for the same reason as Harvard. Some were designed to promote a certain sect or denomination. Others were to teach Christianity in general. Not only did these early institutions provide ministers and missionaries, but they also supplied the early teachers and leaders of the colonies. The curriculum of these colleges included liberal and practical arts, but religion was the core around which the curriculum was organized.

Secularization of Colleges

The scene has changed. Today most of these privately-endowed institutions of higher learning are indifferent to Christianity. The secularization that affected state education affected these colleges as well, and religious emphasis in purpose and curricular content was soon forgotten. Religion was forced out of its central position to be handled by student organizations or second-rate theological schools.

Not only did this trend affect private institutions such as Harvard, Yale, and Columbia, but it also affected some colleges actually established and supported by church groups. In order to compete with state colleges and universities, these church-related schools developed comparable programs, sometimes at the expense of their original purpose of serving the church. In 1923, Arlo Brown depicted the state of the church-related college in this way: "It is not uncommon today to find denominational colleges requiring for graduation 20 to 30 semester hours of foreign language study and advanced mathematics while making no requirement in psychology, Bible, religious education, and similar subjects."[1]

Not all Christian colleges have surrendered to a secularistic trend. Excellent Christian liberal arts colleges like Pepperdine, Wheaton, and Gordon, still place the Christian world view at their center, preparing Christian men and women to live the Christian lifestyle in whatever vocation they pursue.

The Teaching of Religion in American Colleges

The secularistic trend is now being reversed. Both church-related and state institutions of higher learning recognize to a greater extent the need for religious teaching.

Surveys of the Early Part of the Century

One of the endeavors of the Religious Education Association was to promote the teaching of religion in higher educational institutions. W. S. Athearn, a member of this Association, wrote in 1913:

> There is at the present time an organized effort, led by the Religious Education Association, to put courses in religion back into denominational colleges. Only a few church colleges are teaching religion. They are teaching the same subjects that state universities teach, and their students are forced to absorb religion from the atmosphere of the college chapel, the Christian associations, etc. Now that state universities are surrounding themselves with student pastors, Divinity houses, and Christian associations, the denominational colleges must either go out of business or begin to perform a task for society which the state school can not do; the task is to teach religion in every year of the college course.[2]

In 1915, Athearn conducted a survey of the teaching of religious education in 300 American colleges. Sixty-seven of them offered an average of five and one-third courses each in English Bible and literature, and 38 of them offered an average of two courses each in religious education. Only seven colleges offered enough courses in Bible and religious education to constitute a major for the bachelor's degree. These seven were Carleton, Drake, Grinnell, Millikin, University of Chicago, Yale, and Eugene Bible University. Of these, only the University of Chicago, Drake, and Eugene Bible University offered enough courses for a student to major in religious education.[3]

In 1915 and 1916, the Council of Church Boards of Education made an independent study of 203 colleges under its jurisdiction. Of these colleges, only 33 were making adequate provision for permanent instruction in the Bible, and only 138 of these colleges required any Bible for graduation.

Other surveys indicated the weakness of the church colleges in regard to religious instruction. These colleges, sponsored by the churches, were supplying everything but what the churches needed—religious teachers.

Athearn led a one-man crusade against the secularization of colleges and universities organized and supported by the churches. He took surveys and published books (such as *Religious Education and American Democracy* and *A National System of Education*) that related to this problem. He also used the convention and lecture platform to forward his crusade.

Athearn stated that the church-related college must be a school of the church, teaching young adults religion first and then other subjects. These other subjects would never be taught apart from the church's basic religious presuppositions and implications, however. Personality is the supreme emphasis of a church college: all student activities are not for the privileged few, but for all.

In the pamphlet, *Religion at the Heart of the Christian University,* Athearn (by then president of Butler University) stated four distinct tasks that must be achieved by the church college: (1) to preserve the essential disciplines and cultures of the liberal arts college; (2) to give religion and the Bible their rightful places in the college curriculum; (3) to give proper recognition in the college course to religious education and various forms of social service as vocational fields of great personal and social significance; and (4) to prepare college students for satisfactory graduate work in graduate and professional schools in the fields of religion and social science.[4]

Athearn believed that no student in the church college should be allowed to graduate without being prepared for intelligent lay service in the local church. This, he felt, could be done through the students electing a "service minor in Christian service courses in addition to required biblical courses."[5]

The Christian religion and the Bible must be central to the Christian college or university. Whenever the church college is completely secularized, whenever it fails to prepare young people for effective lay service in the local church, it forfeits its right to existence.

Present Trends

Five types of programs have become operative: (1) courses in religion within the curriculum of the state-supported university; (2) a department of religious education within the church-supported university; (3) a Bible college or Bible chair supported by a church or churches, the work of which is accredited by the university; (4) courses offered by independent denominational foundations accredited by the foundations; and, (5) a school of religion supported by the churches offering work accredited by the university.

Seymour Smith made a more recent study[6] of religion in higher education. The study concluded that 95 percent of the major state universities offer religion courses for credit. In the 1920's, tax-supported schools averaged only two and one-half courses per institution; in 1933 the average had moved to five courses; by 1958 the average had reached almost nine courses per institution.

Conservative Christians, however, should not be overly optimistic about this situation. Although state colleges and universities are teaching religion, too often it is the religion of liberal Christianity, not the religion of biblical faith. Only about half of all college students are attending institutions where the gospel is a living force.[7] As long as this situation continues, evangelical churches must continue to foster a higher education that will give preeminence to the Bible and biblical faith. Such institutions as Wheaton, Trinity, Gordon, Bob Jones University, Milligan College, Westmont College, and others are still needed to give this biblical witness to American universities and to provide leadership for evangelicalism.

Professional Training in Christian Education

Theological seminaries came into existence toward the close of the eighteenth century and developed rapidly in the nineteenth. These institutions functioned as professional training schools for the ministry. Courses in Bible, theology, and practical ministries dominated their curriculum. As Christian education became more prominent, seminaries began making some provision for professional training in this field. As early as 1906, a chair of education or Christian pedagogy was established in the College of the Bible, Lexington, Kentucky. Hartford Seminary, under the leadership of Edward Porter St. John, established a School of Religious Pedagogy at about the same time. Other institutions quickly followed the leadership of these two schools. Arlo A. Brown said of the first 15 years of the twentieth century, "There was practically no oppostion to a chair of religious education in theological seminaries after the awakening at the beginning of the century. The installing of such chairs became largely a matter of when the institution could secure first the necessary funds and then the properly trained men."[8]

But what was true of the seminaries was not true in the colleges of the church. The first course in Christian education offered in a college for degree credit was offered at Drake University in 1910. By 1915, only seven colleges offered enough courses for a major in Bible and Christian education. Only the University of Chicago, Yale University, and Columbia University offered enough work for a doctorate with a major in religious education, and these institutions could do so only because of their affiliation with theological seminaries.

It was at this point that W. S. Athearn again exerted leadership. He believed that the church must develop a body of professionally trained religious educators. For a decade, he inspired and directed a creative program of professional training on the college and university level at Boston. In so doing, he became responsible for the upsurge of religious education of training in other university centers and theological seminaries.

Athearn had been called to Boston to serve as the head of a new work in religious education at Boston University in 1916. At first he served as a professor in the graduate school of the University. In the next three years, various training agencies were unified under Athearn's leadership to become the School of Religious Education and Social Service of Boston University. This school aimed at training competent leaders for the fields of religious education, social service, and general church work. By the 1928-29 school year, over six hundred students were enrolled in the School of Religious Education and Social Service.

The Boston school served as a pattern for many other professional training schools. Southern Baptist seminaries, through the influence of Dr. J. M. Price of Southwestern Seminary, developed similar programs in their institutions. Today, almost all theological seminaries offer the M.R.E. degree as well as ministerial degrees. Only Hartford School of Religious Education and the Southern Baptist seminaries offer the D.R.E. Other universities and seminaries offer doctorates in religious education under the Th.D. or Ph.D. or Ed.D. program. Boston University no longer has a School of Religious Education, as all religious education courses are offered in the School of Theology or School of Education. The impact of the pioneer school at Boston under Athearn's leadership did much to popularize and standardize religious education as a profession.

The Rise of Bible Colleges and Institutes

A new form of American education has developed in the last hundred years. Since the 1880's, more than 240 Bible institutes and Bible colleges have been founded, enrolling more than 25,000 students.[9] Though given little place in the history of education, these colleges and institutes have become a decisive force in the education program of evangelicalism.

S. A. Witmer, who served as the Executive Director of the Accrediting Association of Bible Colleges for several years, has chronicled the growth and development of the Bible college movement in his book, *The Bible College Story: Education with Dimension*. He points out that two basic principles have shaped the program of Bible colleges. The first is a thorough commitment by Bible college educators to the Bible as the inspired and authoritative Word of God. The second principle is the mission of the church as expressed in our Lord's Great Commission. The practical purpose of the Bible college is to educate and prepare recruits to implement this work.

Causes for Establishment

The first Bible institutes were established to train lay people for Christian service. The movement developed out of the evangelical awakening that occurred toward the latter part of the nineteenth century. Dwight L. Moody formed the Chicago Evangelization Society in 1886. After his death, this institution was named the Moody Bible Institute. The Nyack Missionary Institute was founded in 1882 by A. B. Simpson. It had a strong missions course as well as the usual Bible and practical courses.

Most of the Bible colleges of today came into being as a reaction to the type of higher education sponsored by liberal churches. The fundamentalist-modernist controversy early in this century had drawn such sharp lines that new institutions were established to perpetuate the fundamentals of biblical faith. Many new denominations resulted from divergences in theology, and many of these new denominations established Bible colleges for the training of ministers and Christian workers.

Though these institutions differ radically in program, course offerings, and facilities, they are alike in many respects:

1. All are wholeheartedly evangelical in theological convictions. Each school is founded on the tenets of the Christian faith commonly accepted by evangelicals.

2. The direct study of the English Bible is given central place in all of these schools. Many schools require a student to have as much as thirty to fifty hours in direct Bible study in their four- or five-year degree program. Others require corresponding amounts for diploma courses (two- or three-year courses).

3. These colleges or institutes emphasize practical Christian service. They provide courses in Christian education, personal evangelism, and preaching. Many have Christian service programs that provide opportunities for students to engage in these activities while they are being taught.

4. These colleges emphasize missions. Some have been established for the express purpose of training missionaries, others have extensive departments of missions, and still others provide technical studies in medicine and radio to help prepare missionary volunteers. As a result of this emphasis, evangelical missionaries on the field outnumber those going out through the denominational boards by about two to one.

5. These colleges encourage additional study. In the early years, most Bible college graduates entered the ministry immediately upon graduation. Seeing a more complex world with intense demands upon ministers, many college leaders now recommend graduate study in conservative seminaries.

Accrediting Associations

In recent years, these colleges have banded together to form a professional association. Under the auspices of the Bible Institute Division of the Commission on Education of the National Association of Evangelicals, a meeting was held in Minneapolis in 1946. Representatives from twenty-eight Bible colleges and institutes formed an association of Bible schools that would serve as an accrediting agency and a channel of communications.[10] The Accrediting Association of Bible Colleges is now recognized by the United States Office of Education as an association accrediting undergraduate colleges in the field of Bible education. More than sixty schools meet strict academic requirements to be fully accredited by the Association. The American Association of Bible Colleges is now a member of the Council on Post-Secondary Accreditation, the organization of accreditation for all American higher educational institutions.

The strength of Bible colleges in certain religious movements can be seen in the following example. Among the Disciples of Christ, liberalistic leadership captured most of the theological schools. Bible colleges were then organized throughout the United States to train ministers and Christian workers for a large segment of conservative Christians. The number of these colleges has increased to over forty institutions, some of them enrolling several hundred students. Fourteen of these are fully accredited, with two others holding candidate status for accreditation. The total number of students now studying in these Bible colleges far exceed the number in the older Disciple institutions who are preparing for Christian work.

The Emphasis Upon Christian Education

Bible colleges have emphasized Christian education for years. Most of these institutions have departments of Christian education in which students can prepare for a teaching ministry. Some of these colleges have degree programs or courses to prepare students for work as Christian education directors, youth workers, or leaders in other phases of education in local churches.

One important development resulting from the Bible institute movement has been the organization of the Evangelical Teacher Training Association. In May, 1931, a small group of men met in the offices of the *Sunday School Times* in Philadelphia. James M. Gray and C. H. Benson represented Moody Bible Institute, Charles G. Trumbull and Philip E. Howard, the *Sunday School Times*, Lew W. Gosnell, the Bible Institute of

Pennsylvania; B. Allen Reed, the National Bible Institute; and Calvin C. Ellis, Juniata College. The group decided to inaugurate an association that would, in association with Bible colleges and institutes, put teacher training on a higher plane than any existing agency was then doing. The Association, through cooperating schools (both at college and seminary level), promotes a Standard Training Course which consists of 432 hours or units of work divided as follows: Bible, 144; Department Specialization, 48; Personal Evangelism, 36; Mission, 36; Biblical Introduction, 15; Child Study, 15; Pedagogy, 15; Sunday School Administration, 15; Bible Geography, 12; and Electives, 96. This would equal twenty-four semester hours of college work.

Since 1931, the Evangelical Teacher Training Association has carried forth its program consistently. Through its member schools it provides a teacher-training program unequaled by any other agency.

Summary

The role of religious education in institutions of higher learning has fluctuated. Medieval universities were Christian educational institutions, but their American counterparts have largely forsaken the original pattern. As the religious education movement gained momentum, churches demanded more religious teaching in higher education. Religious education as a profession has been developed through graduate centers and theological seminaries. The Bible college or institute has arisen as a reaction to Protestant liberalism to foster an evangelical Christianity that is vitally interested in religious teaching. The Evangelical Teacher Training Association, associated with Bible colleges and institutes, has done much for teacher training. The picture is encouraging, particularly for the prospects of religious teaching in American higher education.

Project

Read the bulletins of a Bible college of your choice. How has its curriculum and program changed during its history? What courses does it offer in Christian education?

Selected Bibliography

Athearn, W. S. *An Adventure in Religious Education*. New York: Century Company, 1930.

_______ . *Religious Education and American Democracy*. Des Moines, IA: privately published, 1913.

Benson, C. H. *History of Christian Education*. Chicago: Moody Press, 1943.

Brown, A. A. *A History of Religious Education in Recent Times*. Nashville, TN: Abingdon Press, 1923.

Gaebelein, Frank (ed.). *Christian Education in a Democracy*. New York: Oxford University Press, 1951.

Lotz, Philip H. (ed.). *Orientation in Religious Education*. New York: Abingdon-Cokesbury, 1950.

Ringenberg, William C. *The Christian College*. Grand Rapids, MI: Wm. B. Eerdmans Publishing Co., 1984.

Taylor, Marvin J. *Religious Education: A Comprehensive Survey*. New York: Abingdon Press, 1960.

_______ . *An Introduction to Christian Education*. New York: Abingdon Press, 1964.

Witmer, S. A. *The Bible College Story: Education with Dimension*. New York: Channel Press, 1962.

---

[1]A. A. Brown, *A History of Religious Education in Recent Times* (Nashville, TN: Abingdon Press, 1923), p. 231.

[2]W. S. Athearn, *Religious Education and American Democracy* (Des Moines, IA: privately published, 1913), p. 10.

[3]W. S. Athearn, *An Adventure in Religious Education* (New York: Century Company, 1930), p. 126.

[4]Athearn, *Religious Education and American Democracy,* p. 3.

[5]*Ibid.,* p. 5.

[6]"Religious Instruction in State Universities: A Report of Recent Trends," *Religious Education,* LIII, No. 3 (May-June, 1958).

[7]Frank Gaebelein (ed.), *Christian Education in a Democracy* (New York: Oxford University Press, 1951), p. 134.

[8]Brown, p. 238.

[9]Gaebelein, pp. 157ff.

[10]*Ibid.,* p. 173.

Conclusion

The teaching ministry of the church is not a new star on the religious horizon. From the very beginning of creation, God has provided ways by which a people, His people, could be taught to know and follow Him. The book of Acts, that historical record of the early expansion of the church, reveals a teaching church. All through the ages the church has stood strong, penetrating the darkness of sin, when it has taken seriously its responsibility to teach. But the church has languished in apathy and weakness during those eras when teaching was no longer deemed essential.

God's purpose and program for the church have not changed. Forms have been altered from age to age, but the task is still the same: each generation is to teach the faith to its peers and to its offspring. The task of communicating faith is never-ending. The church is always just one generation away from extinction.

Effective communication of sound doctrine results when strong foundations are built. You have explored those foundations in detail, since they are critical to the programs you will lead. The mission of the church is unique. So is the content the church teaches—the Bible. Your philosophy of Christian education is only now being formulated, but it eventually will guide your choices of programs and materials.

The communication of faith calls for understanding the audience, heeding sound teaching principles, and selecting appropriate methods and materials. You were exposed to up-to-date research findings and practical plans for communicating to particular groups of learners. You have not yet achieved skill in teaching—that will come with further study and extensive practice—but you have the basic tools to do the job.

The teaching function of the local church is made more effective with visionary planning, careful administration, and critical evaluation. Your overview acquainted you with the basic principles and, hopefully, whetted your appetite for added study.

Teaching occurs in the local church, but even so, the congregational task is aided by the wide variety of extra-church organizations that exist alongside the church. Camping, Christian schools, campus ministries, Christian colleges, publishing companies, and other extra-church concerns are cooperative efforts to serve the church or to extend the ministry of the local church. The skilled educator is aware of the available resources.

You have been given a practical overview of the educational task of the church. Most topics have received only cursory examination; all deserve a more detailed analysis. That must wait for advanced study. Meanwhile, you have the beginning tools to share in the marvelous work of God—communicating faith to others (2 Timothy 2:2).

Index

Scripture Index